Lecture Notes in Computer Science 2176

Edited by G. Goos, J. Hartmanis, and J. van Leeuwen

Springer
Berlin
Heidelberg
New York
Barcelona
Hong Kong
London
Milan
Paris
Tokyo

Klaus-Dieter Althoff Raimund L. Feldmann
Wolfgang Müller (Eds.)

Advances in Learning Software Organizations

Third International Workshop, LSO 2001
Kaiserslautern, Germany, September 12-13, 2001
Proceedings

Series Editors

Gerhard Goos, Karlsruhe University, Germany
Juris Hartmanis, Cornell University, NY, USA
Jan van Leeuwen, Utrecht University, The Netherlands

Volume Editors

Klaus-Dieter Althoff
Fraunhofer IESE
Sauerwiesen 6, 67661 Kaiserslautern, Germany
E-mail: althoff@iese.fhg.de

Raimund L. Feldmann
University of Kaiserslautern
Postfach 3049, 67653 Kaiserslautern, Germany
E-mail: r.feldmann@computer.org

Wolfgang Müller
FH Ludwigshafen
Ernst-Boehe-Straße 4, 67059 Ludwigshafen, Germany
E-mail: wolfgang.mueller@fh-ludwigshafen.de

Cataloging-in-Publication Data applied for

Die Deutsche Bibliothek - CIP-Einheitsaufnahme

Advances in learning software organizations : third international workshop ; proceedings / LSO 2001, Kaiserslautern, Germany, September 12 - 13, 2001. Klaus-Dieter Althoff ... (ed.). - Berlin ; Heidelberg ; New York ; Barcelona ; Hong Kong ; London ; Milan ; Paris ; Tokyo : Springer, 2001
(Lecture notes in computer science ; Vol. 2176)
ISBN 3-540-42574-8

CR Subject Classification (1998): D.2, K.6, H.5.2-3, I.2.4, K.3, k.4.3

ISSN 0302-9743
ISBN 3-540-42574-8 Springer-Verlag Berlin Heidelberg New York

Springer-Verlag Berlin Heidelberg New York
a member of BertelsmannSpringer Science+Business Media GmbH

http://www.springer.de

Printed in Germany

Typesetting: Camera-ready by author, data conversion by PTP-Berlin, Stefan Sossna
Printed on acid-free paper SPIN: 10840452 06/3142 5 4 3 2 1 0

Preface

The importance of production and use of high-quality software is still growing, as more and more businesses depend on information technology. Well-educated, highly skilled, and experienced employees characterize the situation in most companies in the developed countries. Increasingly they work together in temporary networks with geographically distributed offices. Using and developing their knowledge is a key issue in gaining competitive advantages. We have learned during recent years that the exchange and development of knowledge (which we call learning) demands a great deal of human interaction. However, it is widely recognized that information systems will, in many cases, enable the sharing of experience across distributed organizations and act as a knowledge repository. A Learning Software Organization (LSO) will turn Intellectual Capital into market shares and profit, as it establishes the means to manage its knowledge.

The LSO workshop series was created in 1999 to provide a communication forum that addresses the questions of organizational learning from a software point of view and builds upon existing work on Knowledge Management and Organizational Learning. It aims at bringing together practitioners and researchers for an open exchange of experience with successes and failures in organizational learning. Right from the beginning, fostering interdisciplinary approaches and providing an opportunity to learn about new ideas has been a central issue of the workshop series. The feedback that we have obtained in recent years has encouraged us to continue our work for a better understanding of the setup and running of Learning Software Organizations.

The discussion today is centered around the establishment of the right culture to promote continuous learning and foster the exchange of experience and the appropriate support with information systems. Should such a culture be introduced first or will it grow with the technological possibilities? Is there a single successful culture or is it something each company has to create on its own? Does the technological support depend on the type of business and products? Is there a general description of knowledge? To all these questions no final answer has been found so far.

In 2000 we held the workshop in conjunction with the International Conference on Product Focused Software Process Improvement (PROFES) because we felt that software process improvement is a key strategy to secure a competitive market position and needs to be closely connected to organizational learning to keep pace in a fast changing business. As the discussions during the workshop underlined this point of view, we decided to combine this year's workshop with the PROFES conference too. Again, the workshop brought together experts from computer science, business, and organization science as well as from cognitive science.

This year the number of submitted papers again increased by 50%. From these, the program committee finally selected 12 for oral presentation and 3 for poster presentation. Additionally, the LSO 2001 program included two keynote talks as well as a panel session.

Many people "behind the scene" helped us to successfully prepare the workshop. As the workshop chairs, we would like to thank all these people. First of all, we have to mention the authors and presenters for their willingness to share their expertise and the members of the program committee who did a great job reviewing the submitted papers. We would especially like to thank our keynote speakers, Scott Henninger and Franz Lehner. Last but not least our gratitude is extended to Dietmar Janetzko for organizing the panel on Knowledge Creating Communities.

We are convinced that LSO 2001 offered a good communication forum both for practitioners and researchers with vital discussions, an exchange of new ideas, and the possibility to establish valuable contacts.

July 2001

Klaus-Dieter Althoff
Raimund L. Feldmann
Wolfgang Müller

Workshop Organization

Workshop Chairs

Klaus-Dieter Althoff, Fraunhofer IESE, Kaiserslautern (Germany)
Raimund L. Feldmann, University of Kaiserslautern, Kaiserslautern (Germany)
Wolfgang Müller, University of Applied Science, Ludwigshafen (Germany)

Program Committee

Andreas Abecker, DFKI (Germany)
Brigitte Bartsch-Spörl, BSR Consulting (Germany)
Ralph Bergmann, University of Kaiserslautern (Germany)
Giovanni Cantone, Università degli Studi di Roma "Tor Vergata" (Italy)
Reidar Conradi, University of Trondheim (Norway)
Birgit Geppert, Avaya Labs Research (USA)
Christiane Gresse von Wangenheim, Universidade do Vale do Itajaí (Brazil)
Scott Henninger, University of Nebraska (USA)
Knut Hinkelmann, University of Applied Science, Solothurn (Switzerland)
Dietmar Janetzko, University of Freiburg (Germany)
Yannis Kalfoglou, Open University (UK)
Stefan Kirn, Technical University of Ilmenau (Germany)
Ralf Klamma, Aachen University of Technology (Germany)
Bernd Krämer, University of Hagen (Germany)
Dai Kusui, NEC (Japan)
Franz Lehner, University of Regensburg (Germany)
Mikael Lindvall, Fraunhofer Center Maryland (USA)
Werner Mellis, University of Cologne (Germany)
Tim Menzies, University of British Columbia (Canada)
Enrico Motta, Open University (UK)
Dietmer Pfahl, Fraunhofer IESE (Germany)
Ulrich Reimer, Swiss Life (Switzerland)
Kurt Schneider, DaimlerChrysler (Germany)
Rudi Studer, University of Karslruhe (Germany)
Carsten Tautz, tec:inno - empolis Knowledge Management Division (Germany)
Ralph Traphöner, tec:inno - empolis Knowledge Management Division (Germany)
Eric Tsui, CSC (Australia)
Angi Voß, GMD AiS (Germany)

In addition to the PC members Ljiljana Stojanovic and Koji Kida helped in reviewing the technical papers.

Table of Contents

Introduction and Motivation

Keynote Addresses and Panel

Planning LSOs

Applications

Analysis

Learning

Additional Papers: LSO 2001 Posters

Announcements

Part 1:

Introduction and Motivation

On the Status of Learning Software Organizations in the Year 2001

Raimund L. Feldmann[1] and Klaus-Dieter Althoff[2]

[1]University of Kaiserslautern, AG Software Engineering, Postfach 3049, D-67653 Kaiserslautern, Germany
r.feldmann@computer.org
[2] Fraunhofer IESE, Department of Systematic Learning and Improvement (SLI), Sauerwiesen 6, D-67661 Kaiserslautern, Germany
althoff@iese.fhg.de

Abstract. To keep pace in the accelerating business, software organizations have to continuously improve their products and processes. Therefore, a culture has to be established that promotes continuous learning and fosters the exchange of experience. This requires an interdisciplinary approach, bringing together ideas and concepts from computer science and information systems, business and organization science as well as cognitive science. In this paper we give a snapshot of existing work related to Learning Software Organizations (LSOs). From our perspective, we list topics currently discussed in research and practice in accordance with the basic steps of a learning cycle.

1 Introduction

IEEE Software magazine's current series of so called *"Country Reports"* [9, 10, 18, 22] clearly states how important the software industry has become for countries around the world. Software is seen as a key element that governs competition at the threshold to the 21st century. To keep pace in the accelerating business, software organizations have to continuously improve their products and processes (i.e., the software and software developing processes). Achieving quantum leaps in improvement, however, requires leveraging the knowledge of highly educated, skilled, and experienced employees. A Learning Software Organization (LSO) establishes the means to manage this knowledge and turns intellectual capital into market shares and profit. On their way towards a LSO, companies have to create a culture that promotes continuous learning and fosters the exchange of experience. This requires an interdisciplinary approach, bringing together experts and/or ideas from computer science and information systems, business and organization science as well as cognitive science. Still, many questions in this field are unresolved and under heavy research as indicated by the growing number of publications in this area.

In the remainder of this paper we shortly describe some available methods and techniques for implementing LSOs (Section 2). After this brief introduction, Section 3 lists ideas reflecting the state-of-the art and state-of-the practice in building LSO as presented at the 3rd International Workshop on Learning Software Organizations (LSO'01) in Kaiserslautern, Germany.

K.-D. Althoff, R.L. Feldmann, and W. Müller (Eds.): LSO 2001, LNCS 2176, pp. 2-6, 2001.

3 Currently Discussed Topics in Research and Practice

After the short introduction, we now take a look at this year's talks given at the 3rd International Workshop on Learning Software Organizations (LSO 2001). We group the contributions according to the four steps of the basic learning cycle:

Step 1: Planning LSOs

In [26] Ralph Trittmann presents a framework for knowledge management, based on organization theory. The framework takes into account technical infrastructure, organizational structure, coordination, and motivation aspects. Based on this information the framework allows to compare knowledge management activities in different organizations. Therefore, when planning knowledge management activities, an organization may use the framework to select the appropriate form of knowledge management for its purposes.

With CORONET-Train Pfahl et. al. provide a methodology for supporting web-based collaborative learning [23]. A network of learning relations between novices, practitioners, and experts is described for enhanced collaboration and to support learning by teaching, coaching, and mentoring. The approach seems to be interesting, especially for organizations with a large workforce.

Requirements for knowledge management support in an academic environment are examined in [15]. The authors list the key areas of knowledge management regarding content, processes, organization, and technical infrastructure issues. The outlined tailored solution can serve as an example for implementing such an environment in other research and development organizations.

Step 2: Applications

Judith Segal provides us in [24] with insight information on the influence of Software Process Improvement (SPI) activities on an organizational memory and learning. The case study discusses the lessons learned of an organization that implemented a manual of software best practice. Some practical deficiencies of an accepted techno-centric model for SPI are illustrated and, therefore, may be avoided in future.

In [28] Angi Voß et. al. present a web-based infrastructure for collaborative data mining. This example tackles the problems of implementing a virtual enterprise organization consisting of different units spread over Europe. Based on an existing organization it is discussed how such a virtual enterprise can be supported in exchanging ideas and information.

Another example from practice is described in [11]. The usage of a skills management system of a Software Consultancy Company is described and pros and cons of the given system are discussed.

Step 3: Analysis

Lessons learned about structuring and describing knowledge in an experience management system are discussed in [21]. Based on three implementation examples the authors analyze what can be improved regarding the organization of knowledge for future implementations.

Automated knowledge elicitation is a promising way to get information out of data sources. The authors of [19] discuss how web-based data mining services can be utilized for this purpose in the context of a learning software organization. For companies that are currently constrained by the high cost of data mining software, the described approach may offer an interesting alternative to access this kind of enabling technology for their data analyzing processes.

A concrete model with a two-level feedback system for learning in software organizations is presented in [20]. The analysis is based on software measurement activities in development projects and takes into account six different areas. Companies may use the analysis results to changes their organization of measurement activities.

Step 4: Learning

To foster process integrated learning Philipp Starkloff and Katja Pook suggest the ADVISOR approach [25]. The approach organizes learning and training around the process chains to increase process awareness among employees. A concrete e-learning system is presented that may be applicable for many other organizations.

In [16] the authors are concerned with task-specific knowledge management in a process-centered environment. The suggested feedback loop allows continuous process improvement and, therefore, integrates learning aspects in the daily work of software developers.

Finally, Matthias Brandt and Markus Nick are concerned with computer-support for reuse of project management experience [8]. A reference model for a project management experience base is given. This reference model may be used to document the learned experience in other organizations as well.

4 Summary and Outlook

Concluding, we can state, that advances in Learning Software Organizations have been gained during the last years. However, in 2001 we are still on our way towards a comprehensive methodology for building and running LSOs more effectively. Additional research work and practical evaluation has to be spent in the coming years.

References

1. A. Abecker, A. Bernardi, K. Hinkelmann, O. Kühn, M. Sintek: Towards a Technology for Organizational Memories, IEEE Intelligent Systems, 1998.
2. D. Aha R. Weber (eds.): In Proc. of the Workshop on Intelligent Lessons Learned Systems at 17th National Conference on AI (AAAI-00), 2000.
3. K.-D. Althoff, A. Birk, S. Hartkopf, W. Müller, M. Nick, D. Surmann, C. Tautz: Systematic Population, Utilization, and Maintenance of a Repository for Comprehensive Reuse. In G. Ruhe, F. Bomarius (eds.), *Learning Software Organizations - Methodology and Applications*, LNCS # 1756, Springer Verlag, 2000.
4. V.R. Basili: Quantitative evaluation of software methodology. In Proc. of the 1st Pan-Pacific Computer Conference, Melbourne, Australia, September 1985.
5. V.R. Basili, G. Caldiera, D. Rombach: Experience Factory; In J.J. Marciniak (ed.), *Encyclopedia of Software Engineering*, vol 1, 469–476; John Wiley & Sons; 1994.
6. V.R. Basili, H.D. Rombach: The TAME Project: Towards improvement-oriented software environments. In *IEEE Transactions on Software Engineering SE-14(6),* 758-773, 1988.

7. A. Birk, C. Tautz: Knowledge Management of Software Engineering Lessons Learned; In Proc. of the 10th Conf. on Software Engineering and Knowledge Engineering; San Francisco Bay; USA. Skokie, Illinois, USA: Knowledge Systems Institute; 1998.
8. M. Brandt, M. Nick: Computer-Supported Reuse of Project Management Experience with an Experience Base. LNCS # 2176, Springer Verlag, 2001.
9. M. Broy, S. Hartkopf, K. Kohler, D. Rombach: Germany: Combing Software and Application Competencies. In *IEEE Software*, 18(4), July/August2001.
10. R. Cochran: Ireland: A Software Success Story. In *IEEE Software*, 18(2), March/April 2001.
11. T. Dingsøyr, E. Røyrvik: Skills Management as Knowledge Technology in a Software Consultancy Company. LNCS # 2176, Springer Verlag, 2001.
12. R.L. Feldmann, C. Tautz: Improving Best Practices Through Explicit Documentation of Experience About Software Technologies. In: C. Hawkins et. al. (eds.), INSPIRE III Process Improvement Through Training and education, The British Computer Society, 1998.
13. A. Goodall (ed.): Survey of Knowledge Management Tools - Part I & II, *Intelligence in Industry*, vol. 8, January/February 1999.
14. T.F. Gordon, A. Voss, G. Richter, O. Märker: Zeno: Groupeware for Discourses on the Internet. In *Künstliche Intelligenz*, Nr. 2 / 2001, p.43-45, ISSN 0933-1875, 2001.
15. C. Gresse von Wangenheim, D. Lichtnow, A. von Wangenheim, E. Comunello: Supporting Knowledge Management in University Software R&D Groups. LNCS # 2176, Springer Verlag, 2001.
16. H. Holz, A. Könnecker, F. Maurer: Task-Specific Knowledge Management in a Process-Centred SEE. LNCS # 2176, Springer Verlag, 2001.
17. C. Johansson, P. Hall, M. Coquard: "Talk to Paula and Peter - They Are Experienced" - The Experience Engine in a Nutshell. In G. Ruhe, F. Bomarius (eds.), *Learning Software Organizations - Methodology and Applications*, LNCS # 1756, Springer Verlag, 2000.
18. D. Ju: China's Budding Software Industry. In *IEEE Software*, 18(3), May/June 2001.
19. S. Krishnaswamy, S. Wai Loke, A. Zaslavsky: Knowledge Elicitation Through Web-based Data Mining Services. LNCS # 2176, Springer Verlag, 2001.
20. C. Lewerentz, H. Rust, Frank Simon: A Model for Analyzing Measurement Based Feedback Loops in Software Development Projects. LNCS # 2176, Springer Verlag, 2001.
21. M. Lindvall, M. Frey, P. Costa, R. Tesoriero: Lessons Learned about Structuring and Describing Experience for Three Experience Bases. LNCS # 2176, Springer Verlag, 2001.
22. D. Moitra: India's Software Industry. *IEEE Software*, 18(1), January/February 2001.
23. D. Pfahl, N. Angkasaputra, C. Differding, G. Ruhe: CORONET-Train: A Methodology for Web-Based Collaborative Learning in Software Organisations. LNCS # 2176, Springer Verlag, 2001.
24. J. Segal: Organisational Learning and Software Process Improvement: A Case Study. LNCS # 2176, Springer Verlag, 2001.
25. P. Starkloff, K. Pook: Process-Integrated Learning: The ADVISOR Approach for Corporate Development. LNCS # 2176, Springer Verlag, 2001.
26. R. Trittmann: The Organic and the Mechanistic Form of Managing Knowledge in Software Development. LNCS # 2176, Springer Verlag, 2001.
27. G. van Heijst, R. van der Speck, E. Kruizinga: Organizing corporate memories. In Proc. of the 10th Banff Knowledge Acquisition for Knowledge-Based Systems Workshop, Department of Computer Science, University of Calgary, Calgary, Alberta, Canada, 1996.
28. A. Voß, G. Richter, S. Moyle, A. Jorge: Collaboration support for virtual data mining enterprises. LNCS # 2176, Springer Verlag, 2001.

Part 2:

Keynote Addresses and Panel

Keynote Address: Organizational Learning in Dynamic Domains

Scott Henninger

Department of Computer Science & Engineering
University of Nebraska-Lincoln
Lincoln, NE 68588-0115
scotth@cse.unl.edu

Abstract. Enabling organizational learning involves more than repositories and search engines. At its core, it involves the design of work practices that balance the desire for innovation with knowledge of past experiences and best practices. This tension is particularly acute in the software industry, which involves the development of a highly variable product that dictates the need for continuous process adjustments.

This paper explores the issues of managing knowledge in dynamic domains requiring significant levels of improvisation within each repetition of the process. The challenge is not one of capturing and finding complete solutions to problems, but the more difficult task of finding and integrating partial solutions that can serve as the baseline for continuous improvement, and hence, organizational learning. Techniques will be explored that couple process and workflow management with knowledge management to capture and build an experiential body of knowledge for software development activities.

1 Introduction

While the Business School concepts of organizational memory [1, 2, 48, 52] and organizational learning [7, 8, 19, 33, 36, 38, 41, 46] have been around for some time, most rely mainly on knowledge exchange between people in organizations. Indeed, these may be the most important and critical components of any knowledge management or organizational learning strategy. But the promise of the computer networked organization is to further strengthen these knowledge exchanges and business processes with enhanced communications tools and information technologies.

The need for tools supporting learning organizations, the primary focus of the Workshop on Learning Software Organizations, are therefore becoming increasingly important to gain competitive advantage, or just survive, in today's fast changing business environment. Designing tools to support learning organizations through methodologies and tools to facilitate the systematic capture and use of organizational knowledge has proven elusive. Knowledge Management has become a hot topic in recent years [26, 43], but is only one piece of the organizational learning processes, as shown in Fig. 1. Workflow systems automate business processes and deliver documents during workflow, but tend to be weak on learning and improvement tools. Experience factory approaches [11] have a workflow conducive to organizational learning, but current tools have largely focused on repository technologies for the

K.-D. Althoff, R.L. Feldmann, and W. Müller (Eds.): LSO 2001, LNCS 2176, pp. 8-16, 2001.

at all stages of the development lifecycle [13, 27]. Accomplishing this involves not only a repository and some search tools, but organizational structures that use, store, and produce experiences that can be used as the basis for future development efforts.

2.1 The LSO Process

Fig. 1 shows the LSO process as a cycle of using software development resources to create new products, which leads to new knowledge creation and in turn becomes new software development resources, normally after an analysis phase that synthesizes and packages experiences to become new development resources. These then become resources to be used as the basis for new product development efforts.

The software development resources can take on various forms, including guidelines, standards, experience packages, pattern languages, manuals, software development ontologies. These are but a few of the proposed and possible kinds of resources available to software developers. Knowledge management tools with broad ranges of resource types remain few and far between, making this a fertile ground for future research.

Analysis tools have received some attention, particularly in terms of lessons learned repositories [3]. Some work has also been done on tools for measuring the effectiveness of repositories [23] and using user feedback to calculate the perceived usefulness of knowledge assets [4]. But little work to date has concentrated on tools to *analyze* emerging knowledge and put into a form that is broadly applicable. Even tools as simple as data mining may be useful here, but some creative thinking is needed on how the artifacts created in project development can be turned into knowledge assets. Domain analysis [5] and other software reuse research may prove useful here.

Of particular interest in this paper is the product creation step in Fig. 1. Although this step has received the most attention in the software engineering field, most approaches view projects as the central unit of study. This is beginning to change, as frameworks, architectures, patterns, domain analysis, and other fields place emphasis on creating resources for product families that cross project boundaries. But these fields have not sought to understand the issues involved in developing new knowledge – experiences packaging [11], if you will – during project execution.

The exploration of how existing knowledge is brought to bear on a problem and used to create new knowledge [39] during product development has yet to be pursued in any kind of scale. This is a critical area for LSO research, as it is central to the process of learning in organizations [42].

2.2 Knowledge Use

One of the most critical elements of support for learning organization is integrating technical solution into daily work activities. Not only are tools needed for knowledge capture and representation, we also need to design work practices that incorporate the use of existing knowledge as a normal part of the workflow. These issues present interesting and important socio-technical issues that cannot be solved in isolation. Technical solutions need to be informed by social and organizational processes or risk being ignored as irrelevant or distracting. Likewise, the ability to improve the social processes of a learning organization depends critically on technology to improve dissemination and generally expand one's sphere of knowledge beyond what exists in fallible working memory or fragile social networks [51].

The underlying problem is not so much of capturing and storing knowledge, but using existing knowledge as the basis for current activities. Forcing the use of repositories do not solve the problem and incentive programs in areas such as software reuse have demonstrated that good solutions are not easy to come by [44]. Part of the problem is as much a matter of human perception as it is reality. It is fascinating how people are unwilling to spend ten minutes to search for something that will take them ten hours to create and debug on their own. Nonetheless, it is clear that the information needs to be readily available at the developer's fingertips in an easily assimilated form before people will begin the often difficult task of understanding someone else's solution to a complex problem.

Our approach has tried to grapple with this problem by creating applicability rules describing the context in which development resources are applicable [31]. If a project finds that cross-platform and cross-browser requirements are best met through using the Java Plug-in, then this knowledge can be encoded in rules that point people to this result. The development team is stepped through a question-answer session designed to elicit project characteristics for the areas known to the repository designers. Relevant resources are then assigned to the project according to chosen characteristics and the rule-based system. This kind of *information delivery*, telling people what information exists instead of waiting for them to discover that it exists and needs to be searched for, is critical to broaden the knowledge sphere of individuals [25]. Agent technology is another obvious area that can be applied some support for helping people use, or at least identify, existing knowledge. Understanding and assimilating found or delivered information to the task at hand is another step in the process of knowledge use, but has received little attention to date.

2.3 Knowledge Creation

Every project is unique in some respect. This is the nature of new product development – and software engineering is somewhat unique in this respect. Most engineering disciplines involve some degree of repetition of components, many involving a manufacturing process that is repeated as exactly as possible. Software development has neither. Component-based approaches are just beginning to appear and inherently address problems lending themselves to domain-specific product families. Manufacturing processes are negligible in cost, process, and effort.

The implication, for our purposes, is that it is not enough to consider the use of existing knowledge. Because software development (and design in general) has so much variance between projects, we need to focus more on the knowledge creation process [26]. One way to look at this is as a process of improvisation, where knowledge is not constructed from a blank sheet of paper, but "involves and partly depends on the exploitation of prior routines and knowledge" [21]. In other words, knowledge creation depends on knowledge use and knowledge use leads to knowledge creation (see Fig. 1).

New conceptualizations of knowledge management are needed that place the knowledge creation process as a central component [26] of the system and methodologies dictating its use. Tools alone will not be enough to solve these inherently difficult problems. But tools developed with an understanding of the intertwined nature of knowledge creation and use will go further to support learning software organizations.

3 Steps Towards the Next Generation

The creation of experience bases for learning software organizations have thus far received the lion's share of attention and research [12, 14, 15, 22, 29]. And it is a common belief is that data mining is the answer to the question of next-generation tools for organizational memories. But a close inspection of Fig. 1 and the previous sections should reveal that search technologies should be the tool of last resort. Finding relevant information is only one step of the process, and search methods should be used only when an LSO tool fails to provide adequate workflow support. Search, information filtering, data mining, and etc., have their place and can play a vital role, particularly in the analysis and knowledge creation phases. But the emphasis in supporting a LSO should be placed on the design of work practices and the tools that support activities by placing key information in the hands of the user when it is needed. This will involve understanding software development work practices better and developing frameworks for tools supporting the social, organizational, and cognitive processes involved.

The creation of knowledge, and indeed the process of creating software systems, is a social process. People work together, collaborate, challenge each others' assumptions, and generally set the knowledge creation process in motion. They create networked communities of practice [16] within the organization that disseminate and exploit existing knowledge and work together to create new knowledge when novel circumstances arise. They collaboratively adapt canonical accounts from manuals and other existing resources to novel situations to create new insights and learn. Tools such as Eureka and other systems that support the creation and dissemination of stories [26] are needed that support collective learning processes and the social construction of knowledge [17].

Coupling repository and knowledge-based technology with software process support has received some attention [24, 40], including the BORE (Building an Organizational Repository of Experiences) work we have been conducting at the University of Nebraska [28, 30]. But much more remains to be investigated. Workflow and software process systems are notoriously inflexible and unable to fully support the kinds of dynamic knowledge creation and innovation found in real-world software development efforts. Support for process deviations [18] are needed, but so are alternative conceptualizations on plans and how people really go about executing plans. Suchman's studies found that people use continuous feedback from the situation to re-evaluate and reformulate their plans [49]. People use the plans only as a guideline - a resource - not as a specification for action. This is very similar to Schön's notion of reflection-in-action [45], which reveals how practitioners combine past experiences and feedback from their actions to formulate plans for next steps. These an other perspectives, such as activity theory [10] which looks at how tools mediate between people and actions, all have potential to shed light on the complex phenomenon of LSO and inform the design of supporting tools.

There are also a number of intelligent and semi-intelligent technologies that are needed to support an LSO process, particularly in the analysis and information delivery stages. An interesting twist on information filtering is current research on social navigation [20, 47], collaborative filtering [37], and recommendation systems [9, 50]. This set of techniques uses statistical analyses of behavior by other users to guide users toward relevant information, whether it be musical tastes, Web pages, or locating experts [35]. This opens up an entirely different set of tools that can provide decision support that is guided and informed by aggregate behavior of others. Not only can such techniques support communities of practice, they can also play an important role in analysis tools that can identify current practices being used and whether or not they should become part of the organization's standard work practices.

These are but a few of the perspectives that have the potential to address the social, organizational, cognitive, and technical issues necessary to begin understanding how tools can be created that meaningfully and profoundly support learning software organizations.

4 Concluding Remarks

The nascent Learning Software Organizations community has established a track record of concern for creating tools that disseminate best practices within organizations. In order to take the next steps, an improved understanding of the interplay between exploiting existing knowledge and generating new knowledge is needed. Tools are needed that support improvisation while basing decision on known best practices. In this paper, I have described some of the issues involved in the LSO process and have outlined potential sources for improving our understanding of using existing resources in dynamically evolving domains. These are just pointers to the first steps that need to be taken to better understand the social, cognitive, and technical processes involved in creating tool support for Learning Software Organizations.

Acknowledgements. This research was funded by the National Science Foundation (CCR-9502461 and CCR-9988540).

References

1. M. S. Ackerman, "Answer Garden: A tool for growing organizational memory," in *MIT Sloan School of Management*. Boston, MA, 1994.
2. M. S. Ackerman and C. A. Halverson, "Reexamining Organizational Memory," *Comm. of the ACM*, vol. 43, pp. 59-64, 2000.
3. D. W. Aha and R. Weber (Eds.), *Intelligent Lessons Learned Systems: Papers from the 2000 Workshop*. Menlo Park, CA: AAAI Press, http://www.aic.nrl.navy.mil/AAAI00-ILLS-Workshop/, 2000.
4. K.-D. Altoff, M. Nick, and C. Tautz, "Improving Organizational Memories through User Feedback," *2nd International Workshop on Learning Software Organizations (LSO 2000)*, Oulu, Finland, pp. 27-44, 2000.

5. G. Arango, "Domain Analysis: From Art Form to Engineering Discipline," *Fifth International Workshop on Software Specification and Design*, Pittsburgh, PA, pp. 152-159, 1989.
6. J. Arent, J. Nørbjerg, and M. H. Pederson, "Creating Organizational Knowledge in Software Process Improvement," *2nd International Workshop on Learning Software Organizations (LSO 2000)*, Oulu, Finland, 2000.
7. C. Argyris, "Double Loop Learning in Organizations," *Harvard Business Review*, vol. Sept-Oct, pp. 115-125, 1977.
8. C. Argyris and D. A. Schön, *Organizational Learning: A Theory of Action Perspective*. Reading, MA: Addison-Wesley, 1978.
9. M. Balabanovic and Y. Shoham, "Referral Web: Combining Social Networks and Collaborative Filtering," *Comm. of the ACM*, vol. 40, pp. 66-72, 1997.
10. J. E. Bardram, "Plans and Situated Action: An Activity Theory Approach to Workflow Systems," *Proc. European Computer Supported Cooperative Work (ECSCW 97)*, Lancaster, UK, 1997.
11. V. Basili, G. Caldiera, and D. Rombach, "Experience Factory," in *Encyclopedia of Software Engineering*: Wiley & Sons, 1994, pp. 469-476.
12. V. Basili, M. Lindvall, and P. Costa, "Implementing the Experience Factory Soncepts as a Set of Experience Bases," *International Conference on Software Engineering and Knowledge Engineering (SEKE '01)*, Buenos Aires, Argentina, 2001.
13. V. R. Basili and H. D. Rombach, "Support for Comprehensive Reuse," *Software Engineering Journal*, pp. 303-316, 1991.
14. A. Birk and F. Kröschel, "A Knowledge Management Lifecycle for Experience Packages on Software Engineering Technologies," *1st International Workshop on Learning Software Organizations (LSO 1999)*, Kaiserlautern, FRG, pp. 115-126, 1999.
15. M. Broome and P. Runeson, "Technical Requirements for the Implementation of an Experience Base," *11th International Conference on Software Engineering and Knowledge Engineering (SEKE '99)*, pp. 87-102, 1999.
16. J. S. Brown and P. Duguid, "Organizational Learning and Communities-of-Practice: Toward a Unified View of Working, Learning, and Innovation," *Organization Science*, vol. 2, pp. 40-57, 1991.
17. J. S. Brown and P. Duguid, *The Social Life of Information*: Harvard Univ. Press, 2000.
18. G. Cugola, "Tolerating Deviations in Process Support Systems via Flexible Enactment of Process Models," *IEEE Transactions on Software Engineering*, vol. 24, pp. 982-1000, 1998.
19. T. H. Davenport and L. Prusak, "Working Knowledge -- How Organizations Manage What They Know," *Harvard Business School Press*, 1998.
20. A. Dieberger, P. Dourish, K. Höök, P. Resnick, and A. Wexelbat, "Social Navigation: Techniques for Building More Usable Systems," *interactions*, vol. 7, pp. 36-45, 2000.
21. T. Dybå, "Improvisation in Small Software Organizations," *IEEE Software*, vol. 17, pp. 82-87, 2000.
22. R. L. Feldmann, "Developing a Tailored Reuse Repository Structure - Experience and First Results," *1st International Workshop on Learning Software Organizations (LSO 1999)*, Kaiserlautern, FRG, 1999.
23. R. L. Feldmann, M. Nick, and M. Frey, "Towards Industrial-Strength Measurement Programs for Reuse and Experience Repository Systems," *2nd International Workshop on Learning Software Organizations (LSO 2000)*, Oulu, Finland, pp. 7-18, 2000.
24. S. T. Fiorini, J. C. S. do Prado Leite, and C. J. de Lucenda, "Reusing Process Patterns," *2nd International Workshop on Learning Software Organizations (LSO 2000)*, Oulu, Finland, pp. 19-37, 2000.
25. G. Fischer, A. Lemke, and T. Schwab, "Knowledge-Based Help Systems," *Proc. Human Factors in Computing Systems (CHI '85)*, pp. 161-167, 1985.

26. G. Fischer and J. Ostwald, "Knowledge Management: Problems, Promises, Realities, and Challenges," *IEEE Intelligent Systems*, vol. 16, pp. 60-72, 2001.
27. S. Henninger, "Accelerating the Successful Reuse of Problem Solving Knowledge Through the Domain Lifecycle," *Fourth International Conference on Software Reuse*, Orlando, FL, pp. 124-133, 1996.
28. S. Henninger, "An Environment for Reusing Software Processes," *Fifth International Conference on Software Reuse*, Victoria, British Columbia, pp. 103 - 112, 1998.
29. S. Henninger, "An Evolutionary Approach to Constructing Effective Software Reuse Repositories," *ACM Transactions on Software Engineering and Methodology*, 1997.
30. S. Henninger, "Using Software Process to Support Learning Software Organizations," *1st International Workshop on Learning Software Organizations (LSO 1999)*, Kaiserlautern, FRG, 1999.
31. S. Henninger and K. Baumgarten, "A Case-Based Approach to Tailoring Software Processes," *International Conference on Case-Based Reasoning (ICCBR 01)*, Vancouver, B.C., 2001.
32. S. Henninger, K. Lappala, and A. Raghavendran, "An Organizational Learning Approach to Domain Analysis," *17th International Conference on Software Engineering*, Seattle, WA, pp. 95-104, 1995.
33. G. P. Huber, "Organizational Learning: The Contributing Processes and the Literatures," *Organization Science*, vol. 2, pp. 88-115, 1991.
34. C. Johannson, P. Hall, and M. Coquard, "Talk to Paula and Peter -- They are Experienced," *1st International Workshop on Learning Software Organizations (LSO 1999)*, Kaiserlautern, FRG, pp. 69-76, 1999.
35. H. Kautz, B. Selman, and M. Shah, "Referral Web: Combining Social Networks and Collaborative Filtering," *Comm. of the ACM*, vol. 40, pp. 63-65, 1997.
36. D. H. Kim, "The Link Between Individual and Organizational Learning," *Sloan Management Review*, vol. Fall, pp. 37-50, 1993.
37. J. Konstan, B. Miller, D. Maltz, J. L. Herlocker, L. R. Gordon, and J. Riedl, "GroupLens: Applying Collaborative Filtering to Usenet News," *Comm. of the ACM*, vol. 40, pp. 77-87, 1997.
38. B. Levitt and J. G. March, "Organizational Learning," *Annual Review of Sociology*, vol. 14, pp. 319-340, 1988.
39. J. G. March, "Exploration and Exploitation in Organizational Learning," *Organizational Science*, vol. 2, pp. 71-87, 1991.
40. F. Maurer and B. Dellen, "Process Support for Virtual Software Organizations," *1st International Workshop on Learning Software Organizations (LSO 1999)*, Kaiserlautern, FRG, 1999.
41. E. C. Nevis, A. J. DiBella, and J. M. Gould, "Understanding Organizations as Learning Systems," *Sloan Management Review*, vol. 36, pp. 75-85, 1995.
42. I. Nonaka and H. Takeychi, *The Knowledge-Creating Company: How Japanese Companies Create the Dynamics of Innovation*. New York: Oxford Univ. Press, 1995.
43. D. O'Leary, "Enterprise Knowledge Management," *IEEE Computer*, vol. 31, pp. 54-61, 1998.
44. J. S. Poulin and J. M. Caruso, "A Reuse Metrics and Return on Investment Model," in *Advances in Software Reuse*. Los Alamitos, CA: IEEE Computer Society Press, 1993, pp. 152-166.
45. D. A. Schön, *The Reflective Practitioner: How Professionals Think in Action*. New York: Basic Books, 1983.
46. P. Senge, *The Fifth Discipline: The Art and Practice of the Learning Organization*. New York: Currency Doubleday, 1990.

47. U. Shardanand and P. Maes, "Social Information Filtering: Algorithms for Automating "Word of Mouth"," *Proc. Human Factors in Computing Systems (CHI '95)*, Denver, CO, pp. 210-217, 1995.
48. E. W. Stein and V. Zwass, "Actualizing Organizational Memory with Information Systems," *Information Systems Research*, vol. 6, pp. 85-117, 1995.
49. L. Suchman, *Plans and Situated Action: The problem of human-machine communication.* Cambridge, UK: Cambridge Univ. Press, 1987.
50. L. Terveen, W. Hill, B. Amento, D. W. McDonald, and J. Creter, "PHOAKS: A System for Sharing Recommendations," *Comm. of the ACM*, vol. 40, pp. 59-62, 1997.
51. L. G. Terveen, P. G. Selfridge, and M. D. Long, "From 'Folklore' To 'Living Design Memory'," *Proceedings InterCHI '93*, Amsterdam, pp. 15-22, 1993.
52. J. P. Walsh and G. R. Ungson, "Organizational Memory," *Academy of Management Review*, vol. 16, pp. 57-91, 1991.

Keynote Address: How Do Companies Learn? Selected Applications from the IT Sector

Franz Lehner

Faculty of Business and Economics, University of Regensburg, Universitätsstr. 31
D-93053 Regensburg, Germany
franz.lehner@wiwi.uni-regensburg.de

Abstract. Organizational Learning is a phenomenon that is hard to grasp. In software development, as in other areas, the chance for significant improvements depends on the ability to learn from past experiences. But even here, organizational learning is not the natural consequence of a project, not even of successful projects. This can be traced back to two reasons. On the one hand, such success is frequently the result of complex interactions during the course of the project, and it is often difficult to establish a time and place relationship between cause and effect. Furthermore, assessment is done on the basis of certain interests, which often only become transparent towards the end of the project. On the other hand, company incentive systems often result in people quickly going on to the next project, and continuing to study a finished project is considered a loss of time. Thus, as expected, the learning effect is low.

After a brief introduction to understanding organizational learning and learning organizations, selected applications and examples from the IT sector will be presented and discussed. At the end, an attempt will be made to relate the results of a current knowledge management study among Germany´s top 500 companies on the theory of organizational memory and success factors for software projects.

K.-D. Althoff, R.L. Feldmann, and W. Müller (Eds.): LSO 2001, LNCS 2176, p. 17, 2001.

Panel: Knowledge Creating Communities

Dietmar Janetzko

University of Freiburg
Institute of Computer Science and Social Research
Department of Cognitive Science, Friedrichstr. 50
D-79098 Freiburg
dietmar@cognition.iig.uni-freiburg.de

Abstract. The paper gives an outline of basic steps required to set up a environments that foster the elicitation of knowledge in communities.

1 Introduction

Traditionally, software that makes use of knowledge (knowledge-based systems, in particular expert-systems), had a focus on single experts. It may or may be not known today that viewing experts as a repository of knowledge was in itself a step back from a more ambitious goal: If Artificial Intelligence was too ambitious to be realized, modelling in a more confined realm, i.e., expertise of single humans, could prove to be the more promising research strategy [2]. This is clearly an example of a fairly standard research strategy well known under the name of divide and conquer.

Surprisingly, quite the opposite approach turned out to be successful, too. Instead of focusing on single experts more recent approaches in knowledge management and also Artificial Intelligence have opened up the perspective and concentrate now on knowledge of communities ("communities of practice"). Compared to Artificial Intelligence, which has been - at least at the beginning of this approach - funded generously, this line of software development has become quite influential without massive protection and support by industry, military, and academia. We call this approach *knowledge creating communities.* Well known examples of knowledge creating communities are web-sites that capture cross-sellings and use them for corporate filtering or portal-sides that collect comments on various products and aggregate this type of knowledge (e.g., by using qualitative methods).

Knowledge creating communities may be described precisely (e.g., members of an organisation or company), but they may also extend to more or less anonymous visitors who share an interest in a web-site [5]. Recently, software production within a true knowledge creating community, viz., the open source community, has attracted much attention [4].

K.-D. Althoff, R.L. Feldmann, and W. Müller (Eds.): LSO 2001, LNCS 2176, pp. 18-20, 2001.

2 Tasks in Knowledge Creating Communities

Clearly, there is a broad range of knowledge creating communities differing both on the level of the type of community and the kind of knowledge provided. Commonalities between them surface, however, when analyzing the knowledge. To actually exploit the knowledge of knowledge creating communities a number of tasks have to be addressed successfully:

Creation of a living community and a culture of knowledge sharing. This is a community that generates behavioural or verbal contributions, which represents the raw material for knowledge. One of the reasons to take a closer look on communities like the open source community is to find out whether or not this apparently efficient way of software production can be transferred to other fields, too. This idea has become know under the name *community building* (e.g., [3]). The basic questions here are to find out (1) whether or not the open source community is the only model of a knowledge creating community and if possible (2) the general mechanisms of such communities.

Installation of enabling technologies. Clearly a community that shares the knowledge is not enough to use the knowledge. There have to be techniques that support capturing or eliciting the knowledge. For high-traffic web-sites, for instance, collaborative filtering has become a good approach to elicit and also exploit knowledge in a community (cf. [1]).

Application of exploitation technologies. These are techniques (e.g., mining techniques) that aggregate the raw data such that the result (viz., knowledge) may fuel other applications. The type of knowledge that may be captured in knowledge creating communities is quite diverse and ranges from, e.g.,

- co-occurencies of concepts to
- rules (e.g., extracted from cross-sellings via corporte filtering), or
- ontologies (e.g., extracted from news posting via qualitative methods), or
- classification grids (e.g., generated by Bayesian Networks).

Tools and methods suitable to capture this kind of knowledge come mostly form text mining. They can be used to discover realtionships in large volumes of text (word processing files, spreadsheets, e-mails, Web-Sites) and analyze them

Representation methodologies. These are approaches at describing and representing community knowledge in a machine readable way (e.g., topic maps based on XML, shareable and reusable Ontology).

References

1. Claypool, M., Makoto Waseda, Ph. L. & Brown, D. (2001). Implicit Interest Indicators. In *Proceedings of ACM Intelligent User Interfaces Conference (IUI)* USA, January 14-17, 2001, Santa Fe, New Mexico,

2. Jackson, P. (1999). Introduction to Expert Systems. Harlow, UK: Addison Wesley.
3. Kim, Amy Jo (2000). Community Building on the Web : Secret Strategies for Successful Online Communities. Berkeley, CA: Peachpit Press.
4. Raymond, E. S. (1999). The Cathedral and the Bazar. Musings on Linux and Open Source by an Accidental Revolutionary. Cambridge, MA: O'Reilly
5. Smith, R. G. & Farquhar, A. (2000). The Road Ahead for Knowledge Management. An AI Perspective. AI Magazine, Winter 2000, 17-40.

Part 3:

Planning LSOs

The Organic and the Mechanistic Form of Managing Knowledge in Software Development

Ralph Trittmann

University of Cologne, Department of Information Systems,
Prof. Dr. Werner Mellis, Pohligstr. 1 , D-50969 Cologne, Germany
www.systementwicklung.uni-koeln.de
Ralph.Trittmann@uni-koeln.de
http://www.systementwicklung.uni-koeln.de

Abstract. This paper presents a framework for knowledge management in software development. The dimensions of the framework are drawn from organization theory. Therefore, it allows for a systematic comparison of knowledge management activities in different companies. By applying established theories from various disciplines, two basic forms of knowledge management can be derived from this framework. The organic form is fitting when the primary intention of knowledge transfer is achieving innovation effects. The mechanistic form is suitable for companies mainly aiming at leveraging existing knowledge. The findings of a survey generally support the existence of the two forms of knowledge management in practice. However, both forms may coexist, when referred to distinct dimensions of knowledge like application domain, methodological, and technical knowledge.

1 Introduction

Software development is often troubled by cost overruns, late deliveries, low product quality, and users' dissatisfaction [1]. Furthermore, various sectors of the software industry are confronted with increasing instability due to continuous changes in technology, unpredictable strategies of competitors, and rapidly changing customer needs [2]. The emerging field of knowledge management could be useful in addressing existing problems and new challenges in software development.

While a lot of knowledge management approaches can be found in literature, the concept of the experience factory is the most popular approach related to the special needs of software development. The experience factory is a logical and/or physical organization that supports project development by analyzing and synthesizing all kinds of experience, acting as a repository, and supplying that experience to various projects on demand [3]. However, published case studies indicate that knowledge management activities of software companies differ significantly from each other [e.g. 4, 5, 6, 7, 8]. Some of the measures reported in these studies are in conflict with the recommendations of the experience factory. Therefore, implementing an experience factory does not seem to be the only form of managing knowledge in software development. The question arises which knowledge management activities are suitable given a certain situation an enterprise finds itself in. Aiming at answering

K.-D. Althoff, R.L. Feldmann, and W. Müller (Eds.): LSO 2001, LNCS 2176, pp. 22-36, 2001.

this question, first of all one has to compare different approaches for knowledge management in practice systematically.

This paper has three objectives: First, to describe a framework allowing for comparisons between various knowledge management activities. Second, to identify distinct forms of knowledge management and to justify their existence by pointing out their different benefits. Third, to evaluate whether the theoretically derived forms of knowledge management actually do exist in practice.

2 A Framework for Knowledge Management

Although there is no generally agreed upon definition of knowledge management, it is nearly undisputed that facilitating the transfer of knowledge is at the heart of knowledge management [9, 10]. Therefore, in the following the terms knowledge management and management of knowledge transfers will be used interchangeably, focusing on intra-organizational transfer. In general, knowledge transfer aims at providing knowledge to staff members so that they are able to better accomplish their tasks. Knowledge transfer consists of the following steps: Identifying knowledge sources or receivers, transforming knowledge into a suitable format for transmission, transmitting the knowledge between sender and receiver, interpreting and applying the transmitted knowledge. Managing knowledge transfers requires various measures supporting the different steps of knowledge transfer, including technical aspects as well as social and psychological aspects [11].

Consequently, a framework for managing knowledge has to deal with these different aspects. Furthermore, the framework must allow for a non-ambiguous classification of knowledge management activities according to defined categories. Last but not least, the framework must not be based on an assumption about "good knowledge management". With such an approach capturing the variety of knowledge management measures would be impossible. Existing frameworks do not address all of these needs. For example, they focus mainly on technical aspects [12], they do not allow for a non-redundant classification of measures [13], or they are based on a normative approach of knowledge management [14].

A framework addressing the needs described above can be developed by applying the scientific findings of organization theory. In this case, so-called organization areas derived from organization theory and suitable for comparing different organizational designs will be used as dimensions of a framework for describing knowledge management. In the following sections, different measures for managing knowledge will be described and structured according to the organization areas technical infrastructure, organizational design, coordination, and motivation.

2.1 Technical Infrastructure

The term technical infrastructure denotes IT-based systems supporting the identification, storage and communication of knowledge. Concerning identification, systems facilitating finding of experts, e.g. so-called yellow pages, can be distinguished from systems offering retrieval mechanisms for documented knowledge. Knowledge can stored by using database schemes. A more informal way of storage is using more or less structured documents like Word-Documents on a file-server. The kind of support for communicating knowledge differs with the richness of the communication medium. The term media richness refers to the degree of personal interaction facilitated by a medium [15]. Within technical systems the highest degree of interaction is obtained at present by video conferencing. An example of a lower degree is E-Mail.

To summarize the above, systems mainly facilitating a codified form of knowledge transfer can be distinguished from systems, which are primarily aligned to a personalized form [16]. In the first case knowledge is separated from its original carrier - the minds of the employees - and is transferred in a written form. These knowledge management systems primarily act as a container for the transferred knowledge. In contrast, brokering between the personal knowledge bases of the employees is the main task of systems supporting a personalized form of knowledge transfer. Here, above all people are interlaced, building a network of bridging ties between previously separated groups or individuals. Knowledge is personally exchanged, either face-to-face or via transfer media of high richness. It needs to be emphasized that these two different forms of IT-based systems represent a polarity, not a dichotomy. There are intermediate stages between the extremities.

2.2 Organizational Structure

In general the organizational structure contains the assignment of tasks to organizational units and the allocation of authority among those units. In the context of knowledge management this means separating knowledge management tasks, assigning them to and building of „knowledge units", and apportioning authority among knowledge units and operational units.

Knowledge management tasks like collecting, analyzing, generalizing, and storing knowledge can be grouped in two different ways. Either those tasks can be combined that concern the same topic (knowledge object), or those that involve the same sorts of activities. While the experience factory is an example of the latter, the former way of combining tasks is performed at sd&m. In this company so-called knowledge brokers are responsible for developing sd&m-specific knowledge related to their topic and maintain a knowledge store related to their specific area of expertise [4]. Topics include requirements engineering, database systems, internet technology, quality management etc.

A knowledge unit can be established in the form of a department or a position. Crucial to the term knowledge unit is the fact that its members are not engaged in tasks of the operational business procedure. Since the experience factory is separated from the project organization it serves as an example for a knowledge unit in the form of a department. Experience communicators at Ericsson Software Technology AB hold knowledge positions [6]. They do not do developers´ work for them. Rather, their main task is to help others to solve their own problems by giving educational answers.

The relationship between knowledge and operational units, i.e. the allocation of authority, can be called supervisory or advisory. The former seems to underlie the concept of the experience factory, since the responsibility for software process improvements is explicitly anchored there. The latter takes place for example at sd&m where the knowledge brokers act as internal consultants [9].

Summarizing the above, a centralized organizational knowledge structure can be distinguished from a decentralized one. The centralized structure is characterized by a functional assignment of tasks to at least one knowledge department, being more or less supervisory related to the operational development organization. In contrast, having implemented a decentralized approach, widely distributed employees act as advisors for software developers, providing help concerning their specific topic.

2.3 Coordination

Coordination needs are a consequence of the division of labor [17]. So-called coordination mechanisms are meant to ensure that the different contributors´ work fits together in such a way, that the software delivered complies with internal and customer requirements. Traditionally, coordination mechanisms focus on timing of activities, planning and control of work products, allocation of staff members etc. But there is a need to coordinate the flow of knowledge in a company as well. Different kinds of expertise are distributed in a company and task requirements in software development cannot be defined in advance in any detail. Consequently, a perfect match between task requirements and the given level of expertise, i.e. the embodied experiences of an employee, is not achievable. Since the required experience may exist elsewhere in the enterprise, there is a need to coordinate supply and demand for knowledge.

These needs can be addressed in a formal or in an informal way. Formal mechanisms aim at defining transfer processes in advance. For example, at Pixelpark a quality manager has to participate in kick-off meetings of development projects in order to introduce up-to-date knowledge into the project [18]. Informal ways of coordination rely on creating occasions, where experience transfer can happen spontaneously. At Ericsson Software these occasions are called flashes and include different kinds of cross-section teams as well as unscheduled meetings or coffee breaks [6].

Coordination mechanisms can also be distinguished concerning the hierarchical position of the transfer partners. At Andersen Consulting best practices as determined by a superior unit are distributed via CD-ROM [19]. This is an example of a hierarchical or vertical coordination of knowledge supply and demand. In contrast, lateral or horizontal mechanisms focus on facilitating knowledge transfer between software developers directly. An example is the so-called space management that is based on the fact that physical proximity eases knowledge transfer.

The different aspects of coordination as discussed above will be summarized to coordination by standardization as a formal and vertical mechanism and coordination by mutual adjustment as an informal and horizontal way of coordination.

2.4 Motivation

Motivation designates the drive of an individual to a certain behavior. Concerning knowledge management, motivation denotes the willingness to share knowledge with others and use others' knowledge for one's own tasks.

According to motivation theory extrinsic and intrinsic motivation can be separated [20]. Employees are extrinsically motivated if their needs are satisfied indirectly, especially through monetary compensation. At Ernst & Young the level and quality of employee's contribution to the document database is part of their annual performance review that is linked directly to salary negotiations [16].

In contrast, motivation is intrinsic if an activity is undertaken for the immediate satisfaction of one's own need. In the business context the ideal intrinsic incentive system is the work context itself, which should be satisfactory and fulfilling for the employees. Measures supporting intrinsically motivated knowledge sharing are those fostering cohesion of the group, leading to so-called "team-spirit". For example, a participative form of leadership, common spare-time activities and abandoning of individual variable pay-for-performance can be named.

The following table 1 summarizes the description of the organization areas of knowledge transfer. It must be emphasized that there are intermediate stages between the so-called 'opposite designs'. I.e. they do not represent a dichotomy, but a polarity.

Table 1. Organization areas of knowledge transfer

Organization areas	Aspects	Opposite designs
Technical Infrastructure	- Identification - Storage - Communication	IT-based systems supporting **codified** knowledge transfer versus systems supporting **personalized** transfer
Organizational structure	- Unit building - Task assignment - Allocation of authority	**Centralized** versus **dezentralized** knowledge units
Coordination	- Defining transfer processes - Creating transfer occasions - Hierarchical position of transfer partners	Coordination by **standardization** versus coordination by **mutual adjustment**
Motivation	- Incentive system - Leadership	Motivation by **extrinsic** versus motivation by **intrinsic** measures

3 Forms of Knowledge Management

As described in the section above, knowledge transfer can be organized in different ways. Beyond that, enterprises actually implement different measures for managing knowledge. This is illustrated by the examples given in order to describe the different aspects of the organization areas of knowledge transfer. The question arises, what reasons do exist for these discriminate measures?

Assuming rational behavior, managers will chose the organizational alternative with the best cost/benefit relation. While the costs of organizational measures can be determined quantitatively, measuring or even estimating the benefits quantitatively seems to be impossible. Consequently, in order to evaluate alternatives to organize knowledge transfer, qualitative criteria have to be used. In the following this will be done by using the concept of the competence configuration.

3.1 Benefits of Knowledge Transfer

In their concept of the competence configuration Roos and van Krogh state that the achievement of competitive advantages results from the synthesis of a firm's particular task and knowledge system to what they call competence configuration [21]. In other words, tasks and knowledge to fulfill these tasks have to fit together.

Transferring internal knowledge can improve the competence configuration of an enterprise in two ways. On the one hand, existing knowledge can be applied to similar tasks, which results in deepening of the knowledge system. On the other hand, through the combination of knowledge from different sources, new tasks or formerly unsolved problems can be handled, i.e. the knowledge system is broadened. Knowledge transfer leading to a deeper knowledge system is associated with a leverage effect of existing knowledge [22]. In contrast, broadening the knowledge system can be called the innovation effect of knowledge transfer. It needs to be emphasized, that there is a transition between the two effects. The more knowledge is transformed by combining it with other knowledge and by applying it to new contexts, the less knowledge will be leveraged and the more innovative a transfer will be.

At the root of the leverage effect is transferring knowledge created in one area into another one in order to solve new but similar tasks or produce better solutions by using the transferred knowledge. In that way, multiply solving similar problems is avoided, repeating failures of the past is prevented, and economies of scale can be realized. In addition, using existing knowledge generally leads to time benefits compared to the creation of new knowledge. And of course, applying knowledge to different tasks may lead to improvement of the knowledge itself. Finally, leveraging knowledge reduces the risk of knowledge losses. Some authors call the leverage effect the reuse economics of knowledge management [16]. The term reuse stresses the main contribution of leveraging existing knowledge for software development, that is increasing efficiency of development.

The innovation effect is based on creating links between formerly unconnected elements of the organizational knowledge system. These links facilitate the creation of new knowledge, needed to solve problems or to master tasks that are new to the company and are too complex to be handled by a single individual. Moreover, using complementary knowledge elements to extend the competence configuration leads to additional synergies. For example, a comprehensive view of the firm is promoted by mutual insights into the task contexts of the transfer partners. In the context of software development, innovation effects should contribute mainly to increased effectiveness.

Looking at these briefly described distinct benefits of knowledge transfers, it seems to be obvious that measures being suitable for realizing leverage effects cannot equally promote innovation effects at the same time. This leads to the thesis that two basic forms of managing knowledge transfer can be distinguished, one facilitating mainly leverage effects and one fostering innovation effects.

3.2 Mechanistic Form of Knowledge Management

The mechanistic form of knowledge management is constituted by a consistent setting of the organization areas facilitating leverage effects of knowledge transfer. Managing knowledge in a mechanistic way means implementing IT-based systems supporting codified knowledge transfers, establishing centralized knowledge units, coordinating knowledge supply and demand by standardization and increasing the willingness to share knowledge through extrinsic incentives. The term 'mechanistic' refers to the 'mechanistic systems' of Burns and Stalker [23]. A mechanistic system is an organizational design being suitable for stable environments, that has a lot in common with the mechanistic form of knowledge management, e.g. the high importance of standards and formalisms.

Aiming mainly at leveraging existing knowledge can be called a rational objective only in the case of limited variability of development tasks. Task similarities can concern the application domain, the development methodologies applied or the technology used to implement the software. The degree of similarity influences the extent to which leveraging existing knowledge is possible, since it determines the demand for certain kinds of knowledge. For example, in a software company specialized at developing software for the insurance industry there will be a great demand of insurance-specific application domain knowledge. Ideally, each development project can benefit from application knowledge gained in earlier projects or in other projects being conducted at the same time.

In this situation transferring knowledge means multiplying existing knowledge to several receivers. In general, multiplication of knowledge can be achieved more easily by codification. Electronically, knowledge can be distributed in shorter time to more potential receivers compared to transferring it personally. But of course, in order to document knowledge, efforts hast to be expended. From the viewpoint of an expert facing high demands on a certain kind of knowledge, it does make good economic sense to document his knowledge instead of answering each request verbally [24]. This especially holds true assuming that in cases of high demand experience exists on how to document the knowledge in a way, that after transmitting it, no further feedback of the expert is required. Therefore, systems supporting storage, identification and communication of codified knowledge will generally be more beneficial for leveraging knowledge than those facilitating personalized transfer.

Central units are able to survey tasks to be done and anticipate problems arising during task execution, if task variability is limited. Therefore, they can act as a mediator between knowledge supply and demand, providing help to those looking for knowledge as well as to those aiming at spreading new insights. Using knowledge from unknown sources requires trust in the quality of the transferred knowledge. Central units can ease trust-building by generalizing knowledge from different sources and verifying the relevance of experiences for certain development projects. In order to increase the reuse of valuable experiences knowledge units should possess the authority to give directives to operational units, i.e. to the development projects. For example, generalizing experience is eased by uniform structures of codified knowledge. Since, due to time restrictions, software developers may be unwilling to adhere to predefined document structures, knowledge units need the power to enforce use of their predefined structures.

Defining processes for knowledge transfer and interrelating them with development processes facilitates leveraging knowledge in different ways. For example, defining points in time where experiences have to be collected, documented or communicated prevents deferring or even suspension of these activities. In general this is likely to occur, since accomplishing these tasks is time consuming and may be perceived by employees as superfluous, probably extending only the duration of the development project. Beyond that, primarily not the current project, but future projects will be the primary beneficiaries of this work. Thus, usefulness of standardization will be increased if defined transfer processes are binding directives. It therefore seems to be obvious that facilitating leverage effects by standardization benefits from establishing powerful centralized knowledge units. Looking at another form of standardization, this synergy may become even clearer. Knowledge transfers can be predefined so that knowledge is pushed to employees, e.g. by electronic means like listservers, workflow-systems or distributing CD-ROMs. By these means leverage effects can be achieved only if the pushed knowledge is closely related to the tasks of the receiver, which requires knowledge units overseeing the different development projects. As the examples given have illustrated, there can also be synergy effects between standardization and centralized units on the one hand and IT-based systems supporting codified knowledge transfer on the other.

While measures of knowledge-push or directives certainly influence knowledge sharing, there remains a dependency on the willingness of the employees to participate in knowledge transfers. In general, intrinsic motivation to share knowledge can be evaluated as a useful, and of course cheap form a motivation, since almost no expenditures for incentives have to be invested. But there are disadvantages, too. Knowledge sharing is not a goal by itself. If it is not task-oriented, willingness to share knowledge can lead to time-consuming activities, reducing general performance in the worst case. Aiming at leverage effects can be viewed as a controlled form of knowledge transfer. I.e. ideally only experiences useful for reuse are collected, edited and transmitted to places where they are needed. In contrast to intrinsic motivation, extrinsic incentives can focus on these desired knowledge transfers. This is true especially in the case of codified knowledge. For example incentives for contributions to knowledge bases can be combined with an evaluation of reuse, quality or helpfulness of that knowledge. Therefore the described interrelation between the organization areas also concern this fourth area of the mechanistic form of knowledge management, that is motivating by use of extrinsic incentives.

3.3 Organic Form of Knowledge Management

While the mechanistic form of knowledge management will be suitable if aiming at leveraging existing knowledge, facilitating innovation effects of knowledge transfer requires other organizational measures. Concretely, IT-based systems have to support personalized transfer, knowledge units should be decentralized, coordination will mainly be achieved by mutual adjustment and motivation should be intrinsic. Burns and Stalker denote an organizational design fitting to a dynamic environment as an 'organic system' [16].

Where one is aiming at innovation effects, task similarity is unlikely. Instead, development projects are facing new and complex development tasks that cannot be accomplished by simply applying experiences from former projects. Rather new solutions have to be developed for the first time, i.e. new knowledge has to be crated. Assuming complex tasks, it is widely accepted that different perspectives foster innovative solutions [25]. These perspectives stem from the different experiences of individuals respectively their distinct knowledge bases. Therefore knowledge transfer leading to innovation effects might be better described as an exchange and discussion of ideas than as a process of request, communication, interpretation and usage of knowledge.

Developing software on the basis of unclear, customer-specific requirements or developing a visionary new standard application are examples of tasks requiring innovative transfers or exchanges. In these situations, specifying the development task and developing the software have to be conducted in parallel. To the perspective of knowledge transfer that means that it remains unclear for a long time, which kind of experience may be helpful, since the underlying problem is poorly specified. Consequently, an exchange between experts in different domains is needed, allowing for open discussion and permanent feedback. I.e. a personalized form of knowledge transfer has to be supported by the IT-based system. For example, looking for experts in different application domains can be assisted as well as linking people via chat rooms or video conferencing.

Given uncertainty and dynamics of tasks in development projects, a central unit cannot assist knowledge transfer adequately, since such a unit will be too distant from developers' tasks. But with the necessary collaboration of experts in different domains conflicts and misunderstandings are likely to occur. Therefore decentralized knowledge units, i.e. specialized roles or positions, can be helpful to mediate between transfer partners. Beyond that, collecting lessons learned and refining knowledge is not obsolete in the case of unclear development tasks. But since in the case of high task dynamics reusing experiences directly is unlikely, these lessons should remain in the minds of certain employees, who are then made widely known as experts.

Several reasons exist, why the organic form of knowledge management relies mainly on mutual adjustment as coordination mechanism. Firstly, research suggests that innovations are hindered by formalization or other kinds of bureaucratic means [23]. Creativity cannot be prescribed, rather conditions facilitating a flow of ideas have to be created. Secondly, if tasks are unclear and dynamically changing, distributing knowledge will be time consuming with a small chance to be beneficial for accomplishing actual tasks. I.e. knowledge transfers have to be horizontal, leaving the responsibility to share expertise at the level of the development staff. Of course, the innovation effects of coordination by mutual adjustment can be lifted. For example physical proximity, coffee breaks and in the case of larger and/or geographically distributed projects IT supporting personalized transfer can act as catalysts. As the latter shows, interrelations between organization areas also occur in the organic form of knowledge management.

While intrinsically motivated knowledge sharing is beneficial for obtaining leverage effects as well as for innovation effects, its importance increases in the second case. Trying to foster motivation to share knowledge at the individual level by extrinsic incentives requires incentives that can be adjusted to an individual's contribution. With knowledge transfers leading to innovation effects, this must be regarded as impossible. The individual's contribution to the joint output cannot be determined or even be evaluated. This becomes more obvious in view of the fact, that large parts of the shared ideas, perspectives and experiences are likely to be tacit [26]. Motivating extrinsically with incentives focusing on the group level is at least problematic, since it cannot impede opportunistic behavior. I.e. single group members may share knowledge at a minimum degree but will be rewarded for the performance of the whole group. Taking into account that extrinsic incentives can destroy given intrinsic motivation (so-called crowding out effect) [20], managers aiming at innovation effects should concentrate on intrinsic motivation measures, facilitating "team-spirit".

The two basic forms of managing knowledge foster different effects of knowledge transfers. While these connections can be argued conclusively as done above, relevance for practical needs remains unclear. The few published case-studies about knowledge management clearly support the point of view presented here. However, no single case study reports about measures concerning all organization areas.

4 Empirical Findings

In order to examine whether the two basic forms of knowledge management actually exist in practice, an empirical investigation via Internet was conducted. It was not intended to get detailed insights into knowledge management at different companies. Rather it was designed to test whether the theory about a connection between the intended type of transfer effects and the form knowledge transfer is organized matches with the design of knowledge management in practice.

4.1 Data Collection

The objective of the investigation required a form of inquiry suitable to collect data from a wide range of enterprises in a short time. Therefore, a survey via internet on the basis of an online questionnaire was chosen for data collection.

In the general part of the questionnaire, information about the characteristics of the respondents' enterprise, the position of the respondents, and the current status of knowledge management activities in their enterprises were solicited. Questions concerning the overall evaluation of the organization areas as described in section 2 were asked in the second part of the questionnaire, using standardized responses. Since both the relevant terms within the area of knowledge management as well as the term knowledge management itself are used in different ways by different people, relying on a questionnaire can lead to subjective bias of the findings. While this cannot be excluded completely, certain measures were taken to at least reduce any bias present. Firstly, multiple answers were allowed with all questions, facilitating testing of consistent interpretation of the terms used. Secondly, respondents were asked to give examples illustrating their general evaluation of the organizational areas. Therefore, we could examine whether the answers were in accordance with the measures actually undertaken. In the last part of the questionnaire, interviewees were asked to name the goals underlying their knowledge management activities.

The questionnaire was placed at the popular knowledge management portal "knowledgeMARKT" (www.knowledgeMARKT.de) and could be answered during a period of six weeks between April and June 2000. Only data from enterprises which had reached at least the implementation stage of planned knowledge management activities was used for data analysis. Moreover, we excluded enterprises where given answers were inconsistent as well as those with obvious differences between general answers and described measures. The data from 28 enterprises related to the software industry were finally evaluated in detail.

4.2 Data Analysis

At first, the reported goals of knowledge management activities were grouped using an affinity diagram. As expected, two groups could be separated. Thirteen enterprises reported aiming primarily at innovation effects. In contrast, fifteen enterprises reported striving to leverage existing knowledge.

In a second step, the evaluations of the organization areas were examined with regard to the different effects of knowledge management in the enterprises. For example it was analyzed how many of the enterprises having established centralized knowledge units aim at leveraging knowledge compared to the number of respondents intending innovation effects. The following table 2 shows the results of the analysis. Since multiple answers were allowed, a non-ambiguous evaluation of the organization areas was not possible in all cases. For example, some respondents reported about relying on centralized knowledge units as well as decentralized ones. This is described by the entries in the last column of table 2.

Table 2. Empirical findings of conducted survey

Organization areas	Opposite designs	Leverage effects	Innovation effects	Ambiguous Evaluation
Technical Infrastructure	Codified transfer (n=5)	**80,00%**	20,00%	75,00% (n=21)
	Personalized transfer (n=2)	0%	**100,00%**	
Organizational Structure	Centralized Units (n=10)	**70%**	30,00%	17,87% (n=5)
	Dezentralized Units (n=13)	38,46%	**61,54%**	
Coordination	Standardization (n=10)	**70,00%**	30,00%	28,57% (n=8)
	Mutual adjustment (n=10)	40,00%	**60,00%**	
Motivation	Extrinsically (n=4)	**100,00%**	0%	53,57% (n=15)
	Intrinsically (n=9)	22,22%	**77,78%**	

Several conclusions can be drawn from the findings of the survey:

1. Aiming at leverage effects of knowledge transfers is generally connected with organizational measures different to those being taken when aiming at innovation effects.
2. Both the mechanistic and the organic form of knowledge management are relevant in practice.
3. While the mechanistic form dominates in enterprises striving for leverage effects, the organic form is preferred by firms focusing on innovation effects of knowledge transfer.
4. This presumed relation between the intended effects of knowledge transfer and a certain setting of the organization areas does not hold true for all enterprises participating in the survey.
5. Many respondents were not able to evaluate their organizational measures non-ambiguously according to the described opposite designs.

Conclusions one to three clearly support the theoretical arguments. However, the fourth and especially the fifth finding does not reflect argumentation. This will be discussed in the following section.

4.3 Interpretation of Findings

Discussion will start with the last point, i.e. the great number of ambiguous answers. A simple explanation may be the problems in using a questionnaire for collecting the data and the fact that the opposite designs described here actually represent a polarity, not a dichotomy. But there may be another, more fundamental reason for the unexpected findings. Three dimensions of expertise are commonly recognized as important in software development: domain expertise (knowledge about the application domain area), methodological or task expertise (knowledge about development methodologies, design principles etc.), and technical expertise (knowledge about a specialized technical area) [27]. Therefore aiming at leverage or innovation effects should possibly not be regarded as an explicit or implicit general objective of knowledge management, but may refer to different dimensions of knowledge. Looking at the situation of an unclear development task there is a need to create new knowledge about the application domain and new technical knowledge may have to be built up as well. However, this may be done while leveraging methodological knowledge such as experiences concerning object-oriented analysis and design, software inspections etc. If this holds true, the general correlation between intended effects and organization forms of knowledge transfer still stays valid. But some software companies may implement organic and mechanistic forms of knowledge management at the same time, each with respect to different dimensions of knowledge. For example, a central knowledge unit may document methodological experiences, while decentralized units strive to build up technical expertise. In this case a respondent of the survey would not have been able to evaluate the organizational structure non-ambiguously. Although all respondents specified only one general objective of knowledge management, there may be another, less conscious goal concerning only one dimension of knowledge. E.g., while generally aiming at innovation effects, leveraging methodological knowledge may be intended at the same time.

However, this explanation does not fit for the second surprising finding of the survey. I.e. why do companies implement organizational measures argued as being more suitable for the other effect of knowledge transfer as for the one reported as objective by the respondents? Of course, companies may simply have implemented improper measures. This possibility cannot be excluded, since no evaluation of the success of knowledge management in the respondents' companies was conducted. But again, a more fundamental reason should be considered. The arguments given concerning suitability of the basic forms of knowledge management are based on the assumption of rational behavior, i.e. striving for the organizational alternatives with best cost/benefit-relations. While benefits with regard to leverage and innovation effects have been described, no cost-analysis of different alternatives has been conducted. For example, codified transfer seems to facilitate leverage effects better than personalized forms of transfer. But if expenditures of codifying exceed the benefit difference between these alternatives, relying on personalized transfer in order to leverage knowledge will be a rational choice. Costs of codifying experiences are influenced by characteristics of those experiences. The less complex knowledge is, the easier it is to document it in such a way that it can be used by the recipient without requiring additional contact with the expert. As experiences are based on former problem-solving, the term complexity refers to the problem and the solution component of experiences. If an expert is not able to explain why he had chosen or developed a certain solution by referring to characteristics of the underlying problem, or if understanding that problem-solving knowledge is dependent from other knowledge elements, then this experience can be classified as complex [28]. While non-complex knowledge can easily be documented, codifying complex knowledge requires high expenditures if it is possible at all. Thus, although aiming at leverage effects, the cost/benefit relation of transferring knowledge personalized may be better than that of codified transfer when knowledge is complex. Therefore, complexity of knowledge can be viewed as an influencing factor. I.e. it might mediate the relation between organizational measures and intended effects of knowledge transfers.

The explanations described for the two surprising findings of the survey are supported by ongoing research at the University of Cologne. Having conducted case studies at software companies on the basis of interviews, it actually seems to be the case that intended knowledge transfer effects are related to different knowledge dimensions and certain factors exist that partially influence the relation between measures and intended effects of knowledge transfers.

5 Conclusion

In this paper, a framework for knowledge management in software development has been presented. Using the organization areas technical infrastructure, organization structure, coordination, and motivation, it allows for systematically making comparisons between knowledge management activities in different companies. By applying established theories, e.g. theories on coordination, media richness, and motivation, two basic forms of knowledge management can be derived. The organic form consisting of a certain setting of the organizational areas is fitting when innovation effects of knowledge transfer are intended. The mechanistic form, on the other hand, is suitable for companies, aiming at leveraging existing knowledge.

The findings of the conducted survey have supported the relation between the intended effects of knowledge transfer and the suitable form of organizing knowledge management. The two distinct forms of knowledge management have been found in practice as well. However, findings also indicate, that different effects might be intended at the same time, when referred to different dimensions of knowledge. Consequently, the organic and the mechanistic form of knowledge management can coexist.

What conclusions can be drawn regarding the experience factory, the most popular concept for knowledge management in software development? In its original form, a codified transfer, a centralized knowledge unit, and coordination by standardization are recommended [3]. While motivational aspects are not explicitly discussed, it clearly describes a mechanistic form of knowledge management aiming mainly at leverage effects. As the experience factory relies heavily upon codified transfer in the form of experience packages, complexity of knowledge is problematic to deal with using this approach, at least from an economic point of view. By integrating yellow pages further development of the concept has taken this aspect into account [29]. I.e. referring to the technical infrastructure organic and mechanistic measures coexist. While the experience factory still emphasizes codified transfer, it is interesting to discuss whether equally supporting codified and personalized transfer should be considered as an option for managing knowledge.

On the one hand, this will clearly expand the possibilities for finding existing knowledge, and reported empirical results indicate that complementary useful knowledge is retrieved when applying both forms of knowledge transfer [30]. On the other hand, the question arises how much knowledge actually has to be retrieved in order to accomplish a task with "good-enough quality"? While equally implementing systems for codified and personalized transfer will increase the effectiveness of knowledge transfer, it certainly will increase the cost of building up and maintaining the technical infrastructure as well. Designing the technical infrastructure according to certain dimensions of knowledge and taking into account the respective objectives probably makes better economic sense. However, further research needs to be done. E.g., the framework will have to be refined, allowing for more detailed explanations on and recommendations of managing knowledge in software development.

References

1. Jones, C.: Patterns of Software Systems Failure and Success. International Thomson Computer Press, London (1996)
2. Anderson, C.: A World Gone Soft: A Survey of the Software Industry. IEEE Engineering Management Review, 24 (4) (1996), 21-36
3. Basili, V.R., Caldiera, G., Rombach, H.D.: Experience Factory. In: Marciniak, J.J. (eds.): Encyclopedia of Software Engineering, John Wiley & Sons, New York (1994), 469-476
4. Brössler, P.: Knowledge Management at a Software House: A Progress Report. In: Bomarius, F. (eds.): Proceedings of the Workshop on Learning Software Organizations, June 16th, Kaiserlautern (1999), 77-83
5. Houdek, F., Kempter, H.: Quality patterns - An approach to packaging software engineering experience. ACM SIGSOFT Software Engineering Notes, 22(3) (1997), 81-88
6. Johansson, C., Hall, P., Coquard, M.: Talk to Paula and Peter - They are Experienced. In: In: Bomarius, F. (eds.): Proceedings of the Workshop on Learning Software Organizations, June 16th, Kaiserlautern (1999), 69-76
7. Davenport, T.H., Probst, G. (eds.): Knowledge Management Case Book: Siemens Best Practices, MCD, Munich (2001)
8. American Productivity & Quality Center (eds.): Arthur Andersen. Tech. Report, APQC, Houston (1997)
9. Davenport, T.H., Prusak, L.: Working Knowledge: How Organizations Manage What They Know. Boston (1997)
10. Heppner, K.: Organisation des Wissenstransfers: Grundlagen, Barrieren und Instrumente. Gabler, Wiesbaden/Germany (1997)
11. Roehl, H.: Instrumente der Wissensorganisation. Gabler, Wiesbaden/Germany (2000)
12. Althoff, K.-D., Müller, W., Nick, M., Snoek, B.: KM-PEB: An Online Experience Base on Knowledge Management Technology. In: Blanzieri, E., Portinale, L. (eds.), Advances in Case-Based Reasoning - Proc. 5th European Workshop on Case-Based Reasoning, Springer, Berlin (2000), 335-347
13. Probst, G., Raub, S., Romhardt, K.: Wissen Managen: Wie Unternehmen Ihre wertvollste Ressource optimal nutzen. 3rd ed., Gabler, Wiesbaden/Germany (1999)
14. North, K.: Wissensorientierte Unternehmensführung: Wertschöpfung durch Wissen. 2nd ed., Gabler, Wiesbaden/Germany (1999)
15. Straub, D., Karahanna, E.: Knowledge Worker Communications and Recipient Availability: Toward a Task Closure Explanation of Media Choice. Organization Science, 9 (2) (1998), 160-175

16. Hansen, M.T., Nohira, N., Tierney, T.: What´s your Strategy for Managing Knowledge? Harvard Business Review, 77(2) (1999), 106-116
17. Mintzberg, H. The Structuring of Organizations. A Synthesis of the Research. Prentice-Hall, Englewood Cliffs (1979)
18. Schindler, M.: Wissensmanagement in der Projektabwicklung: Grundlagen, Determinanten und Gestaltungskonzepte eines ganzheitlichen Projektwissens-managements. Eul, Lohmar/Germany (2000)
19. Romhardt, K.: Die Organisation aus der Wissensperspektive: Möglichkeiten und Grenzen der Intervention. Gabler, Wiesbaden/Germany (1998)
20. Osterloh, M., Frey, B.S.: Motivation, Knowledge Transfer, and Organizational Forms. Organization Science, 11 (5) (2000), 538-550
21. Roos, J., Von Krogh, G.: Figuring Out Your Competence Configuration. European Management Journal, 10 (4) (1992), 422-427
22. Bendt, A.: Wissenstransfer in multinationalen Unternehmen. Gabler, Wiesbaden/Germany (2000)
23. Burns, T., Stalker, G.M.: The management of innovation. 3rd ed., London (1971)
24. Trittmann, R., Mellis, W.: Wissenstransfer in der Softwareentwicklung: Eine ökonomische Analyse. In: Oberweis, A., Sneed, H.M. (eds.).): Software-Management, Proc. Fachtagung der Gesellschaft für Informatik e.V. (GI), Oktober 1999 in München, B.G. Teubner, Leipzig (1999), 27-44
25. Högl, M.: Teamarbeit in innovativen Projekten: Einflußgrößen und Wirkungen. Gabler, Wiesbaden/Germany, 1998
26. Nonaka, I., Takeuchi, H.: The Knowledge-Creating Company. Oxford University Press (1995)
27. Faraj, S, Sproull, L.: Coordinating Expertise in Software Development Teams. Management Science, 46 (12) (2000), 1554-1568
28. Trittmann, R., Brössler, P.: Effizienter Wissenstransfer in der Softwareentwicklung: Der sd&m-Ansatz. In: Eppler, M., Sukowski, O. (eds.): Fallstudien zum Wissensmanagement: Lösungen aus der Praxis, Net Academy Press, St. Gallen (2001), 163-188
29. Decker, B., Althoff, K.-D., Nick, M. & Tautz, C.: Integrating Business Process Descriptions and Lessons Learned with an Experience Factory. In: Schnurr, H.-P. et al. (eds.): Professionelles Wissensmanagement - Erfahrungen und Visionen, Shaker, Aachen (2001), 54-58
30. Tautz, C.: Customizing Software Engineering Experience Management Systems to Organizational Needs. Fraunhofer IRB Verlag, Stuttgart (2000)

CORONET-Train: A Methodology for Web-Based Collaborative Learning in Software Organisations

Dietmar Pfahl, Niniek Angkasaputra, Christiane M. Differding, and Günther Ruhe

Fraunhofer Institute for Experimental Software Engineering (IESE)
Sauerwiesen 6, D-67661 Kaiserslautern, Germany
{pfahl,angkasa,differdi,ruhe}@iese.fhg.de

Abstract. Skills, knowledge, and motivation of the software engineering workforce are essential prerequisites for maturing software development. But lack of human resources has become an obstacle for growth of the software industry. The CORONET approach aims at relieving the difficult situation by facilitating an innovative methodology and tool support for web-based collaborative learning at the workplace. This paper describes the most important features of the learning methodology CORONET-Train. An empirical evaluation of learning effectiveness in industrial environments has been planned. Results will soon be available.

Keywords: Collaborative Learning, Software Engineering, Competence Development, Web-Based Training, Work-Based Learning, Learning Network

1 Motivation and Background

The demand for specific technology training is growing significantly. Continuous education of the workforce has become an important facilitator of software process improvement [2] and organisational learning [5, 13]. However, university education and classroom-based professional training courses cannot solve the problem alone due to the limited number of people they can reach.

In the software industry, worldwide, the demand for both specific technology training and continuous education is growing significantly. Human resources have become a bottleneck for industrial growth [1]. Skills, knowledge, and motivation of the organisations' employees are essential prerequisites for maturing software development. Workplace learning is arising from an embedded-in-work situation and is oriented on developing skills and knowledge of best practices. Particularly, this is true for the application domain of SE methods and techniques.

Knowledge is considered a crucial resource of any organisation that should be managed carefully. Systematic management of knowledge in a strategic domain like software development is of dramatic importance as a competitive factor for individuals and organisations.

K.-D. Althoff, R.L. Feldmann, and W. Müller (Eds.): LSO 2001, LNCS 2176, pp. 37-51, 2001.

The social processes necessary to continuously create and share tacit as well as explicit knowledge are underestimated and not sufficiently understood and supported currently. Nonaka and Takeuchi [9] have pointed out with their knowledge spiral (socialisation, externalisation, combination, and internalisation) that knowledge creation lives from a balance in processing (creation and sharing) of tacit as well as explicit knowledge. In this process both types of knowledge are of equal importance and are transformed into each other. Socialisation, externalisation, combination, internalisation are the core activities of a Corporate Knowledge Management System and must therefore be accompanied by processes and facilities supporting group interaction.

The European research project CORONET (Corporate Software Engineering Knowledge Networks for Improved Training of the Workforce), which started in February 2000 and will run until April 2002, aims to provide a comprehensive methodology, CORONET-Train, and a technical platform for web-based collaborative learning within software organisations.

The structure of this paper is as follows. In Section 2, a brief introduction into the CORONET project given, its goals and involved partner organisations are presented. Then, in Section 3, the characteristics of the CORONET Learning Environment are outlined. The CORONET-Train methodology, which is the focus of the paper, is described in Section 4. The planned industrial application and evaluation of the CORONET Learning Environment is briefly outlined in Section 5. Conclusions are presented in Section 6.

2 The CORONET Project

The overall challenge of the CORONET project is to improve the effectiveness of training of the workforce in an efficient and sustained way. This challenge is addressed in the CORONET project by achieving the following objectives:

- Development and implementation of a new learning approach CORONET-Train;
- Development and implementation of a new hypermedia learning environment to support CORONET-Train;
- Improvement of hypermedia content production by reuse of existing knowledge packages for methods and techniques in the SE domain;
- Industrial validation of the new learning approach. The integrated approach CORONET-Train is tested in different industrial environments;
- Empirical demonstration of the benefits of CORONET-Train: A common reference model to analyse the costs and benefits of collaborative learning in industrial software organisations will be developed.

These challenges and objectives require comprehensive competences that come from the selected project partners of the CORONET consortium. The methodology development partners Fraunhofer IESE and University of New South Wales (UNSW) contribute expertise in software and knowledge engineering, knowledge management, web-based courseware development, hypermedia didactics, evaluation, and cost-benefit modelling and analysis. The technology development partners Centro de

Computação Gráfica (CCG), Atlante, Fraunhofer IGD, and Institute for Information Processing and Computer-Supported New Media at the University of Technology Graz (IICM) contribute expertise in software and knowledge engineering, learning environments, web-based courseware development, and multimedia. The application partners DaimlerChrysler (DC) and HIGHWARE sarl (HW) contribute expertise in software and knowledge engineering, knowledge management, work-based learning processes and didactics. In addition to the project consortium, a Pedagogic Advisory Board (PAB) was formed of independent experts from academia in order to consult the consortium in questions related to didactics and work-based learning and to review essential project deliverables. The CORONET project activities are co-ordinated by Fraunhofer IESE.

3 The CORONET Learning Environment

The CORONET learning environment may be seen as a combination of an innovative learning methodology, CORONET-Train, accompanied with a software system, i.e. the CORONET platform, supporting the methodology. These two components are closely coupled and will be referred to as the CORONET system.

The CORONET system in turn may be seen as a combination of the following components [14]:

Learning Resources;
Tools;
Learning Scenarios;

CORONET learning resources may be seen as any resources accessible via the web, i.e. documents of different types, persons working online or having an internet account, news groups, discussion forum, brainstorming forum, databases, etc.

CORONET tools provide a context-dependent access to learning resources, and what is essential: the tools support construction of new learning resources via collaboration and flexible reuse. For example, any document can be seen in the context of a training course, mentoring session, discussion forum, etc. The document can be extended with comments or related to another document without actually modifying the document. The document can be reused as a part of another course, as a contribution to a discussion, and so on.

CORONET learning scenarios are sequences of learning processes that use learning resources and tools for accomplishing a particular learning task. Learning processes and their combination are defined via so-called application scenarios, which can be seen as predefined user views.

The CORONET system has been designed to support collaborative learning at the workplace using the Internet technology. The innovative aspects of the CORONET system as compared to existing learning environments are as follows:

1. The CORONET system combines knowledge management and collaborative eLearning. Thus, the CORONET system essentially supports learning in corporate knowledge network environments including collaborative work with human subject-matter experts.

2. The CORONET system facilitates not only delivery, but also collaborative construction of learning resources. New resources are automatically constructed on-the-fly as a result of any collaborative activity (discussions, brainstorming sessions, workshops, annotations, mentoring sessions, etc.) or of reuse.
3. The CORONET system combines a wide spectrum of pedagogical and didactical approaches: Different collaborative learning strategies may be applied on different competence levels, and cover three categories of web-based collaborative learning at the workplace:

The combination of these innovative features makes the CORONET system a powerful learning environment for software organisations that supports all four phases of Nonaka and Takeuchi's experience spiral.

4 The CORONET-Train Methodology

The overall goal of the learning methodology CORONET-Train is to facilitate collaborative learning of software engineers at the workplace in a systematic and demand-focused way. CORONET-Train aims at a long-termed and career oriented development of not only domain-specific knowledge and skills (for an example see [10, 16]) but also meta-cognitive and social competence [6, 12].

In the domain of SE there is a special need for this kind of learning because:

SE is mainly a team-oriented work-process and consequently, learning on the job should be embedded in to comparable social processes.

Technical and knowledge development in the domain of SE are characterised by fast growth and high dynamic change; this requires not only continuous learning, but also the ability to co-operatively manage the multiple problem-solving and learning demands in this domain.

Multiple and complex tasks in the SE process require the developer to specialise and take different perspectives on the process; in order to learn this, software-engineers should get acquainted with these multiple perspectives and how to co-operatively handle them.

Efficiency of learning has to be improved in general. In the context of the tremendous resource bottleneck in the SE domain, this task becomes even more important.

In response to these needs, CORONET-Train has been designed to offer the following features:

1. Long-term competence development: CORONET-Train is a long-term, career-path oriented approach of competence development, focusing on SE subject-matters.
2. Collaboration through networking: Beyond the adaptation to competence levels, the different groups of users are linked through learning networks within and between competence levels.
3. Integration of learning by training and work-based learning: Facilitated by CORONET-Train, the interlocking of learning process and work can happen in different ways, for example:

Learning contents of training (web-based) originate from real work situation; authentic problem constellations can be generated.

Learners participate in "real project" work processes, they can take over real tasks or parts of tasks within a running project in order to learn.

Brainstorming sessions are triggered by a real work problem. The results of the session are directly applied in the work situation.

4. Reciprocal learning: Practitioners and experts can learn while teaching, coaching [11], and mentoring [8] novices and practitioners, respectively.

4.1 Long-Term Competence Development

CORONET-Train defines five roles: Learner, Manager, Author, Knowledge Engineer, and Technical Support (Administration). The role "Learner" has many facets, therefore, this role is further subdivided into eight sub-roles: Knowledge Worker, Trainee, Coachee, Mentee, Moderator, Trainer/Tutor, Coach, and Mentor. Every software engineer in the organisation is a Learner and may have various responsibilities according to the roles he/she assumes. In general, a software engineer is a knowledge worker with regard to a particular subject-matter area in which he/she wants to acquire or generate knowledge and skills.

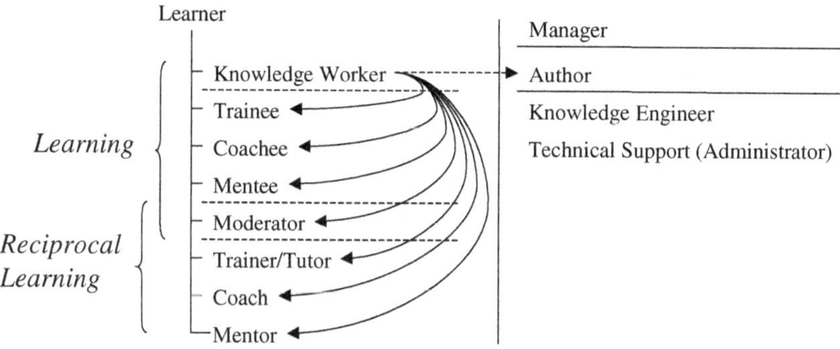

Fig. 1. The CORONET-Train role model

Depending on his/her particular learning needs and the learning processes chosen, a Knowledge Worker can temporarily switch into another role (indicated by arrows in Fig. 1). In the role of Trainee, Coachee or Mentee, a Learner receives help in acquiring knowledge and skills with regards to a particular subject-matter. In the role of Trainer/Tutor, Coach or Mentor, a Learner helps others acquire knowledge and skills in a particular subject-matter ("learning"), and – on the other hand – by doing so, develops his/her own problem-solving and teaching/coaching/mentoring competence ("reciprocal learning"). The role "Moderater" supports both subject-matter related knowledge development and reciprocal learning.

Related to the task of generating learning materials (i.e. courseware) is the role "Author". Authoring can either be done by Knowledge Workers, or by dedicated staff in a SE training organisation.

The remaining three roles in Fig. 1 are related to the introduction of CORONET-Train in an organisation and the set-up and management of the CORONET system

(Manager), the maintenance of the CORONET knowledge base (Knowledge Engineer), and the provision of technical support and system administration services (Technical Support).

Related to a particular subject-matter, the CORONET role "Learner" can assume one of the following competence levels:

Novice: A novice has at most rudimentary theoretical knowledge and no practical knowledge (so called skills) and experience in the subject-matter area.

Practitioner: A practitioner has basic to advanced theoretical knowledge and at most rudimentary practical knowledge and experience in the subject-matter area.

Expert: An expert has advanced theoretical knowledge and comprehensive practical knowledge and experience in the subject-matter area.

Following the underlying principle of systematic career-path oriented competence development, a Learner proceeds from level "Novice" to level "Practitioner" and eventually to level "Expert".

In addition to subject-matter related competence development, CORONET-Train also supports the development of problem-solving competence and social competence, with particular focus on teaching, coaching and mentoring competence (cf. Fig. 2). The design of CORONET-Train stimulates learning towards a growth in all three competence dimensions. This is achieved by following the principle of scaffolding and fading [15], and by using the strategy of reciprocal teaching.

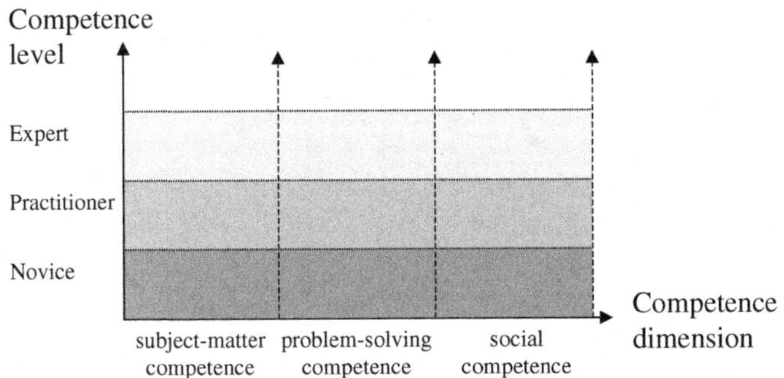

Fig. 2. Competence levels versus competence dimensions

Only when the requirements of a competence level in all three dimensions are satisfied on the basis of defined conditions, an individual has fully achieved a particular competence level. Note that the number of competence levels can be tailored to the needs of a particular organisation. In some organisations the definition of less than three competence levels might be sufficient. In others, a refinement might be appropriate.

In general, the mapping of functions or professional roles (SE roles) to competence levels is under responsibility of the role "Manager". The only exception is the role Moderator, which is assigned dynamically on a voluntary basis. The Manager does the mapping by judging the competence of an individual regarding all the competence dimensions (subject-matter competence, problem-solving competence, and social competence) with regard to the SE subject-matter area of interest.

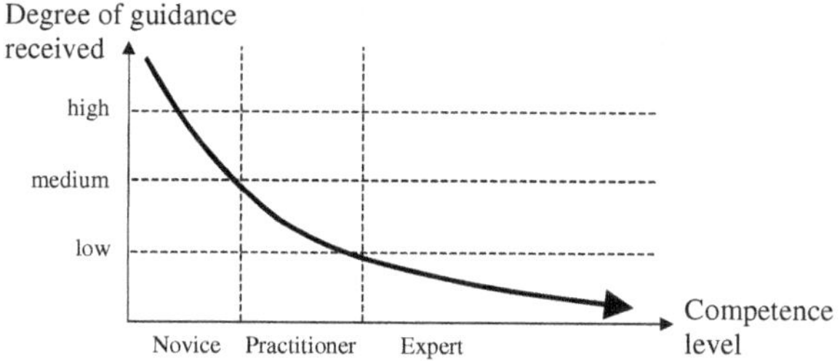

Fig. 3. Degree of guidance received versus competence level

Due to the application of the principle of scaffolding and fading, CORONET-Train provides an increasing grade of self-directed learning as the usage of the CORONET environment proceeds. When Learners enter the CORONET system at the "Novice" level, they are recommended to start with pre-structured training sessions. They will receive support from the higher competence level Learners. After the first introduction into the SE subject-matter of interest, Learners are expected to take more and more responsibility for their own learning processes, and the learning processes of others (work-based learning and reciprocal learning). This is reflected by the various types of dyadic learning relations explained on Section 4.2.2. The relation between decrease of guidance received and competence growth is shown in Fig. 3.

4.2 Collaboration through Networking

CORONET-Train focuses on the collaboration in learning networks. These learning networks can consist of knowledge workers, supportive roles (e.g., trainers, tutors, etc.), and other knowledge sources (e.g., training materials, documents, directories, knowledge repositories, etc.). The key elements of collaborative learning with CORONET-Train include:

- Learning groups and networks
- Dyadic learning relations of Novices, Practitioners, and Experts.

4.2.1 Learning Groups and Networks

Communication between knowledge workers is organised through subject-matter related learning groups. Three types of learning groups exist: Public Groups, Peer Groups, and Training Groups (cf. Fig. 4).

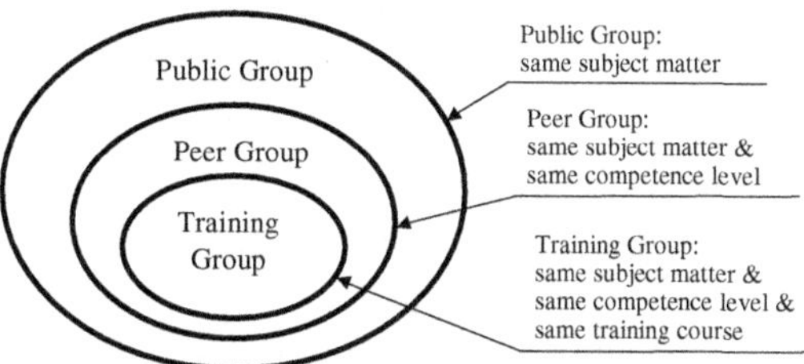

Fig. 4. Types of learning groups in CORONET-Train

All groups are centred on a SE subject-matter. Participants in a particular web-based training course establish Training Groups. Their purpose is the exchange of knowledge and information between trainees, as well as the discussion of problems or the sharing of opinions. Typically, participants of a training course, and thus the members of the Training Group, are at the same competence level. The Peer Group is a natural extension of a Training Course, since it is established by knowledge workers who are at the same competence level. Its purpose is similar to that of a Training Group, but without any specific orientation towards or dependency on a particular training course. The Public Group is open to everybody interested in the related subject-matter. Its purpose is to facilitate communication between competence levels. In particular, it can be used by knowledge workers to raise issues related to their work and available subject-matter materials, and to receive feedback from experts and practitioners in this field.

Note that a Learner can be a member of several learning groups. The set of learning groups forms a learning network.

4.2.2 Dyadic Learning Relations

CORONET-Train encourages the establishment of several types of dyadic communication relationships between Learners through the application of the collaborative learning methodology. Two types of dyadic relationships are identified. The first type, training, is associated with Web-Based Training (Learning by Training). The second type, coaching/mentoring, takes place continuously during the daily project work (Work-Based Learning), independently from participation in a dedicated training course. Each relationship has a mode, either receiving or providing. A Learner assumes roles according on which dyadic relationship is being applied. The dyadic learning relations complement the various possibilities to access learning materials (WBT courseware, documents, guidelines, standards, etc.) and the communication with peers and other knowledge workers within subject-matter related learning networks.

Certain learning relations are bi-directional. By providing teaching/tutoring or coaching/mentoring services to other Learners at the lower competence level, a Knowledge Worker automatically becomes a Learner – not primarily with regards to the subject-matter but with regard to problem-solving and social competence (including leadership skills). In CORONET-Train, this sort of learning is called "reciprocal learning".

Learners at competence level "Novice" (N) may have up to two dyadic relationships (cf. Fig. 5). By taking a training course, a Learner switches naturally from Knowledge Worker to Trainee and receives support in his learning activities from a Trainer/Tutor. In the daily project work, the Knowledge Worker becomes a Coachee and receives guidance in problem-solving, knowledge acquisition, and skill development from a Coach.

Learners at competence level "Practitioner" (P) may have up to four dyadic relationships (cf. Fig. 6). Two relationships are the same as the ones described for Novice, but different in the degree of guidance. As more advance relationships, a Practitioner Learner may assume a Trainer/Tutor role and provide teaching or tutoring services as well as become a Coach and provide coaching services to Knowledge Workers at Novice level.

An important quality of CORONET-Train is that it encourages the Knowledge Workers to become pro-active learners and to learn by effectively utilising the knowledge community through the CORONET system. The learning need and the current situation of the Knowledge Worker will act as a natural guidance for the Knowledge Worker to find the most suitable learning method to proceed. The Knowledge Worker should recognise:

the subject-matter topic to be studied,
the available time frame that can be reserved for learning,
the mode in which learning will be performed (active/passive).

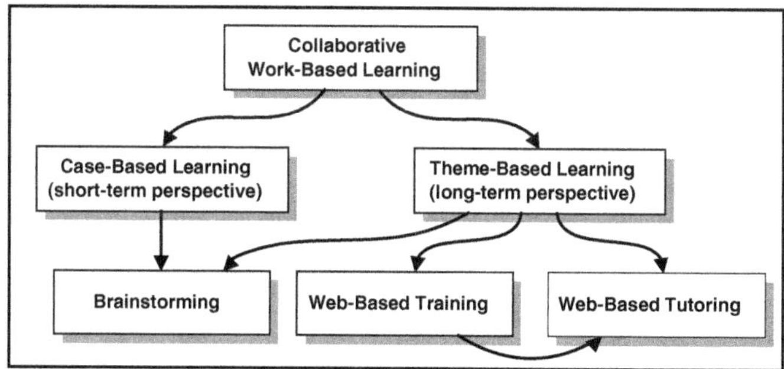

Fig. 9. Interrelation between CORONET-Train learning methods

For each learning method: situation description, recommended knowledge sources, and learning processes are defined. The learning processes are adapted to different competence profiles of the potential users and to specific learning situations and needs (e.g. short-term perspective versus long-term perspective). The advancement of a learner related to a particular subject-matter evolves along three competence levels. The forming of learning groups is described in one of the learning processes. All learning processes are then split into tasks related to the tool functionality access.

Knowledge Workers who have the short-term learning perspective will choose the learning method "Case-Based Learning". They do not have enough time neither to learn a subject-matter extensively nor to attend a training course. In the worst case, they do not know how to handle the project-related case they are working on. The learning method "Brainstorming" will be effective in this situation as the Knowledge Worker can initiate a brainstorming session to discuss the problem with others.

Knowledge Workers who have the long-term learning perspective will choose the learning method "Theme-Based Learning". Subsequently, other learning methods can be applied, such as "Web-Based Training", "Web-Based Tutoring", and "Brainstorming". The goal of the long-term learning is derived from actual project tasks.

Reaching a leaf node in the map of learning methods (i.e. "Web-Based Tutoring" or "Brainstorming") does not necessarily mean that the learning process stops afterwards. The Knowledge Worker may switch seamlessly to another learning situation.

4.4 Reciprocal Learning

Besides Work-Based Learning and Learning by Training, CORONET-Train supports so-called Reciprocal Learning. Reciprocal Learning means learning by teaching, coaching or mentoring. Instead of subject-matter related knowledge and skill acquisition or problem-solving, reciprocal learning aims at the development of social competencies, such as leadership abilities, or coaching, mentoring and teaching competence. This reciprocal learning is reflected by the bi-directional relations of the dyadic learning relations explained in Section 4.2.2.

5 Application and Evaluation

CORONET-Train is applied and evaluated in the context of the CORONET application providers, DC Research Center in Ulm, Germany, and HW in Paris, France. Evaluation goals are defined in close collaboration with DC and HW. The evaluation studies are performed by DC and HW.

5.1 Application Partners

From a requirements and evaluation point of view, the two application partners are complementary. At DC, the focus of CORONET usage is clearly on the work-based learning side, whereas HW focuses on the support of learning by training activities.

Typical DC users are knowledge workers who need to solve concrete problems in their daily work. For many problems, related knowledge is only available in the form of tacit knowledge. Therefore, they need access to an expert who shares his/her knowledge with them, or to peers who experience a similar knowledge need. The access of experts and associated knowledge sharing is supported by the CORONET system.

Typical HW users are being trained in a particular subject-matter. During or after the training course, while they apply what they have learned, they wish to discuss the subject-matter with other trainees and their trainer. Such discussions are supported by the CORONET system.

5.2 Evaluation Plans

Evaluation aims at characterising the effectiveness of the CORONET system. This strategic evaluation goal need to be translated into operational evaluation goals, which are defined from different perspectives: the methodology provider perspective and the application providers' perspective, i.e., DC and HW.

From the methodology provider's point of view, it is important to know how well the demonstrator supports the CORONET-Train methodology, so that specific improvement areas can be identified in the methodology or in the demonstrator and addressed in the second project cycle. This is investigated by evaluation goal 1.

A major goal of CORONET is to support learning. Therefore, evaluation goal 2 investigates learning issues. However, this evaluation goal can only be investigated in practice by investigating how learning takes place at the application providers' sites. Therefore, evaluation goal 2 is implemented by evaluation goals 2a and 2b. Fig. 10 depicts the resulting goal hierarchy. The leaf goals of the goal hierarchy have been detailed using the GQM approach [3] and Kirkpatrick's four-level approach to evaluating training [7]. Data will be collected automatically, with online-questionnaires, and by interviews.

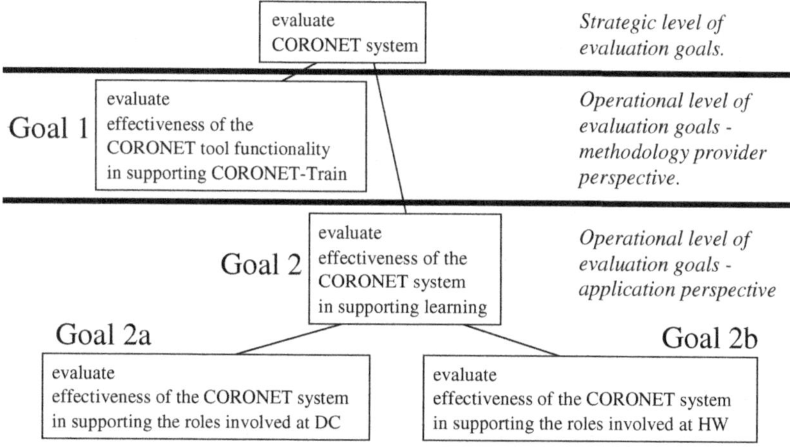

Fig. 10. Evaluation goal hierarchy

Industrial evaluation activities are conducted at the application partners sites of DC and HW. Both DC and HW plan individually tailored evaluation studies.

The overall evaluation goal at the DC site is to evaluate the principal effectiveness from the perspective of the roles involved at DC. These are mainly Knowledge Worker, Coach, Coachee, and Knowledge Engineer. This means on the one hand to check whether the functional elements implemented in the demonstrator are suitable to support the collaborative learning tasks in the DC environment. On the other hand, the effectiveness of the demonstrator from the perspective of the roles involved at DC will be evaluated.

The main evaluation goal at HW is to evaluate the effectiveness of the demonstrator to support exchange between Trainees and Trainer about the usage of previously trained project management techniques in the operational context of their customers. Evaluation studies are conducted in two different companies in France.

6 Conclusion and Future Work

Even though the CORONET project is still at an intermediate stage, most of the innovative didactical concepts related to collaborative learning at the workplace are yet available in the form of the CORONET-Train methodology and a prototype of the CORONET platform.

It is expected that with CORONET-Train, software organisations will be able to improve knowledge acquisition and skill development of their workforce, and thus enhance their software process improvement capability. The main innovations of CORONET-Train are:

Support for long-term competence development.
Enhanced collaboration through networking.
Integration of learning by training and work-based learning
Reciprocal learning (learning by teaching, coaching, mentoring)

With these innovations, CORONET-Train will support software organisations in their continuous improvement efforts, particularly by:

Standardising and stabilising the current SE work practices.
Enabling and fostering of communication, collaboration, and experience exchange.
Offering of demand-oriented web-based training services.
Providing support for sharing and maintaining, as well as identifying and retrieving subject-matter related knowledge.
Dissemination of relevant external knowledge sources.

The first evaluations of both CORONET-Train methodology and CORONET platform started in June 2001. Based on the results of these evaluations an enhanced second version of the CORONET system will be developed and evaluated until end of April 2002. In parallel, a thorough cost-benefit analysis will be conducted.

Acknowledgements. The work presented has partly been funded by the Information Societies Technology Programme of the European Union (IST-1999-11634). Essential input for the definition of the methodology CORONET-Train has been received from Ulrike Behrens, Olivier Bécart, Andreas Birk, Ines Grützner, Niclas Schaper, Nick Scherbakov, Kurt Schneider, Thilo Schwinn, Silke Steinbach-Nordmann, and Michael Stupperich. John D'Ambra, Heike Frank, Ross Jeffery, Michael Ochs, Thilo Schwinn, Olivier Bécart, and Gilles Vallet participated in the development of the evaluation plan.

References

1. Analyse und Evaluation der Softwareentwicklung in Deutschland (English: Analysis and Evaluation of Software Development in Germany). German Ministry of Education and Research (Bundesministerium für Bildung und Forschung) (December 2000)
2. V.R. Basili, G. Caldiera, H.D. Rombach, "Experience Factory", in: Marciniak JJ (ed.), Encyclopedia of Software Engineering, Vol. 1, pp. 469-476, John Wiley & Sons, 1994.

3. L.C. Briand, C. Differding, H.D. Rombach: Practical Guidelines for measurement-based process improvement. In: Journal for Software Process improvement and practice, Vol. 2, No. 4 (December 1996) 253-280.
4. A. Collins, J.S. Brown, S.E. Newman: Cognitive apprenticeship: Teaching the crafts of reading, writing and mathematics. In: L.B. Resnick (Ed.): Knowing, learning and instruction. Essays in the honour of R. Glaser , Hillsdale (NJ), Erlbaum (1989) 453-494
5. A.J. DiBella, E.C. Nevis: How Organizations Learn – An Integrated Strategy for Building Learning Capability, Jossey-Bass Publishers, San Francisco (1998)
6. K. Dovey: The Learning Organization and the Organization of Learning – Power, Transformation and the Search for Form in Learning Organizations. In: Management Learning, Vol. 28, No. 2, (1997), 331-349
7. D. L. Kirkpatrick: Evaluating training programs – The four levels (2nd edition), Berrett-Koehler Publishers, San Francisco (1998)
8. M. Murray, M.A. Owen: Beyond the Myths and Magic of Mentoring: How To Facilitate an Effective Mentoring Program, San Francisco, CA: Jossey-Bass (1991)
9. I. Nonaka, H. Takeuchi: The knowledge-creating company. New York, Oxford University Press (1995)
10. T.J. Ostrand, E.J. Weyuker: A learning environment for software testers at AT&T. In: Proceedings of the 2nd workshop on learning software organizations, Fraunhofer IESE, Kaiserslautern, Germany (2000)
11. J.A. Raelin: Work-Based Learning – The New Frontier of Management Development, Prentice-Hall, New Jersey (2000)
12. G. Reinmann-Rothmeier, H. Mandl: Teamlüge oder Individualisierungsfalle? Eine Analyse kollaborativen Lernens und deren Bedeutung für die Förderung von Lernprozessen in virtuellen Gruppen, Forschungsberichte LMU, 115, Lehrstuhl für empirische Pädagogik und pädagogische Psychologie (November 1999)
13. G. Ruhe, F. Bomarius (eds.): Learning Software Organization - Methodology and Applications, Springer-Verlag, Lecture Notes in Computer Science, Volume 1756 (2000)
14. G. Ruhe, D. Pfahl, J. D'Ambra, C. Differding, R. Ferreira, J. Hornung, V. Mogha, B. Kieslinger, N. Scherbakov, M. Stupperich: Annual Report. Public Project Report, Project IST-1999-11634 (February 2001)
15. R. Schulmeister: Grundlagen hypermedialer Lernsysteme: Theorie-Didaktik-Design, Addision-Wesley, Bonn (1998)
16. E.J. Weyuker, T.J. Ostrand, J.A. Brophy, R. Prasad: Clearing a career path for software testers. In: IEEE Software (March 2000) 76-82

Supporting Knowledge Management in University Software R&D Groups

Christiane Gresse von Wangenheim[1], Daniel Lichtnow[2], Aldo von Wangenheim[2], and Eros Comunello[3]

[1]Universidade do Vale do Itajaí/CES VII, Rod. SC 407, Km 04,CEP 88122-000 São José/SC, Brazil. *Tel:* +55 (48) 281.1517. *Fax:* +55 (48) 281.1506.
gresse@sj.univali.br
http://www.sj.univali.br/~gresse.

[2]Universidade Federal de Santa Catarina
Trindade, 88049-200 Florianópolis, Brazil. *Tel:* +55 (48) 331.7552. *Fax:* +55 (48) 331.9770.
{lichtnow,awangenh}@inf.ufsc.br
http://www.inf.ufsc.br/~awangenh.

[3]University of Kaiserslautern
PO Box 3049, D-67653 Kaiserslautern, Germany.
Tel: +49 (0)631 205 3363. *Fax:* +49 (0)631 205 3357.
eros@informatik.uni-kl.de.

Abstract. One important success factor for Software Research and Development organizations is their ability to systematically manage knowledge and information. Based on our experiences, we examine the specific characteristics and the activities that need knowledge-based support in software R&D organizations in academic environments. A tailored KM solution is outlined considering knowledge content, process, organization and technical infrastructure. The approach is currently being established and evaluated in the context of an international research project.

Keywords: Knowledge Management, Corporate Memory Management Systems, Experience Factory

1 Introduction

Software Research and Development (R&D) organizations aim at developing complex software products and services outstanding in terms of innovation and creativity. Typically, they are composed of multiple interacting communities, each possessing highly specialized knowledge in an environment characterized through rapid changes, shorter development cycles and increased quality demands. In this context, knowledge - the experience, insights, and practical know-how and skills that humans possess and which guide their decisions and actions - is an important asset that makes individual and organizational intelligent behaviour possible and is basic to innovation and creativity. Therefore, the ability to share and leverage knowledge

K.-D. Althoff, R.L. Feldmann, and W. Müller (Eds.): LSO 2001, LNCS 2176, pp. 52-66, 2001.

across the a Software R&D organization has been recognized as important for the success of the organization.

In this context, Knowledge Management (KM) [9],[25] and Organizational Learning (OL) [10],[18],[23] have emerged as explicit areas of pursuit for managing organizations, focusing on how organizations can capitalize what they know, understand what they need to know, and how to make maximum use of the knowledge, and also learning from its application, typically using advanced technology [9],[19].

KM improves knowledge circulation and communication in the organization supporting effective and efficient decision making and the creation of innovative and creative solutions, allowing an organization to retain critical expertise and to avoid loss of an expert's know-how after his retirement or migration. KM enables the exploitation of the experience acquired from past projects and to keep lessons learned in order to avoid the repetition of mistakes and allows nonexperts to retrieve expert advice when needed. It reduces the duplication of effort by efficiently building on previous work. KM enables the consolidation of corporation-wide knowledge into competencies and shortens the learning curve for new technologies, empowering organizations to adapt quickly to changing opportunities [20].

In Software R&D organizations, KM is frequently done in an ad-hoc, informal manner, where the decision to reuse is made by individuals, and the type of knowledge reused is usually limited to personal experiences. Relevant knowledge is often not directly explicitly available, being only available implicitly in the heads of a few employees of the organization. Making this implicit knowledge explicit or sharing it is difficult. Another problem is to access valuable information when required and use it in an efficient and cost-effective manner due to information overload. Thus, to maximize productivity and quality gains through reuse of experience, KM has to be systematized.

This paper addresses the problems faced regarding KM in Software R&D organizations in academic environments, as current R&D methodologies do not adequately address and support the capture and use of relevant information and knowledge. Our work is applied in the context of an international research project, The *Cyclops* Project [8]. This R&D project aims at the development and transfer of new methods, techniques and tools in the area of Medical Image Analysis, being performed by an international R&D consortium consisting of the Federal University of Santa Catarina (Brazil), Taubaté University (Brazil), University of Kaiserslautern (Germany), GMD FIRST (Germany) and medical and industrial partners of both countries, representing an heterogeneous and geographically widespread environment.

The paper is structured as follows: in section 2, we examine the characteristics and specific problems encountered by academic R&D organizations and in Section 3, we describe the research and development activities for which we claim knowledge-based support ought to be provided. A KM solution customized to the identified characteristics, problems and needs is outlined in Section 4. Section 5 describes our current state of research and indicates future research directions.

2 Characteristics of University Software R&D Groups

The principal focus of academic R&D organizations in the Software domain is on research in computer science and the development of prototypical software systems. In this context, research means comprising creative work undertaken on a systematic basis in order to increase the stock of knowledge and the use of this stock of knowledge to devise new applications. Research in the area of computer science today is often technology rather than theory driven. This leads to the development of prototypical software systems which are implemented in order to demonstrate the research solution to be documented and shared. In the domain of our research project, the principal focus is on applied research in the areas of Intelligent Medical Image Analysis, Workflow Management in Medicine, Medical Image Databases and Teleradiology.

In this context, the main objectives of University R&D Groups are twofold:

- on the organizational level, they aim at developing complex software products and services outstanding in terms of innovation and creativity.
- on the individual level, they aim at supporting students to perform intellectually challenging academic projects as part of an honours degree.

This requires support for learning on both levels: organizational and individual, especially as one of the principal objectives of an university environment is to develop knowledge and capabilities.

R&D organizations are typically characterized through highly specialized knowledge and advanced technologies in specific research areas. Researchers need to have sound theoretical knowledge and practical experiences on the specific research topic as well as on research methodologies in order to effectively and efficiently perform research work and software development, as illustrated in Figure 1.

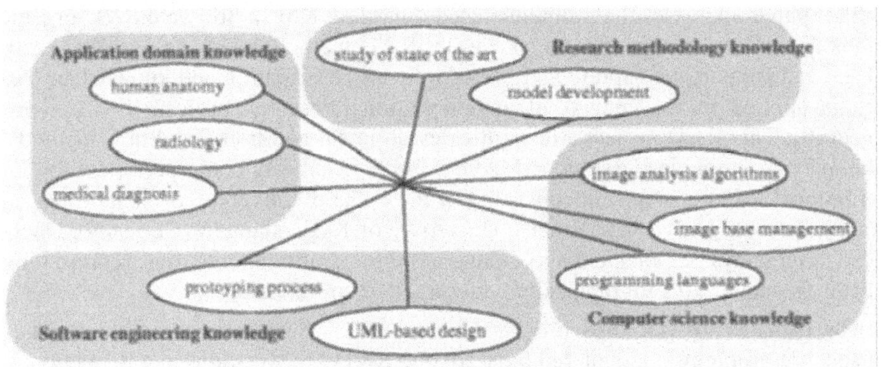

Fig. 1. Examples of knowledge areas of interest

Regarding specifically software research and development in university environments, we can further observe the following characteristics:

Cross-functional and institutional collaboration: R&D organizations are typically composed of multiple interacting communities involving cross-functional and institutional linkages. Different participants join a research project with differing viewpoints. This includes, in the Cyclops research group, for example:

- researchers in Computer Science,
- researchers in Medicine and medical doctors, and
- representatives from radiological equipment and medical software companies.

This also shows the need to bring together participants from across multiple collaborating organizations, where, expertise and skills might be distributed both within and outside the organization. For example, for a research project in the Cyclops project, it is common to employ expertise in specialized areas such as radiology from medical clinics or, for example, through collaborating universities in Brazil and Germany. These cooperating organizations may be geographically distributed in Brazil or world-wide. Especially through the close interaction among these cross-institutional and functional teams, synergy effects contribute to research progress. However, such a collaboration especially requires to organize, integrate, filter, condense and annotate relevant information and to facilitate knowledge sharing and dissemination among the team members.

Constant turnover: University research groups are characterized through a constant turnover of participants, as students generally leave the group when finishing their Master or Ph.D. degrees. This is a major threat to the collective knowledge, since much of the knowledge is situated in the minds of individuals. If there is no repository for knowledge other than personnel, turnover leads to reduction in the organizational knowledge. This includes explicit knowledge (e.g., documents, reports etc. which have not been stored in a centralized database) as well as tacit knowledge which has not been explicitly articulated and stored.

Knowledge leverage: In general, new group members which join the group have different levels of knowledge and capabilities, e.g., a new researcher in the Cyclops Project may have knowledge on image analysis but not on human anatomy or the programming language Smalltalk. In addition, new group members have problems to get an overview on the research done in their area (including also the identification of experts) within or outside the organization. In order to enable the realization of effective research work, members have to acquire the knowledge relevant for the execution of their research project. Such a workplace learning requires to be flexible so that it can be easily adapted to changes in the environment, e.g., wrt. the research areas of interest.

Reinvention of solutions: Often it has been observed that, due to missing information, solutions that might have already been solved either within or outside the organization are reinvented. For example, if within a specific research project a software method for the spiral-CT image segmentation has been developed which could be reused in another project, it is normally re-implemented as its availability remains unknown. In order to prevent this, information and knowledge on existing solutions have to be systematically stored and easily accessible in order to enable their reuse.

Repeated mistakes: Another problem is that often mistakes are repeated due to the inability of organizations to identify or transfer lessons learned, e.g., using Fourier routines for problems where only Wavelet techniques have the power to perform effective texture analysis. In order to prevent this, tacit knowledge on solution strategies applied in the past to solve problems has to be captured explicitly and be accessible when required in order to provide expertise that already exist within the organization.

Resources: Academic environments have limited financial and human resources, which for example does not allow the establishment of additional infrastructural support or special training of new group members.

Constant evolution: The software R&D domain is characterized through continuous evolution of knowledge and rapid technology advances. Therefore, a body of relevant information and knowledge has to be continuously built and updated by constantly gathering new experiences each time a research project is planned and executed.

These goals and characteristics of Software R&D organizations in University environments show that comprehensive KM-based support is required.

3 Which Activities Need Knowledge-Based Support?

The principal activities of software R&D groups in an academic environment can be supported through knowledge and information:

- **Literature search and study** requires knowledge on where to find literature, to distinguish between relevant and irrelevant literature and on how to study literature effectively.
- **Writing research proposals** requires knowledge on the present state of art & practice and the specific research area and knowledge on how to formulate research proposals.
- **Meeting, presenting and discussing ideas** requires organizational support on scheduling meetings, knowledge on how to prepare and present research work and social skills wrt. discussions.
- **Development of theoretical models** requires knowledge on the state of art & practice and the application domain as well as knowledge on research methodologies, on similar research projects and on who, internal or external to the organization, has expertise in the specific area and on solutions which could be reused.
- **Development of prototypical software systems** requires knowledge on software engineering, the systematic development of prototypes as well as capabilities regarding the areas of interest and knowledge on who has expertise or worked on a similar problem and reusable solutions.
- **Writing and publishing scientific papers** requires knowledge on the state of art & practice, the application domain as well as writing skills.
- **Cooperating with research organizations**, industrial and application partners requires the integration of different background knowledge and the sharing of research results, (tele-) meetings and social communication skills.
- **Organization of research** or industrial projects requires knowledge on research programs, disciplines for the planning of projects and the execution of projects.

- **Attending conferences** requires information on upcoming conferences related to the research area of interest and funding possibilities.
- **Organization of events** requires knowledge on planning and execution procedures of events, funding and sponsoring possibilities, etc.
- **Teaching of knowledge** wrt. the research area of interest could be supported through overviews on information sources, tutorials, etc.

These requirements show that it would be beneficial to connect the individual researchers of the organization in a way that they could easily communicate and share any of the above listed type of information or knowledge.

4 Applying KM to a Software R&D Organization in an Academic Research Environment

As pointed out in Section 2, Software R&D organizations in university environments reflect learning on the organizational and individual level. Organizational learning is defined as a skilled process in which both explicit and tacit knowledge is created, acquired, and transferred wrt. the goals of the organization. During individual learning, the knowledge of one single person expands, in a process, in which experiences are transformed into knowledge, through observing phenomena, analysing them, developing models and theories about them and testing these theories an models in practice [16]. In order to effectively and efficiently support learning in university software R&D organizations, the processes necessary to continuously create and share knowledge across the organization have to be supported systematically. This is the goal of KM: to deliver the right information or knowledge at the right time, at the right place, in the right format, satisfying the quality requirements at the lowest possible cost [24]. In order to operationalize KM in software R&D organizations in university environments, relevant know-how has to be continuously build up by gathering new explicit and tacit knowledge during the planning and execution of R&D activities. A logical and physical structure for the continuous build-up of know-how in a software organization is the Experience Factory (EF) approach [5], [6]. The EF environment complements the project organization by enabling the continuous learning on software development from experiences from their software projects and corporate-wide communication of software know-how, thereby promoting the creation of organizational know-how and the establishment of core competencies of the organization. The EF proposes a methodological framework for analysing and synthesizing all kinds of experiences, acting as a repository for those, and supplying these experiences to various software projects on demand. These organizational experiences cover all types of knowledge assets which can support the planning or execution of software projects. Besides internal knowledge sources including explicit knowledge, for example, expertise and lessons learned on software engineering technologies, documents on medical knowledge, deliverables (e.g. software code parcels) or process guides (e.g. on how to give presentations) as well as tacit knowledge in the heads of the researchers, the EF framework can be extended to external knowledge sources, such as the Internet, and in our specific context to knowledge gained through university lectures (see Figure 2).

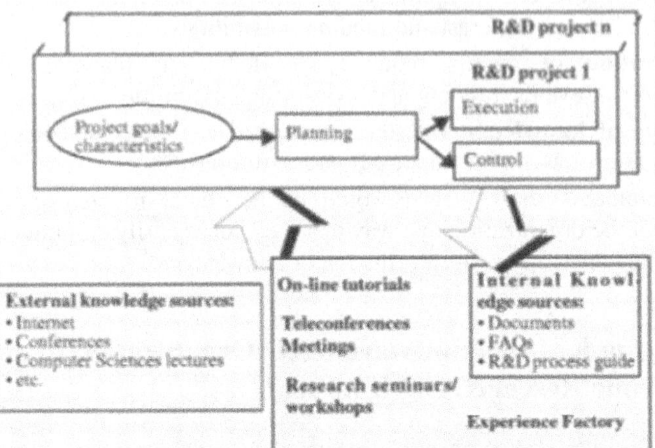

Fig. 2. Experience Factory Organization in University Software R&D Groups

For successfully building knowledge management capabilities within an organization in practice, four key areas have been identified:

- **Knowledge content**: identification and modelling of the valuable knowledge available to be used.
- **Organization**: structuring of the organization for knowledge exchange between human agents, including managerial and motivational aspects.
- **Processes**: definition of the processes to create, build, transform, organize, deploy and use knowledge effectively.
- **Technological support**: definition of tools supporting the creation and sharing of knowledge.

In the following sections, we describe each of these key areas outlining a KM solution customized to the characteristics of university software R&D organizations.

4.1 What Kind of Knowledge Is Reusable?

A main goal of KM is to capitalize existing information and knowledge. This includes sources which are explicitly available in the organization, i.e., documents or tacit knowledge in form of personal experiences, which may be externalized, e.g., by inciting the members of the organization to write lessons learned on solution strategies applied or external knowledge.

The kind of knowledge relevant in software R&D activities can be determined based on the KM goals of the organization, which define goals to be achieved through the sharing and communication of information and knowledge throughout the organization. These KM goals need to be connected to strategic goals of the organization, its specific characteristics and needs. The KM goals can be comprehensively defined in terms of the object to be reused, the purpose for which the object is reused, the activity to be supported, the role, who reuses the know-how and the context in which reuse takes place. Examples of goals include:

- to **reuse documents** in order to support literature study from the viewpoint of a researcher in the research organization,
- to **reuse lessons learned** in order to prevent the repetition of failures in the implementation from the viewpoint of a developer at the research organization,
- to **retrieve similar FAQs** in order to create generalized guides for frequently reoccurring problems, e.g., on the understanding of image analysis techniques from the viewpoint of the knowledge engineer at the research group Cyclops.

Based on the relevant knowledge in R&D activities (as described in Section 3) and the respective reuse goals, the following types of knowledge can be considered of interest:

Documents records (and files) constituting a personalized library including published literature, as well as, publications of members of the organization. The document records state referential information (such as title, author, year of publication) as well as comments and annotations (e.g., indicating the relevance of certain chapters). In addition, the record indicates the location where the document is available (e.g., university library) or, when available in electronic form, enables the upload and storage of the respective file. Such a library facilitates the access to relevant documents and helps to manage documents produced by the organization.

Project documentation including project proposals, plans and reports on research and industrial projects as well as students academic projects. The availability of those project documentations provides examples on plans facilitating the development of new ones and supports the execution of future projects.

On-line tutorials on topics relevant for the specific research environment. The availability of on-line tutorials enables researchers to learn on the specific topic independently and whenever necessary.

Frequently Asked Questions (FAQ) state a question and its answer provided by an expert. A collection of FAQs permits to automatically answer repetitively occurring questions. This facilitates the access to practical knowledge (e.g., on how to create a database connection to an application) and liberates experts to focus on more complex problems. A form to represent lessons learned in an accessible form is to describe them also in form of FAQs, by indicating a question which could be answered by the lesson and describing the lesson as answer to this question.

How-to-do recipes describing step-by-step how repetitively occurring tasks have to be done (e.g., how to connect a laptop to a X-ray computer). These recipes enable inexperienced researchers to perform these tasks without requiring the assistance of an expert.

WWW maps listing and commenting relevant Web sites for a specific research area, e.g., on the standard DICOM. WWW maps guide the location of WWW sites of interest. They allow a more efficient access to relevant Internet sites that otherwise would be difficult and time-consuming to find.

Yellow pages capture human-resource capabilities and indicate experts wrt. specific research topics. The Yellow pages allow members to know whom to contact when they otherwise cannot find a satisfactory solution.

Starter´s kits summarizing and commenting information or knowledge relevant to a beginner wrt. a specific research area (e.g., introducing the programming language Smalltalk by referencing introductory texts, a tutorial and basic technical manuals, and indicating mailing lists and human experts). These pages allow newcomers to effectively and efficiently discover the respective research area.

News messages are any notes or comments of relevance to the research organization (e.g., to notify the availability of a new software version). The systematic management of these messages enables the communication of news and keeps the members informed.

Software parcels packaging and commenting software code or executables which have been developed within or are available outside the organization. Reusing these parcels prevents the re-implementation of readily available software and, thus, can reduces the development effort and improve the quality of the software.

R&D process guides are process models or guides on software R&D activities describing the activities to be performed (e.g., prototype development), model the outputs to be produced (e.g., on the structure and content of a master thesis) and describes how to do the activities. (e.g., on how to write a paper).

Conference calendar is a calendar indicating and commenting conferences of relevance to the research organization. The explicit availability of conference information facilitates the planning of conference participations and keeps the members informed.

The information and knowledge represented in the CM cover all relevant research areas wrt. the specific R&D organization, such as application domain (e.g., radiology, human anatomy), computer science and software engineering (such as image interpretation algorithms, software process model) as well as research methodologies (e.g., on literature revision).

4.2 KM Process in R&D Environments

The KM process can be basically divided into three phases [9]: knowledge generation, knowledge codification and knowledge transfer.

Knowledge Generation aims at the generation of knowledge from various sources. Knowledge can be generated through knowledge acquisition from external sources such as conferences or through university courses related to the specific research areas. Inside the organization, knowledge can be created by bringing together people with different perspectives via research seminars, meetings or teleconferences.

Knowledge Codification aims at putting organizational knowledge into a form that makes it accessible to those who need it. Its purpose is to locate and capture organizational knowledge relevant wrt. the knowledge management tasks, to make it explicit and to organize and represent it in a form which allows its access, delivery and manipulation. Knowledge capture requires systematic procedures for acquiring, organising and structuring organisational knowledge. Knowledge from external sources can, for example, be acquired each time a group member discovers a WWW site or a scientific paper of interest on the Internet. Knowledge acquisition from internal sources can include the exploitation of explicit knowledge already available in the organization (e.g., technical reports or project documentation) or to externalize tacit knowledge and to capture it in some kind of knowledge representation. For example, tacit knowledge can be externalized by writing down lessons learned or by explicitly describing research projects and the expertise of group members. For frequently re-occurring problems, how-to-do recipes can be developed as well as process guides. Knowledge can also be captured by documenting human-based knowledge management. For example, each time a question is answered by a human expert a possibility to acquire new problem-solving knowledge arises.

The acquired knowledge has to be represented and stored to make it accessible and useable to people in an organisation by explicitly modelling objects and their relationships. It may takes different forms with variations in emphasis and formalisms, such as knowledge maps, hypertexts, cases, etc. In addition, the existing knowledge can be synthesized and/or generalized in order to prevent the proliferation of knowledge items and to improve the usability of the available knowledge.

Knowledge Transfer aims at developing strategies to encourage and enable the exchange of knowledge within the organization. Knowledge transfer can be done through person-to-person communications, e.g., through workshops, or through a distributed technical infrastructure which allows to access relevant information and knowledge across the organization.

Executing this knowledge process in a cyclical way results in rapidly growing, well-evaluated, up-to-date, and demand-oriented learning contents of corporate learning systems [1],[7]. Besides these basic phases of KM, in order to cover a continuous knowledge life cycle, maintenance and evolution of the stored knowledge and knowledge management processes is explicitly needed [3]. Maintenance and evolution aims at continuously improve the provided support based on feedback from its application in practice (e.g., regarding the researchers' satisfaction) and the adaptation of the knowledge and information in accordance to changes in the environment.

4.3 Organization of KM in R&D Environments

Effective knowledge management requires a solution integrating management and technological infrastructure.

4.3.1 Technical Infrastructure

To operationalize the Experience Factory in practice, KM requires a technical infrastructure, denoted Corporate Memory Management System (CMMS) [13]. A CMMS includes Corporate Memories (CM) which are the central repository of all the information and knowledge relevant to the KM task in an organization as well as tools to manage this knowledge-base. The tools need to support the access to the right information or knowledge, the continuous acquisition of new experiences and their integration and storage as well as the continuous adaptation and maintenance of the CMMS to the specific environment..

Today, a wide range of Information Technologies are being used to implement CMMSs in general [2],[3], as well as for the software domain [21]. These technologies include e-mail and group support systems, databases and data warehouses, browsers and search engines, intranets and internets, knowledge base systems and intelligent agents. Although, the approaches are numerous, none of these technologies itself offers a comprehensive support. In order to develop a CMMS that effectively contributes to KM in software R&D organizations, requires the integration of various approaches. For example, RetrievalWare [22] integrates natural language concepts and keyword searching and profiling. IKnow [14], includes natural language querying, mechanisms for the acquisition of new information and supports the continuous improvement of the retrieval performance. Other systems (e.g., Answer Garden [4]) integrate human experts into the KM process by forwarding questions which could not been satisfactory answered by the CMMS.

Based on our experiences, we propose a hybrid approach for an effective technical infrastructure to KM integrating techniques from various areas, such as Case-Based Reasoning, Information Retrieval and Information Filtering [11]. Our approach focuses on the support of the user through an intelligent assistant system, acquiring, providing, maintaining and distributing relevant information and knowledge (see Figure 3).

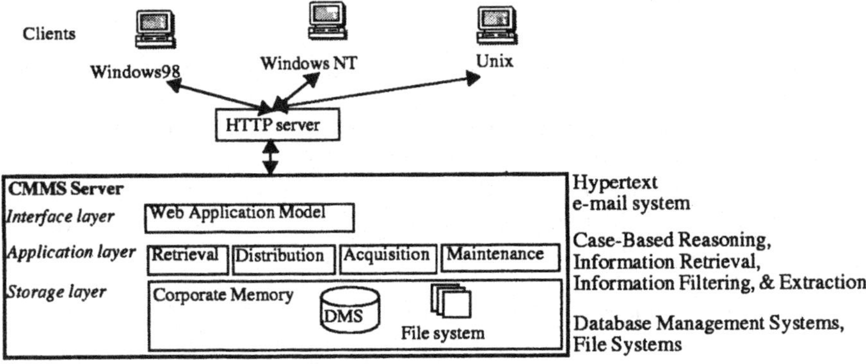

Fig. 3. CMMS Architecture

Various types of reusable information or knowledge (as described in Section 4.1), denoted as CM assets, are stored in the CM. The CM assets are indexed wrt. their specific content as a basis for effective and efficient retrieval.

Besides the CM assets, general domain knowledge is represented in the CM defining terminology and basic concepts of the specific research areas (e.g., the programming language Smalltalk or human brain anatomy). It includes:

- **Classification of relevant knowledge areas**: indicating relevant research areas and their relationships (e.g., Smalltalk (Smalltalk Database Connection, VisualWave, Distributed Smalltalk), Telemedicine (PACS, Teleradiology, DICOM), etc.) enabling a hierarchical classification of the CM assets.
- **Vocabularies**: indicating indicative expressions of the research areas for the indexation of CM assets. For example, the vocabulary on the programming language Smalltalk includes, the terms "class", "SortedCollection", etc.
- **Thesauri**: indicating associative or hierarchical relations between terms in the given domain, e.g., in the context of the programming language Smalltalk the terms "Collection" and "SortedCollection" are considered as similar.

- **Bilingual dictionaries**: indicating the translation of domain-specific terms. In our specific application, we focus on Portuguese-English dictionaries. Here, example terms are "class -> classe" or "OrderedCollection -> coleção ordenada".

In addition, general vocabularies on the Portuguese and English language are represented as a basis for spelling correction of natural language queries.

The CMMS provides manifold support enabling the access to various types of information, knowledge or human experts for various purposes (e.g., facilitate a research on the state-of-art or guide the solution of a programming problem), from different viewpoints (e.g., developer, medical researcher). Search mechanisms (such as e.g., keyword search, similarity-based search) enable the effective and efficient retrieval of useful assets or to guide the access to human experts. Based on the user´s query, the CM is searched and the most relevant CM asset(s) are returned. If the CMMS does not provide a satisfactory retrieval result, the user can automatically direct her/his query to a human expert of the respective research area via e-mail. Once the answer is available, it is automatically send to the user and by composing the user´s query and the answer provided by the expert, a new CM asset is created and integrated into the CM (see Figure 4).

The search mechanisms allow the formulation of queries in natural language (e.g., in Portuguese and English in case of the Cyclops Project) and enable multilingual retrieval (e.g., searching also for English assets for queries formulated in Portuguese). In addition, the CMMS also assist researchers in finding information and knowledge that satisfies long-term goals (e.g. being aware of new publications in the area of radiological 3D reconstructions) through the pro-active distribution of knowledge wrt. to an user´s specific interests (e.g., informing about new published papers wrt. her/his research area).

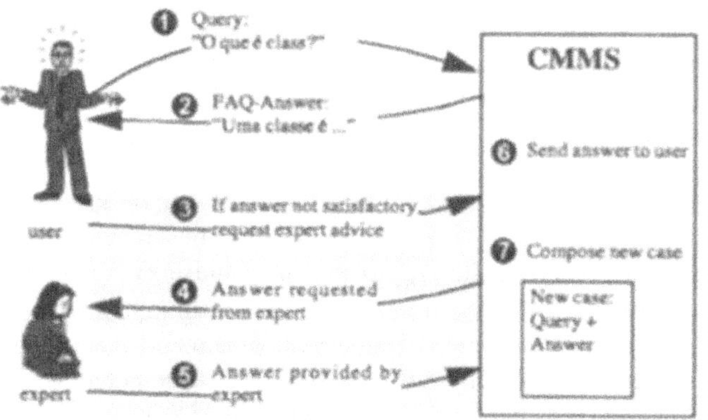

Fig. 4. Interactive retrieval process

In the context of a software R&D organization, relevant information and knowledge is not completely available when creating the CM. Therefore, KM in software R&D organizations requires support for the continuous evolution of the knowledge base and has to be able to deal with incompleteness and inconsistency. This includes the continuous acquisition of new assets as integrated part of the R&D activities (i.e., reporting a FAQ on an recently occurred programming problem) and the indexing and integration of the new acquired assets into the existing CM. In addition, support for the maintenance of the knowledge assets, the general domain knowledge, as well as the improvement of the access mechanisms is provided based on feedback from its application in practice, e.g., through usage protocols. For further details on the technical infrastructure we refer to [11],[12].

4.3.2 Management Infrastructure

The actual establishment of KM in Software R&D organizations needs to be embedded into a management infrastructure that provides funding and strategies to consolidate reuse and learning. Following the EF approach, the organization is divided into project organization and EF. The project organization includes several R&D projects which primary focus is on the development of research or prototypical software systems. Within these projects, information or knowledge from external knowledge sources or the EF is reused and new gathered experiences are collected. In contrast, the EF aims at enabling the reuse of information and knowledge. Therefore, it focuses on supporting the generation, codification, coordination, sharing and maintenance of the knowledge and provides a technical infrastructure for the performance of these tasks. In accordance with the EF approach, every member of the research group has the responsibility to generate, collect and use available information and knowledge relevant to the research project. For example, a member of the Cyclops project who discovers how to establish a database connection within a Smalltalk image has the responsibility to write a lesson learned describing the required steps or a student working on her/his master thesis has the responsibility to include all literature references studied into the CMMS.

Furthermore, for each research area of interest in a specific organization (e.g., on the standard DICOM or the programming language Smalltalk), a domain expert is allocated. His/her responsibility is to create a starter's kit wrt. the specific research area and to revise CM assets which have been negatively commented by the users of the CMMS. In addition, the domain expert is responsible to answer FAQ questions from her/his colleagues related to his/her specific area of expertise.

In addition, a knowledge engineer, responsible for the creation and maintenance of the EF is required, who analyses, revises, evaluates and improves the EF. S/he is also responsible for initiating the development of more generic knowledge based on the observation of frequently re-occurring problems. The knowledge engineer also supports the researchers on request in retrieving and acquiring experiences.

A major problem regarding the introduction of KM in practice is the motivation of the members of the organization to explicitly document and share their knowledge. In order to be successful, KM activities related to the documentation of information and knowledge have to become part of the regular R&D tasks of the organization requesting from all members to share their experiences. This includes for example, the continuous documentation of studied literature or discovered web sites of interest. Students have to present what did work and what did not in their research, diagnosing the problems they encountered and the solution strategies they applied in research seminars as well as by documenting project reports.

5 Outlook and Future Research

For continuous learning in a software R&D organization, systematic knowledge management customized to the specific characteristics and needs is important. In this paper, we describe the requirements for appropriate KM support in software R&D environments based on our experiences in the Cyclops research project. We describe the key areas of KM regarding the required content, processes, organization and technical infrastructure. Currently, we are establishing an EF in the Cyclops project. This includes the organization of weekly research seminars and semestral workshops, regular research topic-specific discussions as well as the implementation of a technical infrastructure. The current implementation of the CMMS focuses on the retrieval (search by navigation and attribute search) and the collection of documents and WWW sites. In addition, mechanisms for the handling and retrieval of FAQs via content-based searching on Portuguese natural language queries have been implemented [12] as well as techniques for the maintenance of the general domain knowledge (including Portuguese domain vocabulary, dictionary and thesaurus on Smalltalk issues). Based on a first evaluation after two months of application in the Cyclops project (limited to the research group at the Federal University of Santa Catarina), we received a positive feedback regarding the usefulness of the CMMS. During the first month, we basically focused on motivating the collection of assets, as the application practically started without any asset stored in the CM. This resulted in the collection of about 140 assets during the first month and a total number of 180 in the second month. Regarding the number of accesses to the CMMS, we observed a rather low number (about 20) during the first month due to the fact that in the beginning only few assets were available. But, in the second month this number increased to about 60 accesses and we are expecting this to continue as more assets become available. Based on further results of its performance and perceived usefulness, we intend to continue the implementation of the CMMS and to broaden the scope of research areas covered. In addition, we are also developing a R&D process guide for the Cyclops project based on the Quality Improvement Paradigm integrating incremental prototyping and Extreme Programming concepts. Future research also includes the development of intelligent knowledge-based techniques regarding information extraction, filtering and retrieval.

Acknowledgments. The authors would like to thank A. Bortolon, D. D. Abdalla, E. M. Barros, P. Dellani and F. Secco for their support and the anonymous reviewers for their helpful comments.

References

[1] K.-D. Althoff et al. Systematic Population, Utilization, and Maintenance of a Repository for Comprehensive Reuse. In G. Ruhe, F. Bomarius (eds.) Learning Software Organizations. Springer Verlag, 2000.

[2] A. Abecker, S. Decker. Organizational Memory: Knowledge Acquisition, Integration, and Retrieval Issues. Proc. of the Workshop on Expertsystems, Germany, 1999.

[3] A. Abecker et al. Toward a Technology for Organizational Memories. IEEE Intelligent Systems, 13(3), June 1998.

[4] M.S. Ackerman, T. W. Malone. Answer Garden: A Tool for Growing Organizational Memory. Proc. of the Conference on Office Information Systems, Cambridge, MA, 1990.

[5] V. R. Basili, G. Caldiera, H. D. Rombach. Experience Factory. In John J. Marciniak, ed., Encyclopedia of Software Engineering, vol.1, pp. 528-532. John Wiley & Sons, 1994.

[6] V.R. Basili, M. Lindvall, P. Costa. Implementing the Experience Factory Concepts as a Set of Experience Bases. Proc. of the 13th International Conference on Software Engineering and Knowledge Engineering, Argentina, 2001.

[7] A. Birk, F. Kröschel. A Knowledge Management Lifecycle for Experience Packages of Software Engineering Technologies. G. Ruhe, F. Bomarius (eds.) Learning Software Organizations. Springer Verlag, 2000.

[8] The Cyclops Project (www.inf.ufsc.br/cyclops)

[9] T. H. Davenport, L. Prusak. Working Knowledge - How Organizations Manage What They Know. Harvard Business School Press, 1998.

[10] P. F. Drucker. The Post-Capitalist Society. Butterworth-Heinemann Ltd., 1993.

[11] C. Gresse von Wangenheim, D. Lichtnow, A. von Wangenheim. A Hybrid Approach for Corporate Memory Management Systems in Software R&D Organizations. Proc. of the 13th Int. Conference on Software Engineering and Knowledge Engineering, Argentina, 2001.

[12] C. Gresse von Wangenheim, A. Bortolon, A. von Wangenheim. A Hybrid Approach for the Management of FAQ Documents in Latin Languages. Proc. of the 4th Int. Conference on Case-Based Reasoning, Vancouver, Canada, 2001.

[13] C. Gresse von Wangenheim, C. Tautz. Summary of the Workshop on Practical Case-Based Reasoning Strategies for Building and Maintaining Corporate Memories at the 3. Int. Conference on Case-Based Reasoning, Germany, 1999.

[14] IKnow (www.knowlix.com/products/iknow.htm).

[15] KnowledgeX (www-3.ibm.com/software/swprod).

[16] D.A. Kolb. Experiential Learning. Prentice Hall, 1984.

[17] J. Laffey, R. Machiraju, R. Chandhok. Integrated Support and Learning Systems for Augmenting Knowledge Workers. Proc. of the World Congress on Expert Systems, Orlando, FL, 1991.

[18] I. Nonaka, T. Takeuchi. The Knowledge-Creating Company. Oxford University Press, Cambridge, UK, 1995.

[19] D. O'Leary. Knowledge Management Systems: Converting and Connecting. IEEE Intelligent Systems, May/June 1998.

[20] C.K. Prahalad, G. Hamel. The Core Competence of the Corporation. Harvard Business Review, 68(3), May 1990.

[21] G. Ruhe, F. Bomarius (eds.) Learning Software Organizations, Springer Verlag, 2000.

[22] RetrievalWare.(www.excalib.com/products/rw/index.shtml).

[23] P.Senge. The Fifth Discipline. Currency Doubleday, 1990.

[24] K.M. Wiig, R. de Hoog, R. van der Spek. Supporting Knowledge Management: A Selection of Methods and Techniques. Expert Systems with Applications, 13(1), 1997.

[25] K. M. Wiig. Knowledge Management: Where did it come from and where will it go?, Expert Systems with Applications, 13(1), 1997.

Part 4:

Applications

Organisational Learning and Software Process Improvement: A Case Study

Judith Segal

Faculty of Maths and Computing, Department of Computing, The Open University, Walton Hall, Milton Keynes, MK7 6AA, UK
j.a.segal@open.ac.uk

Abstract. This paper describes a longitudinal study of an organisation over a period of eighteen months as it initiated and then implemented a manual of software best practice. The organisation consists of end-users, in the sense that, although developing software is an integral part of their job, they are not professional software developers. Although the organisation itself was unaware of current trends in Software Process Improvement (SPI) or theories of organisational learning, our case study affords us insights into some practical deficiencies of the accepted techno-centric model of a SPI programme. We argue that such a model imposes unnatural work practices on an organisation and fails to take account of how process improvements might occur spontaneously within a community of practice.

1 Introduction

This paper is concerned with investigating the contribution that a software process improvement programme might make to organisational memory and learning. Our discussion is grounded in data from a case study, a longitudinal study of an organisation as it attempted, over eighteen months, to introduce a manual in order to control the quality of its financial modelling by assuring its processes and procedures. The modelling is effected using both a proprietary software modelling and a generic spreadsheet package, and the people who construct the models are professional, or would-be professional, financial consultants. Such people may be termed 'computing end-users', that is, people who are not computing professionals, but for whom the use of computers, and the writing of software, is an integral part of their job. As might be expected from end-users, there was little awareness within the organisation of software development standards, still less of models of software process improvement (SPI) and current thinking on organisational learning. As we shall see in section 4 herein, the manual was introduced as an ad-hoc measure in an attempt to address the perceptions of senior management as to how embarrassing software failures might be avoided. Although our data are situated in a particular organisation over a particular period of time, we believe that analysing them from the perspective of models of SPI and theories of organisational learning, can give valuable insights into SPI and the contribution that an SPI programme affords to such learning. Our data support the view that the accepted SPI model might be too techno-centric, in that it might force unnatural ways of working; place too much emphasis on metrics and insufficiently

K.-D. Althoff, R.L. Feldmann, and W. Müller (Eds.): LSO 2001, LNCS 2176, pp. 68-82, 2001.

recognise the importance of communities of practice in sharing and creating knowledge.

Before we describe our case study in detail, we shall discuss some recent related research in section 2. The background to our case study is given in section 3. In section 4, we describe the initiation and implementation of the manual. Section 5 is concerned with the aims of the manual, ideal scenarios of usage by which the aims might best be achieved, and the differences between the ideal and the actuality. In section 6, we discuss these differences and what they might suggest about the implementation of SPI programmes, and their contribution to organisational learning.

2 Background: Some Recent Relevant Research

In this section, we begin by discussing what are, in our view, the salient characteristics of end-user software development. We continue by discussing the link between organisational learning and SPI programmes and describe some recent empirical studies of SPI. We conclude by considering the less formal but very important role of communities of practice in creating and sharing knowledge.

2.1 Characteristics of End-User Software Development

Here we discuss two salient characteristics of end-user software development: autonomy and error-proneness. Regarding autonomy, the advent and explosion of use of PCs over the past two decades might be seen as liberating end-users from the tyranny of the computing professional. With the help of application development packages specifically aimed at end-users, such as spreadsheets, or by using reusable customisable software components, end-users can, in theory, develop their own software as they need it, and alter it at will in line with changing requirements. However, there are (at least) two basic problems with end-user software development. The first problem is that there may be cognitive difficulties with the enabling software which are not immediately apparent. Hendry and Green [1] noted that while spreadsheets might be very easy to develop, they are rather difficult to comprehend, making them difficult to debug, modify, extend or reuse. The use of reusable software components poses its own cognitive difficulties, for example, how does one know which component will fit one's need? The second problem is that end-users typically lack software engineering knowledge, that is, they are unlikely to know sound practices for developing and checking their software. These two problems, the inadequacy of the enabling software and lack of practice knowledge, might explain why much end-user developed software is faulty, Panko, [2]. Many people argue for more organisational controls on end-user computing, see, for example, Taylor et al. [3], although there is evidence that such controls are rare, and even where they do exist, are not always adhered to (Hall, [4]).

We now turn our attention away from end-user software developers and discuss the current trend among professional developers towards implementing software process improvement (SPI) initiatives with the primary purpose of assuring the quality of software by assuring the quality of the processes involved in its development. As we shall see, SPI programmes can also provide a framework for maintaining an organisational memory of processes.

2.2 Software Process Improvement Programmes

Here, we firstly discuss a model of software process improvement (SPI) and then describe some recent empirical studies on the implementation of SPI programmes.

2.2.1 A Model of Software Process Improvement

Fig.1 illustrates a generic model of software process improvement. An organisation defines its organisational procedures, processes and standards with a view to improving software quality. These procedures/standards/processes are then tailored to individual projects, and the person responsible for quality control ensures that they are followed by the project team. Process metrics are collected in a variety of settings. Process improvements may be suggested, with a view to, for example, reducing any large variation in a metric. The improved process becomes the defined standard, and the cycle begins again. The metrics are then used to determine whether the new process is, indeed, an improvement on the old.

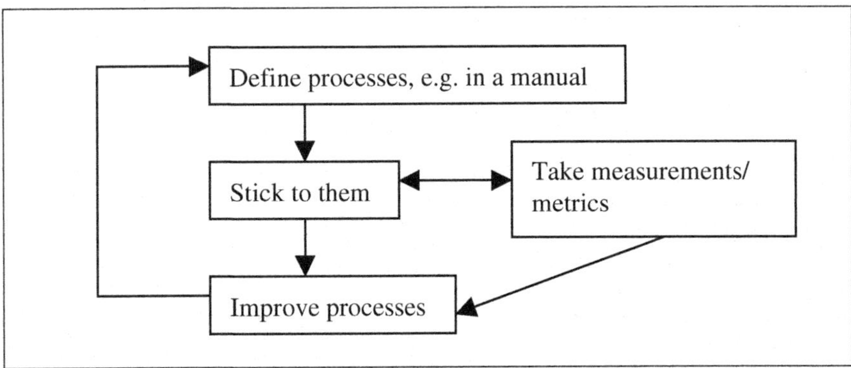

Fig. 1. A generic model of software process improvement (SPI)

This generic model might also be viewed as providing a framework for organisational learning about processes. Defining the processes and procedures may be viewed as creating an organisational memory; improving the processes, as organisational learning. We should emphasise that this view of SPI, as a framework for organisational learning, is not that taken by much of the literature on this topic. Rather, the literature focuses on the original purpose of SPI, which is to improve software quality by way of assuring software development processes.

In the literature, there are both practical and theoretical concerns voiced about the SPI model as illustrated in Fig.1. One practical concern is that organisations might focus on one part of the model at the expense of another. There is consensus in the literature on SPI that continuous process improvement is essential to the establishment of a quality culture in a software development organisation, see, for example, Fox & Frakes [5], Curtis [6] and Sweeney & Bustard [7]. The concern is that, in practice, SPI programmes might concentrate on the definition phase to the detriment of continuous improvement. This concentration might be fostered by certification bodies, such as TickIT [8] which certify that the quality assurance procedures of an organisation, as documented in the organisation's quality manual, conform to a specific standard, such as ISO 9001. With this single-stage certification, once an organisation can show potential customers its certificate, unless the organisation is convinced of the necessity of a quality culture for its own sake, there is not much incentive for it to continually improve its processes/procedures, at any rate, not until the time for re-certification comes round again. In contrast to single stage certification, the Software Engineering Institute, at Carnegie-Mellon University in the USA, has developed a five stage (level) model, the Capability Maturity Model, CMM, to be used both for raising and appraising the process maturity of an organisation. At the first level, both the quality of the software product and the development processes are unpredictable. By the final level, continuous process improvement is integrated into the organisation. For both single and multi-stage certification, there is the concern that organisations may focus on gaining the certification as a marketing badge, rather than on establishing a quality culture.

As to theoretical issues regarding SPI, there is a concern that both the generic SPI model and specific SPI implementations may be too techno-centric. This reflects the apparent consensus in the literature that large software failures can rarely be ascribed purely to technical causes, such as technically inadequate procedures. Organisational and human factors (cultural; psychological; social) often play a major role. See for example, [9] – [12].

Notwithstanding the practical and theoretical issues described above, software process improvement continues to be an important mechanism in improving software quality, and there have been several empirical studies concerning the implementation of an SPI programme, which we shall now describe.

2.2.2 Empirical Studies of SPI Programmes

One of the most frequently cited papers in this area is that of Herbsleb et al., [13], which examined the efficacy of CMM (described briefly above), together with the factors associated with a successful, or conversely, a failing, SPI programme. This examination was based on data gathered from case-studies, questionnaires and CMM assessments. Other relevant studies include those of Hall & Wilson, [14], who conducted a series of interviews with middle managers and developers; McGuire, [15], investigating a team of experienced software developers over the transition period as CMM was introduced, and Sweeney and Bustard, [7], who recorded their experiences of implementing a quality management system in an MIS department. These studies identify four recurring themes: the vulnerability of SPI efforts to deadlines and external pressures; the necessity for adequate allocation of time and resources; the importance of the role and attitude of executive management, and the necessity of viewing an SPI initiative in terms of organisational change.

Considering the four themes in turn: in a survey reported in Herbsleb, over 40% of respondents agreed, or strongly agreed, with the statement "[SPI had] been overcome by events and crises". This vulnerability of SPI to external pressures was also observed by Hall & Wilson, whose interviewees reported that the ability to meet deadlines is often perceived as being more valued by the organisation than the construction of a quality product. The necessity of adequate allocation of time and resources is reported both in Herbsleb et al., where over 70% of survey respondents agreed, or strongly agreed, with the statement that SPI has "often suffered due to time and resource limitation", and in Sweeney & Bustard. The importance of the role of executive management is noted in several studies. Hall & Wilson, comment on the profound influence that the attitude of senior management has on practitioners regarding a quality culture; Sweeney & Bustard assert that visible support from management is crucial to the success of any improvement programme; Herbsleb et al. comment on the importance of senior management actively monitoring SPI progress, and Curtis takes the view that 'lack of executive support is the single biggest reason that improvement programs fail'. The support of executive management can, however, be equivocal. Hall & Wilson note that senior management is often suspected of 'jumping on the bandwagon' and merely paying lip-service to quality issues. Finally in this section, we note a cognisance in the literature that implementing a successful software process improvement programme involves organisational change, see, for example, McGuire, and that the nature of this change needs to be better understood, Herbsleb et al.

SPI is a formal activity: we shall now turn our attention to the less formal but very important activity of knowledge creation and sharing within a community of practice.

2.3 Knowledge Sharing and Creation in Communities of Practice

There is more to organisational knowledge than that which can be explicated in a manual. Cook & Brown, [16], distinguish four different types of knowledge: individual and group explicit knowledge, which might be defined and captured in a manual, and individual and group tacit knowledge. An example of individual tacit knowledge is the ability to ride a bike; group tacit knowledge includes emerging conventions and metaphors by which the group works together and shares ideas. Cook & Brown also distinguish between knowledge and knowing, which they characterise as the deployment of knowledge in physical or mental action. They claim that the interplay between knowledge and knowing can lead to the creation of new knowledge and new forms of knowing.

Communities of practice are groups of people who perform similar tasks, have similar goals and work (probably) in some proximity to each other. An example of such a community, as given in Brown & Duguid, [17], are the photocopier repairers who all work for the same company. The importance of such communities in sharing and creating knowledge as part of their work practice, and in informal social settings, is well recognised in the literature: Brown & Duguid give a very readable account of this phenomenon. The question arises as to how to capture such knowledge, created collaboratively and spontaneously. Mulholland et al., [18], describe the design and implementation of tools for capturing unobtrusively the knowledge created spontaneously as an intrinsic part of communal work practice in an industrial environment. They do not, however, comment on the efficacy of the tools.

Having discussed the characteristics of end-user software developers, and the two perspectives, SPI and organisational learning, by which we wish to interpret our data, we now turn our attention to our case study.

3 The Case Study: Background

Before we introduce the organisation at the heart of our case study, we briefly discuss our methodology. The investigator's initial aim was merely to observe what happened. As to standpoint, her original intention was to interpret the data within the framework of software process improvement: later, she reinterpreted it from the viewpoint of organisational learning. Data were gathered as follows: over the eighteen month course of the study, from July 1999 to December 2000, the investigator conducted 16 semi-structured interviews at all levels of the organisation. and followed them up with several phone-calls. The initiator and maintainer of the manual were both interviewed three times over this period; five partners in the organisation, four modellers, together with their project manager, were each interviewed once.

Our case study involves a financial consultancy in which bespoke software models lie at the core of the business. Fincon[1] is a financial services consultancy of about 130 people, of whom about 100 are professionals, or would-be professionals. In order to be admitted to the relevant professional body, students (invariably University graduates) have to pass in the region of 14 exams, of which, at present, none is concerned with software modelling. Fincon appears to be confident of its standing in the marketplace. Over the period of the interviews, the investigator formed the distinct impression that Fincon had no need of any marketing badge that external certification, as discussed in 2.2.1 above, might provide.

There are basically three levels to the organisational structure of Fincon: the students; the consultants, and the partners. Most of the software modelling, which is at the core of many projects, is done by the students, that is, graduates in the course of taking their professional exams. When these are all passed, the qualified professionals become consultants, and with experience, may manage projects. The highest level of the organisation is that of the partners, each of whom typically directs more than one project at a time, and is rarely involved directly in the modelling. Among the partners is the unit manager.

Most of Fincon's work is unpredictable, intellectually challenging, judgement and knowledge intensive, and undertaken under great pressure. An example might be that Fincon is retained to advise a financial services company on a proposed product line. Financial models and simulations play a large part in such projects. Fincon's product is a report presented to the clients, which says, for example,: 'based on these particular assumptions, and these software models and simulations of the company and the product, we advise you –'. The choice of both the set of assumptions and the type of model depends on the professional judgement and expertise of the Fincon practitioners. Because these projects are unpredictable both in when they arise and in their duration, it is very difficult for Fincon to plan work which is not directly client-related, such as the implementation of a software process improvement initiative.

There are two software packages used specifically in developing the models, a proprietary package, which we will refer to as PMP (Proprietary Modelling Package), and a generic spreadsheet package, Excel. PMP was developed in-house in the middle 1990s with the intention of encapsulating the organisation's knowledge of modelling financial services companies at that time. During the course of the study described in this paper, the use of PMP posed several problems. The financial services industry is in a constant state of flux, so the tasks for which PMP was designed were constantly changing. Unfortunately, PMP consists of 'black box' modules and it is not possible for users to modify the source code. In addition, the modules of PMP are very complex with many different options and switches, and it is

[1] Obviously an assumed name!

difficult to ascertain exactly what each module does, with respect to each setting. Users typically try to find a module which most nearly accomplishes what they want, and effect any modifications by the use of Excel.

Having described the background of our case study, we now go on to discuss the initiation, implementation and use of a manual of software modelling processes.

4 The Case Study: The Initiation and Implementation of the Manual

4.1 The Initiation

There was no client pressure for the instituting of a manual of software processes and procedures, neither was there any element of 'jumping on the bandwagon': as might be expected in an end-user organisation, Fincon had little awareness of current trends in software process improvement. Rather, the manual was conceived as one man's response to a particularly embarrassing case of software failure. The case study begins with a partner of Fincon, subsequently referred to as the 'partner champion', who faced what he described as "the worst week of my professional life" after a bespoke software model, constructed by Fincon, collapsed in front of important clients. On investigation, it transpired that the immediate reason for the model's collapse concerned a particular module of the in-house system, PMP: there was a clash between what the documentation described it as doing; what the modeller understood it to do, and what it actually did do, under a specific set of circumstances. As to underlying reasons, the partner champion decided that they were twofold. Firstly, the company had grown to the extent that it could no longer be assumed that everybody knew, and adhered to, the company's software modelling standards and checking procedures. These standards and procedures, though shared by experienced employees, were nowhere made explicit. Secondly, there was the problem that as modellers grew more experienced in constructing models, they tended to move on to more managerial and directorial jobs, in which modelling played little direct part, taking with them their modelling knowledge, and, especially their knowledge of the complex in-house software modelling system. The partner champion decided that both reasons could be addressed by the implementation of a software modelling quality control manual.

4.2 The Implementation

The partner champion's first act was to seek the agreement of the unit manager to proceed with implementing the manual. That agreement having been forthcoming, the partner champion sought and gained approval for the project from the rest of the partners and from the project managers. The students/modellers were then informed that a manual was on its way.

The partner champion now put together a manual team, consisting of himself; a consultant who became the maintainer of the manual, and gradually took over complete control; and a modeller with responsibility for training in-comers on the use of PMP. This team agreed the overall structure of the manual, and, drawing on their knowledge of each individual's expertise, invited other people within the organisation to contribute to particular sections. The team attempted to encompass different perspectives within the organisation, by sending each section to three people, at junior, middle and senior level, to review. In the event, most responses were from people at the junior (student, modeller) level. They tended (of course) to write sections from their own, operational perspective, and so many of their contributions were of the form 'In order to achieve _, select _ menu from PMP and _ menu option. Be careful when using this option as _' This was extremely useful in disseminating information about the vagaries of PMP, but was somewhat removed from the original intention of the manual, to standardise checking procedures.

As to the diffusion of the manual throughout the organisation, the original paper version was launched early in 1999 with a copy being given to all but support staff. The manual was used for training purposes for incoming students, and also on some projects with a large element of modelling. The maintainer of the manual identified such projects with the help of the resource manager, and tried to persuade the project directors/managers thereon to use the manual, with mixed success. Informal feedback was obtained by the manual maintainer chatting to the users. An electronic version of the manual, on the organisation's intranet, appeared in the spring of 2000. This electronic launch was accompanied by meetings and demonstrations at which all people involved in modelling were expected to attend. Subsequently, whenever a change was made to the manual, for example, a new section or tool added, the whole organisation was informed by means of email.

Having described the initiation and implementation of the manual, we now consider its aims, and the extent to which these aims seem likely to be achieved.

5 The Aims of the Manual, and the Relationship between Realisation of the Aims and Manual Usage

The overriding aim of the manual, as agreed by all the parties involved, is to effect an improvement in the quality of the financial models constructed using PMP and Excel. There are various sub-aims by which this might be achieved. These sub-aims were not explicitly stated, but emerged from the various interviews. We shall describe them in 5.1, discuss the ideal scenarios under which they could best be realised in 5.2, and, in 5.3, describe how the situation at Fincon differed from the ideal.

5.1 The Aims of the Manual

In the course of the interviews, three main aims of the manual were identified: capturing best practice; ensuring the consistency of procedures; and the provision of an instrument for training and troubleshooting. Capturing best practice is clearly very important in organisations like Fincon, which are heavily dependent on ever-changing knowledge; in which individuals move, or are promoted, and take their knowledge with them, and in which the size and/or rate of growth of the organisation, makes informal lines of communication and informal knowledge networks, potentially unstable. As to consistency of procedures, Fincon is an organisation in which it is the exception, rather than the rule, for modellers to stay with a project for its entirety. Rather, modellers leave and join projects part-way through, according to demand. If all such projects are conducted using the same procedures, then it is easier for people to join projects and also to review and/or reuse them. In addition, making checking procedures consistent was the original aim of the manual, and should improve users' confidence in the model. Regarding the provision of an instrument for training and troubleshooting, it is clear that a manual of best practice has the potential to form the basis of a training programme, and to act as a trouble-shooting guide. Although, as we stated in 4.1., Fincon had little awareness of current trends in SPI, it should be noted that capturing best practice (as in: *Define processes*) and ensuring the consistency of procedures (as in: *Stick to them*) are both important features of the generic SPI model in Fig.1.

5.2 Realising the Aims: The Ideal Scenario

Before describing the actual situation at Fincon, we shall discuss the ideal scenario of manual usage both at the individual and organisational level. Later, in section 6, in the light of our data described in 5.3, we shall discuss just how 'ideal' this scenario actually is. We omit here any use of the manual as a basis for a formal training programme, since we have no information on this.

Fig.2 depicts an ideal scenario for an individual modeller. S/he has a task to do; s/he looks up the associated procedures and processes in the manual (so as to ensure consistency throughout the organisation). If s/he thinks s/he knows a better procedure, s/he informs the maintainer of the manual, who evaluates it and incorporates it into the manual, if necessary, thus keeping the manual up to date with process improvements. Otherwise, s/he attempts to follow the procedure in the manual. But the information in the manual might not suffice to enable her/him to complete the task. In this case, like the photocopiers in Brown & Duguid, s/he turns for help to her/his colleagues, the community of practice. Eventually some sort of solution (or compromise) emerges, enabling the modeller to complete her/his task. This solution/compromise is passed to the maintainer of the manual for evaluation, and possible inclusion in the manual.

At the organisational level, all projects with a large modelling element should use the manual (to ensure consistency of procedures); at the end of a project, the modelling should be reviewed and any process improvements noted and passed to the maintainer of the manual (so as to ensure that the manual is kept up-to date); and, finally, the maintainer of the manual should be given sufficient time and resources to do his job effectively.

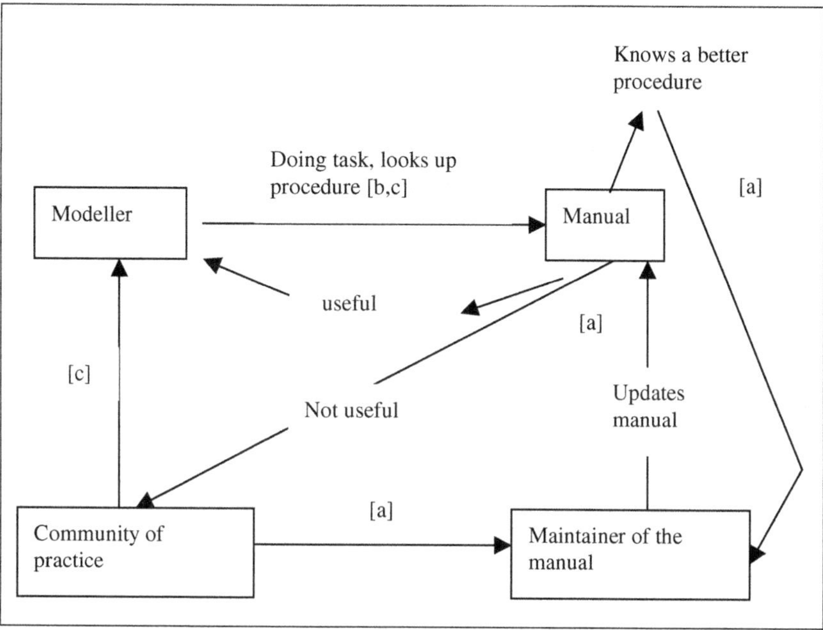

Fig. 2. The ideal individual scenario. Key: [a] relates to activities concerned with keeping the manual up-to-date; [b] relates to activities concerned with consistency of procedures; [c] relates to activities concerned with training and trouble-shooting

5.3 The Actual Use of the Manual

Here, we consider first the individual, and then the organisational, perspective.

The actual use of the manual by the individual modellers, as elicited from interviews, is illustrated in Fig.3. As we can see, there are big differences between this and Fig.2. If modellers think they know how to do a process/procedure to complete a task, then they do it, without consulting the manual to check how it compares with the documented procedure. As to the manual as an instrument for trouble-shooting, if a modeller doesn't know how to complete a task, then his/her first port of call is usually not the manual, but his/her colleagues in the community of practice. Fincon is clearly an organisation with a strongly co-operative culture at the modelling level. Informal knowledge networks are strong and information freely given. All four of the modellers interviewed talked of moving desks to be nearer to people with whom they were working closely, or for whom they felt they had (an informal) training responsibility. Although the manual was not deemed as important as the community of practice in resolving impasses, it was appreciated as a confidence provider (one could look up information in private in the manual without being made to look an ignoramus in front of one's peers); as a provider of refresher overviews, and of arcane details (such as the data formats required by specific modules of PMP); and as a way of structuring conversations with other people seeking help, when the modeller being applied to for assistance could refer to specific sections of the manual.

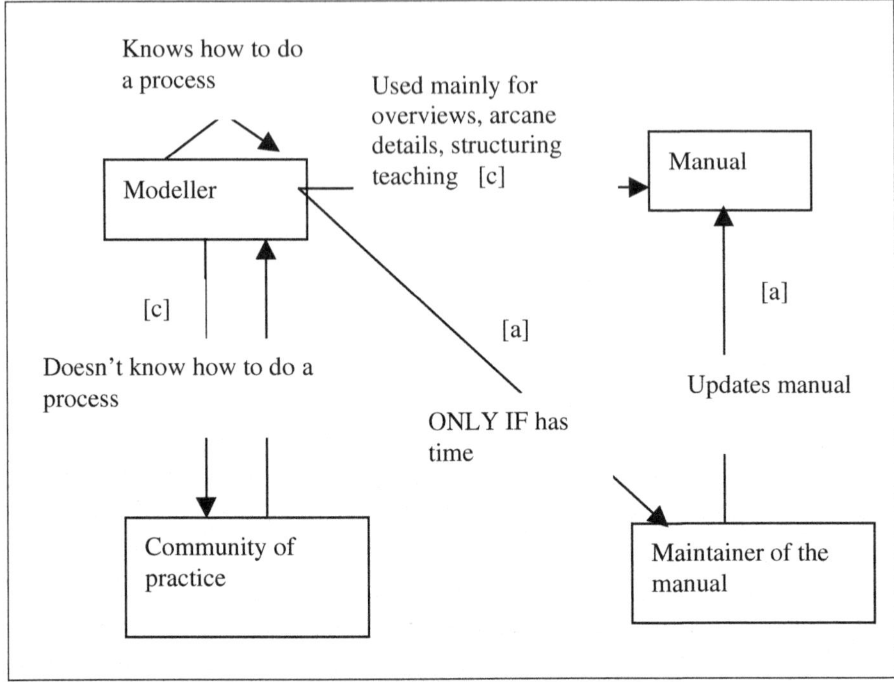

Fig. 3. Actual individual usage. *Key: as above, [a] relates to activities concerned with keeping the manual up-to-date; [c] relates to activities concerned with training and trouble-shooting. No activities relate to ensuring the consistency of procedures*

Having considered consistency of procedures, and training and trouble-shooting, we turn our attention to the third aim of the manual, to maintain an organisational memory of best practice. This was problematical. The maintainer of the manual had provided a feedback button on each section of the on-line manual, but as of half-way through the case study, the feedback button had been used only once in a few hundred hits. In the interviews with the four modellers, it became clear that they saw the upkeep of the manual as being primarily the responsibility of the maintainer of the manual and his team. Three of the four modellers had been involved in the original writing of the manual, but indicated that, once they'd made their contribution, they didn't then check that it had actually been incorporated. All, when pressed by the interviewer, had ideas as to how the manual might be improved/updated; none had passed these ideas on to the manual team. On occasion, as reported by the maintainer of the manual to the investigator, other modellers did spontaneously offer some updates to the manual. This happened when some modellers found themselves in a hiatus between projects and decided that they could usefully fill their time by making a generic tool from a piece of code which had been used effectively in a specific project, and then make this tool available via the on-line manual. However, the modellers lacked the experience to know whether a tool had the potential to be of use generically, and if it had, how to transform it from a tool which had been effective on a particular project, into one which could be useful more generally. They were thus heavily dependent on guidance from the maintainer of the manual, which, of course, increased the calls on his time.

We now consider the organisational perspective. In section 5.2 above, we identified that in order to best achieve the aims of the manual, the organisation should ensure the use of the manual on all projects with a strong modelling element; should review the modelling element of each project on its completion and pass on any identified process improvements to the maintainer of the manual, and should provide the latter with adequate time and resources in which to do his job.

The actuality was quite different from the ideal. Firstly, the use of the manual on projects was not mandatory. The investigator interviewed one project manager, who had been identified by the maintainer of the manual as managing a project with a large modelling element on which the manual had been heavily used. It was clear from this interview that the manager viewed the manual not as an instrument for ensuring consistency, but rather as a reference tool, that the modellers could use if they wished. As to reviewing the modelling element of a project in order to identify any novel elements, this rarely, if ever, happened. At the conclusion of a project, attempts were made to capture any new knowledge that had emerged about financial matters, for example, about tax, but not about the modelling process. Finally, the allocation of time and resources to the maintainer of the manual were, over the course of the case study, never sufficient. Client work always came first and maintaining the manual had to be fitted round this. Even in the case of the modellers generalising their tools (see above), because of the pressures of client work on both the modellers and the maintainer, work which took 2 weeks in total in fact stretched over 6 or 8 weeks.

In this section, we have described the differences between the actual use of the manual and what we identified as its ideal usage. Notwithstanding these differences, we should emphasise that Fincon is a very successful organisation and that embarrassing software failures, of the type described in 4.1. above are very rare. Given this fact, we now consider the extent to which our 'ideal usage' is realistic in practice, and ponder on the general insights afforded by our study.

6 Discussion and Conclusions

6.1 Accounting for the Differences between the Ideal and Actual Scenarios

We shall consider the differences firstly from an individual, and then from an organisational, perspective.

We note that several facets of Fig.2 appear unreasonable from the point of view of the modeller and his/her community of practice. For example, consider the activity labelled [b] in Fig.2, by which the modeller ensures that the procedure s/he is about to use is in the manual, that is, the organisational documentation. This activity does not appear in Fig.3. And from the point of view of the modeller, this absence is entirely reasonable. If s/he has used the same procedure successfully many times before, and thus has faith that it does the required job, why should s/he waste precious time checking it against the manual? As to the responsibility of the individual modeller and his/her community of practice for keeping the manual up to date, our data show that the situation is more complex than suggested by activities [a] in Fig.2. The data suggest that the modellers did not see maintaining the manual as being an intrinsic part of their job; rather, they appeared to regard it as something they did when they had time. The work of Mulholland et al, [18], in providing tools to capture knowledge as an intrinsic part of usual work practice, might make a difference here. Our data also make plain the need for heavy involvement from the maintainer of the manual and his team, which requires the provision of adequate dedicated time and resources. Our final comment on Fig.2 is that it is unreasonable to expect the manual to supplant the community of practice as a repository of knowledge. The manual can only provide explicit knowledge such as arcane details, and not the tacit knowledge discussed in 2.3; in addition, the information presented in the manual might be difficult to apply to a specific situation, see, for example, [19].

Considering the organisational perspective, we noted in section 5.3 three differences between the actual and ideal scenario: the use of the manual was not mandatory on projects; reviews of the processes used in completing a project in order to identify novel elements rarely happened, and the maintainer of the manual was not given sufficient time and resources to fully maintain the manual. The first difference might have been due to the professional culture of the organisation (one doesn't tell fellow professionals what to do); or it may have been lack of appreciation that the manual might be used as a tool to ensure consistency of procedures organisation-wide. As we noted in section 5, this, together with the other aims of the manual, was not made explicit. We have already noted that the project manager viewed the manual primarily as a reference tool; in interview, the unit manager appeared to view it primarily as a training instrument. He took the position that ensuring consistency of procedures was an individual, rather than an organisational, concern and was all a matter of time. Eventually, he suggested, all modellers would have used the manual in their initial training, and hence all would use the same procedures consistently. Mirroring the concern expressed in 2.2.1, that SPI programmes might focus solely on process definition, this opinion fails to take account of any improvement in procedures since the initial training period.

The fact that processes were rarely reviewed at project completion in order to identify novel elements, might be due to external pressures, for example, to start the next project, or to an assumption within the organisation that the capture of modelling knowledge is not as important as that of financial. This assumption is evidenced in the interview with the project manager: he talked of *intellectual knowledge* being concerned with financial information whereas modelling knowledge was just *techniques*; he also said "everybody in theory knows how to do modelling.".

Finally in this section, we discuss the issue of lack of time and resources dedicated to maintaining the manual. The data suggest that this is mainly due to external pressures. These pressures, inevitable in a successful consultancy, made it difficult to do anything which wasn't directly related to a specific client project. Even where resources were available, maintaining the manual competed with activities concerned with marketing and extending the organisation's capabilities in some professional area. Executive management tended to take the view that in this competition, the latter activities were more important than the former.

We now consider what this case study might teach us about the implementation of SPI programmes in general and the relationship between SPI and organisational learning.

6.2 Discussion: Lessons from the Case Study

This case study concerns an organisation attempting to address the threat of software failure by way of a manual. In 6.1 above, we identified three reasons why the ideal and actual scenarios of usage of this manual might differ. These are: unreasonable expectations imposed by the ideal scenario; external pressures, and the attitude of the management towards the manual. Concerns about external pressures and management attitude were also voiced in the studies in 2.2.2: we believe that the most useful insights from our case study derive from a consideration of the ideal scenario in Fig.2.

We have identified two such insights, both concerned with the techno-centricity of the general model of SPI, in Fig.1. The first is that it might impose unnatural work practices on practitioners: it is easy to understand why a practitioner who believes s/he knows how to achieve a particular task, might feel resentful at being required to check that her/his procedure is in some organisational repository. The second concerns the organisational learning aspect of SPI. Fig.1. does not, in our view, place enough (or, indeed, any) emphasis on the capture of process improvements which might arise spontaneously through a community of practice. Rather, it relies on metrics in order to identify situations where process improvements might be helpful. It is difficult to see how this reliance on metrics would have helped the organisation of our case study, since each project undertaken by Fincon is unique.

We hope that we have demonstrated that individual case-studies, situated in a particular organisation over a particular period of time, can provide unique insights into the efficacy of general theories and models. Our plans for the future are to continue a programme of case-studies of end-user organisations, and also to investigate the effect of integrating the use of knowledge capture tools into work practice, as suggested by Mulholland et al. [18].

References

1. Hendry D.G. & Green T.R.G: Creating, comprehending and explaining spreadsheets: a cognitive interpretation of what discretionary users think of the spreadsheet model. Int. J. Human-Computer Studies **40** (1994)1033-1065.
2. Panko R: What we know about spreadsheet errors. Journal of End User Computing, **10(2)** (1998) 15-21
3. Taylor MP, Moynihan EP & Wood-Harper AT. End user computing and information system methodologies. Information Systems Journal **8** (1998)85-96
4. Hall MJJ. A risk and control-oriented study of the practices of spreadsheet application developers. Proceedings of the 29th Annual Hawaii International Conference on System Sciences. (1996) 364-373
5. Fox C & Frakes W. The quality approach: is it delivering? Comm ACM. **40(6)** (1997) 25-9
6. Curtis B. Which comes first, the organisation or its processes? IEEE Software. **15(6)** (1998) 10-13
7. Sweeney A & Bustard D. Software process improvement: making it happen in practice. Software Quality Journal **6** (1997) 265-273
8. British Standards Institute. The TickIT Guide (1995)

9 Hovenden FM, Yates S, Woodman M & Sharp HC. The use of ethnography with discourse analysis in the study of software quality management systems. Software Quality Management II, Vol. 1: Managing quality systems. BCS Software Quality Management Specialist Group, Edinburgh (1994) 557-572

10. Clegg C, Axtell C, Damodaran L, Farbey B, Hull R, Lloyd-Jones R, Nicholls J, Sell R & Tomlinson C. Information Technology: a study of performance and the role of human and organization factors Ergonomics **40(9)** (1997) 851-871
11. Doherty NF & King M. The consideration of organizational issues during the systems development process: an empirical analysis Behaviour & Information Technology. **17(1)** (1998) 41-51.
12. Robinson H, Hall P, Hovenden F, Rachel J. Postmodern Software Development. The Computer Journal. **41(6)** (1998 363-375.
13. Herbsleb J. Zubrow D. Goldenson D. Hayes W. & Paulk M. Software quality and the capability maturity model. Comm. ACM. **40(6)** (1997) 30-40.
14. Hall T & Wilson D. Views of software quality: a field report. IEE Proc-Softw. Eng. **144(2)** (1997) 111-118
15. McGuire EG. Factors affecting the quality of software project management: an empirical study based on the Capability Maturity Model. Software Quality Journal **5** (1996) 305-317
16. Cook SDN & Brown JS. Bridging epistemologies: the generative dance between organizational knowledge and organizational knowing. Organization Science **10(4)** (1999) 381-400
17. Brown JS & Duguid P. The Social Life of Information. Harvard Business School Press. Boston, Mass (2000)
18. Mulholland P, Domingue J, Zdrahal Z & Hatala M. Supporting organisational learning: an overview of the ENRICH approach. Information Services & Use **20** (2000) 9-23
19. Arnfeld A & Rosbottom J. Improving the availability and cost-effectiveness of guidelines for guideline users: towards a structured approach. Behaviour & Information Technology. **17(3)** (1998) 135-140

Collaboration Support for Virtual Data Mining Enterprises

Angi Voß[1], Gernot Richter[1], Steve Moyle[2], and Alípio Jorge[3]

[1] GMD.AiS, Schloß Birlinghoven, D-53754 Sankt Augustin, Germany
{angi.voss, gernot.richter}@gmd.de

[2] Oxford University Computing Laboratory, Wolfson Building, Parks Road, Oxford, OX1 3QD, United Kingdom.
steve.moyle@comlab.ox.ac.uk

[3] LIACC-University of Porto, Rua do Campo Alegre, 823, 4150 Porto, Portugal,
amjorge@liacc.up.pt

Abstract. RAMSYS is a web-based infrastructure for collaborative data mining. It is being developed in the SolEuNet European Project for virtual enterprise services in data mining and decision support. Central to RAMSYS is the idea of sharing the current best understanding to foster efficient collaboration. This paper presents the design and rationale of Zeno, a core component of RAMSYS. Zeno is a groupware for discourses on the Internet and, for RAMSYS, aims to provide a "virtual data mining laboratory" to aid data miners in collaboratively producing better solutions to data mining problems.

1 Introduction

Organizational learning and knowledge management are two sides of the same coin. The knowledge, which a company tries to acquire, develop and disseminate, shall be used in daily work to improve productivity and ultimately competitiveness. Tacit knowledge, which is effective at work, is often hard to make explicit and therefore left untapped, although it is assumed to be highly valuable [9]. Collaborative work, where people can watch each other and possibly discuss their actions, is ideal for sharing, disseminating and even improving tacit knowledge.

Now, what changes if collaboration is not taking place in face-to-face situations, but at distributed geographical sites? The collaborators can watch and communicate with each other only through telecommunication media. These exchanges can and even should be recorded, they have to be recorded and processed in a way that makes it easy to join the team at any time, or to resume work after shorter or longer individual absences. Therefore we expect that tools and methods for distributed collaboration provide a basis for capturing knowledge (from experiences) and, vice versa, that tools and methods for applying knowledge can help to improve collaboration.

This paper will describe how collaboration in a virtual enterprise for data mining can be supported [6], hoping that the ideas can, at least partially, be carried over to distributed software organizations.

K.-D. Althoff, R.L. Feldmann, and W. Müller (Eds.): LSO 2001, LNCS 2176, pp. 83–95, 2001.

In order to be successful, an enterprise must learn. It must improve its processes i.e. understand when to apply which procedures, models, tools and techniques, and it must get to know its competence, i.e. what kind of products it can deliver how efficiently and effectively. In the case of data mining, the products are services and the enterprise must understand what data mining problems it can handle. To develop a competence profile is particularly difficult in virtual organisations, which are geographically distributed, whose member companies may fluctuate and do not know each other well.

The data mining enterprise we are going to describe is in the process of formation. Organizational learning is on the agenda, but has not yet started so that we can only briefly summarize the issue that have been identified. In particular, the transition from concrete experiences in the form of accomplished projects to knowledge, which has been assessed, generalized and prepared for reuse, is an open issue.

2 Towards a Virtual Enterprise in Data Mining

The leading edge of European data mining expertise is currently spread over a number of data mining units consisting of research laboratories and companies across Europe. Each one of these data mining units has developed areas of specific expertise to solve particular data mining problems. Frequent on-site collaboration, often required in solving data mining problems, is made difficult by geographical distance and costs. These issues are of fundamental importance to the European Union funded SolEuNet Project [11]. The SolEuNet Project aims to develop a virtual enterprise that produces data mining and decision support services to enhance European business competitiveness.

Customers of SolEuNet will be able to pose their data mining problem to a multitude of experts from academic and commercial partners, located in six European countries. The experts will apply their methods to solving the problem — but also communicate with each other to share their growing understanding of the problem. It is here that collaboration is key. We will describe plans to support collaboration through a web-based groupware, but will not touch on other important matters such as legal status, intellectual property rights, contracting and payment.

2.1 The Data Mining Process

Data mining is the automatic extraction of non-trivial and actionable knowledge from large or very large databases [1,3]. The databases can be transactional relational databases, text corpora, the Web or any other data repository. The extracted knowledge is typically represented as logical and/or mathematical models. Although in this paper data mining is equated to knowledge discovery in databases (KDD), some authors prefer to consider data mining as one step in a larger KDD process.

Data mining processes broadly consist of a number of phases. These phases, however, are interrelated and are not necessarily executed in a linear manner. For example, the results of one phase may uncover more detail relating to an "earlier" phase and may force more effort to be expended on a phase previously thought complete.

The definition of the phases varies. The SolEuNet consortium is committed to using the CRISP-DM methodology — CRoss Industry Standard Process for Data Mining [2]. The methodology has been developed by a consortium of industrial data mining companies as an attempt to standardise the process of data mining. In CRISP-DM, six interrelated phases are used to describe the data mining process: business understanding, data understanding, data preparation, modelling, evaluation, and deployment. Figure 1 presents an overview of how data preparation (phase 3) and modelling (phase 4) are embedded in the CRISP-DM reference model. The other phases are of minor relevance to this paper. The net of (alternating) graphical symbols models relationships between active (boxes) and passive (bubbles) functional units of a system or process [10]. Bubbles represent states such as the availability of data, reports, ideas, models, or the ability of an event or process to continue, or the situation that an event has occurred. Boxes represent state transitions such as an action that creates a result (possibly a prerequisite for another action) or a decision where to proceed (which path to take in the system model).

Modelling is the process of extracting input/output patterns from given data and derive models that allow such patterns to be reproduced from given input. Of course, modelling relies on the preceding data preparation phase which covers all activities to construct the final data set from the initial raw data. This includes table, record and attribute selection as well as transformation and cleaning of data for modelling tools. In the modelling phase, various modelling techniques are selected and applied and their parameters are calibrated to optimal values. The resulting models are then tested and interpreted from a more technical point of view (as opposed to the point of view applied in the evaluation phase).

2.2 Collaborative Data Mining

In SolEuNet, each data mining project will be developed by a number of data mining units in a network of expertise. Each unit represents a work site operated by an expert, an expert team, or a technical support team. Some members of the units form the management committee. In terms of the CRISP-DM methodology, the management committee has to manage the entire project and is responsible for the first two phases, business understanding and data understanding. These tasks yield a detailed specification of the problem and the available data, as input for the other groups, who compete or cooperate in solving the next tasks of modelling. The final tasks of evaluation and deployment are again left to the responsibility of the management committee. Collaboration is most promising during the data modelling phase.

The process of analysing data through models has many similarities to experimental research: first the modeller (cf. a scientist) applies his/her analysis

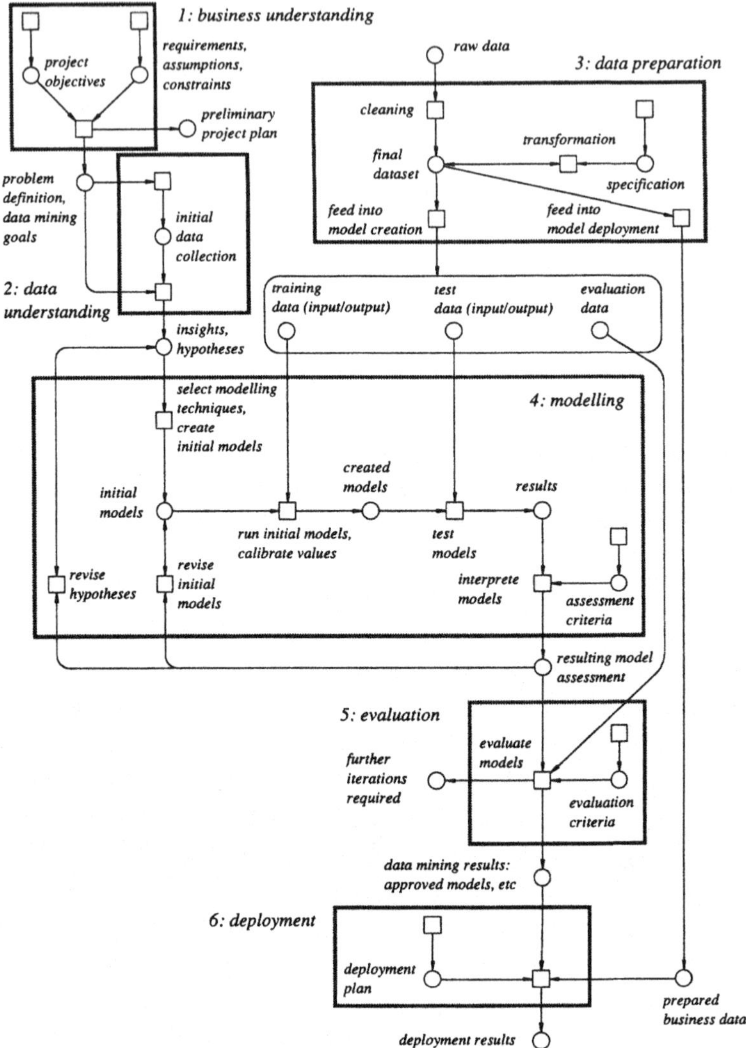

Fig. 1. Data preparation and modelling in the CRISP-DM model.

techniques to the data (cf. experimental results) to produce a model (cf. a new theory). These models (cf. theories) are tested for significance, and then refined (maybe in the light of new evidence). Like the process of scientific discovery, data mining can benefit from different techniques used by multiple researchers who collaborate to improve their combined understanding. This collaborative approach is what SolEuNet aims to provide.

According to [8] collaboration shall be based on the following principles.

Light Management: Project objectives, requirements, problem definition, and evaluation criteria should be clear from the beginning of the project to all participants. Consequently, it is the task of the management committee for each problem to ensure that information flows within the network and that a good solution is provided. However, the management committee will not control directly the work of each unit.

Start at any time: From time to time it may be necessary in solving a data mining problem that extra expertise is necessary, or becomes available. Consequently all the problem information necessary to start problem solving should be available at all times. This includes problem definition, data, evaluation criteria and any specific knowledge already produced by project participants.

Stop at any time: Problem solving should be conducted by each unit so that a working solution (model) is available whenever the management committee requests an intermediate result or even has to stop experimentation. One approach would be that participants follow a sort of "simplicity first" strategy for modelling: simpler models are tried first, and more complex models are compared to the simpler ones.

Problem Solving Freedom: Members of the network have varied expertise, techniques, and tools. It is hoped that these complement each other in the data mining process. Each unit is in the best position to decide which approach to follow for the given problem. The management committee may give specific suggestions but does not prescribe problem-solving approaches. In this way, experts are not constrained as to which techniques to employ.

Knowledge Sharing: As each modeller experiments and produces new knowledge on the problem, this should be immediately shared with all the participants in the data mining project (e.g. ideas, data modifications, models, evaluation results).

Security: The data and information relating to any data mining problem is likely to contain sensitive information, which may not be revealed outside the project. The lightly managed network structure must ensure that access to project information is strictly controlled and monitored.

These principles of collaboration and the CRISP-DM methodology as adapted for SolEuNet lead to the requirements for a support system called RAMSYS, a "SYStem for RApid remote collaboration in data Mining projects".

3 System Requirements

Through its tasks, the CRISP-DM methodology provides a framework for organising the work of the units and the deliverables. Every task can be assigned to one or more (competitive) units. The deliverables produced by each unit should be associated with its individual assignment. The management committee may then compose or select from the competitive results the final deliverable of the task. As the structure of tasks, assignments and deliverables records who did (or has to do) what in a project, it is an important instrument for achieving the principle of "light management" (see Section 2.2).

The principles of "problem solving freedom" and "knowledge sharing" require a combination of tools that allow the groups to share data, data transformations and metadata, to apply models to training data and to assess or evaluate models using evaluation data. We call this the "data mining laboratory". The principles "start / stop at any time" call for a means that, at a glance, provides an overview of how and why something was done. On an idea board the rationale (justifications, the why) for the experiment can be constructed. Here the units may exchange ideas about expected outcomes, promising models or alternative parameter settings. Here they may also discuss and explain successes and failures. An experimentation area visualises the history and current status of experimentation. It allows the units to record what actions should be performed, are being performed or have been performed on which data. The recording of experiments should not cause additional overhead. Therefore the experimentation area should be operationally coupled with the data mining laboratory. Ideally it should provide an intuitive, convenient access to the tools and results in the data mining laboratory.

According to the principle of "security", access to all the data, documents and tools should be in a secure way, and via ftp or http.

3.1 Idea Board

On the idea board the users (here a "user" is typically a data mining expert assigned to a particular data mining problem) share ideas about which final results (patterns, relationships, insights) to expect, which models to apply, or which transformations to execute on the data. Ideas may be commented, raise questions or inspire new ideas, leading to a network similar to an idea map or a concept map. Each of the contributions should have a subject, a text body, and possibly file attachments. Users should be offered a two-dimensional graphic interface, as well as a list that can be sorted by author or modification date.

3.2 Data Mining Laboratory

Clearly, for data management the laboratory must include database management components. They will manage an increasing set of tables. To facilitate "blind" assessment of any submitted models, the "outcome" attributes of some records (called the "test set") will not be accessible to the data miners. Not only the data tables, but also the collection of metadata is made available. This includes descriptions of the data items and their interrelationships (e.g. database schemas). New columns or tables may be created by transformations. Since they may be time-consuming and may even have to be carried out by a specific unit, transformations may have to be requested and be computed offline. Transformations should be specified using a script language. The application of centrally available models may be specified similarly. Models that have to be applied locally may be requested by providing more informal descriptions.

3.3 Experimentation Area

The experimentation area contains two kinds of objects: objects that represent actions, and objects that represent their input and output. We call them action objects and data objects. Action objects may be transformations, model applications, and assessments of models (i.e. applications of models to test data). Data objects may be views, metadata, and results of model applications and assessments. Data objects and action objects are interrelated with input/output relationships, they may be connected to metadata, and to ideas that capture their intentions.

Each action object is associated with a tool in the laboratory. By "activating" the action, users may invoke the tool. The tool, in turn, may (successively) update the action object with metadata and status information, and it may create new output objects.

Transformations, model applications and assessments that may not be achieved through a tool in the laboratory have to be requested from an appropriate unit. The "tool" associated with such a request action would then organise the telecommunication between the requesting unit and the unit that can perform the desired action locally.

It should be possible to organise data objects into a hierarchy of resources for experimentation and action objects into a hierarchy of experiments. For instance, an experiment could consist in calibrating the same model with different views, and could later be extended by assessments of the resulting versions of the model with evaluation views.

Users may navigate through the hierarchies of data and action objects. The links between action objects and data objects should be displayed in a two-dimensional graph. Since the graph may become very large, it should be possible to show only the paths leading to a selected node. Also, users should get a list sorted by types, modification dates or other properties.

3.4 Task Management

The six top tasks (phases) of the CRISP-DM methodology and their sub-tasks (generic tasks and specialised tasks) form a hierarchy. In the course of a data mining project, each task gets associated with one or more assignments. An assignment of a task should specify the unit, a budget, a deadline, etc. Assignments may (or should) relate to ideas that motivate, justify or describe the approach chosen in this assignment. The deliverables of each unit should be associated with the assignment. Since a task may have competitive assignments, it is the job of the management committee to compose from the various deliverables the output of a task and store it with the task.

Users may navigate through the task hierarchy to assignments and deliverables, and follow links to the ideas. Alternatively, they may see a list sorted by due date, date of last modification, unit or other properties.

3.5 The Portal

All services should be integrated into a Web portal. At the start page, users have to identify themselves before they get access to the list of projects they are engaged in. Each project should provide a summary of recent changes and buttons to branch to the task, experiment and idea parts of the project. Each of these parts should provide a summary of news, full-text search, and the different presentation styles described before.

4 A System Based on the Zeno Groupware

In order to reduce time and costs, SoEuNet tries to realise the RAMSYS system with existing tools that are available free of charge, ideally as open source. Zeno, a groupware for discourses on the Internet is already being used as collaboration platform in the SolEuNet Project [15]. The new version of Zeno, due this summer, will be available under an open source license. This new version comes with a simple, generic framework for representing different kinds of discourse and their subject matters, such as conflict resolution, consensus building, consulting, group decision making, or participatory problem solving [5,15]. In the following we will cast tasks and the different parts of the articulation level into Zeno's new framework.

4.1 The Journal Server

Application-specific data structures, such as elaborated in the previous section, can be mapped onto two Zeno-specific concepts, journals and articles. Journals and articles resemble folders in their ability to contain other information resources, but differ from them due to their special functionality in the context of Zeno. The notion of a "journal" covers both the private records of individuals and the records of various kinds of public discourse, including newspapers, periodicals and, interestingly, the records of deliberative and legislative bodies. Zeno offers journals as organisational units and articles as content units for collaborative work. Following the metaphor of a journal, Zeno distinguishes the roles of editors, authors and readers. Editors of journals determine access rights, form and layout, the types and characteristics of articles, the rules of composition and admissible (cross-)references. Authors compose and revise articles, creating new versions as needed.

Journals and articles may be nested, which makes up the primary or compositional structure, which is always a tree. In addition, an arbitrary secondary or referential structure may be established by references to and from articles, journals or Web-addressable content. The latter comprises documents as elementary units of content, and folders as mere containers for Web resources.

An *article* does not contain organisational information like a journal. It can carry some information of its own, in its head and body. The body of an article serves as a note, a short communication, a covering letter, or a summary. It

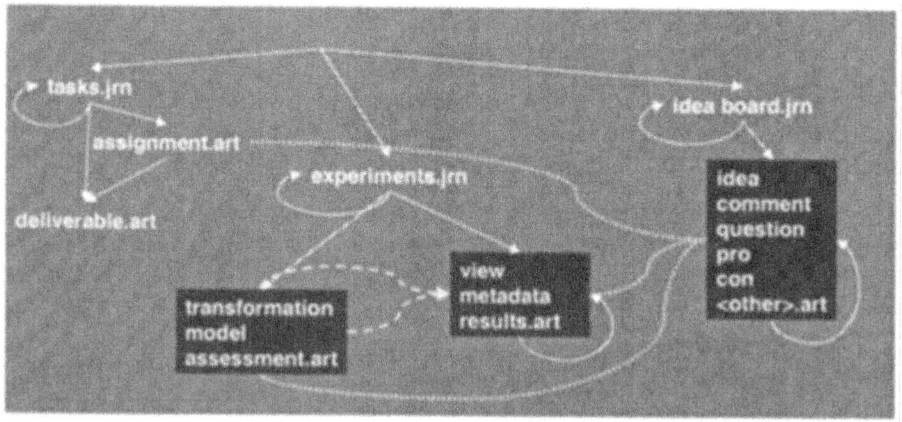

Fig. 2. Primary and secondary structure of a RAMSYS project journal.

may be written in plain text including URLs. The head, consisting of a set of attributes, serves as a form sheet for further information about the article. By default, Zeno will maintain creation, modification and expiration dates, author, and publishing status. The structure of article heads may be customised for different types of articles, and each journal may declare different types of articles. Articles may have arbitrary attachments of any MIME type. Articles may also have subordinate articles or be linked with other articles serving as follow-up articles, replies or other components.

Since each data mining project may be carried out by a different consortium, every data mining project must be carried out in a project-specific context. This context is provided by a project-specific journal. The journal can be created by copying a template for RAMSYS projects. A project journal contains three sub-journals (or sections): for tasks, experiments and ideas. The project journal should be created by the management committee, who would proceed to define the access rights and attach the documentation produced during the first tasks to the deliverables of the first tasks.

Data objects and action objects, introduced in Section 3.3, are mapped onto articles, which results in journals composed of data articles and action articles. Figure 2 shows the schema for the primary and secondary structure of a RAMSYS project journal. The solid arrows point to admissible successor articles Dashed depict secondary input/output links between data articles and action articles. Other secondary associations may be drawn between the articles; e.g., the dotted arrows indicate links between contributions to the discussion and the articles referred to.

In order to associate tools with what was called action objects in Section 3.3, the Zeno framework as described so far has to be extended. Beside their structure, articles may also have a behaviour, both of which can be customised for the different types of articles. Every article has a default property that contains the full path name of a class implementing its behaviour through methods. These must will conform to the conventions of Java beans so that they are open for inspection. This features makes it easier to develop customizable user interfaces for articles with behaviours. These interfaces will provide special commands to invoke, control or terminate the tools. Vice versa, the tools can access the journal server via its Web-API. Thus, the tools can create new articles for views, results or metadata below the top-level data article, and connect them with the action article via links.

4.2 WebDAV: Store for Journals

Zeno's information resources are managed with a DAV server. DAV, or WebDAV, stands for Web Distributed Authoring and Versioning. It is a proposed IETF standard consisting of extensions to HTTP/1.1 to support remote authoring of Web pages [14]. DAV distinguishes two kinds of resources, collections (of resources) and elementary resources, also known as non-collections. A DAV resource represents any network data object or service that can be identified by a URL. While concepts for versioning are still under discussion, the proposal already covers links between resources, XML properties for meta-information on resources, locks to control access to resources and avoid lost updates, and name space operations to copy and move resources. Zeno's journals and articles are mapped to DAV collections and documents to non-collection resources.

4.3 User Interface

Zeno comes with generic user interfaces. With the Web interface users can navigate through the hierarchy of journals, and along the primary and secondary structure of a journal. With the Pad, a client side GUI, users will be able to directly manipulate journals and articles, expand and contract journals, drag and drop, and inspect the content of a selected journal or article.

With the Pad, users have four options for viewing the content of a journal. They may see the tree representing the primary structure of the journal. The look and feel and the interaction is similar to the Windows explorer. Or users may get a listing of articles, which may be sorted by the standard attributes. Thus they can see at a glance who wrote/modified which articles, which articles are new, or find articles of a particular type. The third option is the map, a two-dimensional presentation of the articles with their primary and secondary structure. The icons of the articles and the colours of the edges can be selected by the editor. The graph displayed on the map can be restricted to the nodes that are reachable from a selected article along the primary and secondary structure. The fourth option lists the full content of the journal, not just its articles, but also the sub-journals, folders and documents.

Previous experiences have shown that for specific purposes, custom-tailored interfaces are more appropriate than generic ones. Therefore, a Web portal for RAMSYS should be custom-developed. The pages can easily embed Zeno functions from a library, e.g. for listing the content of a journal, for full-text search,

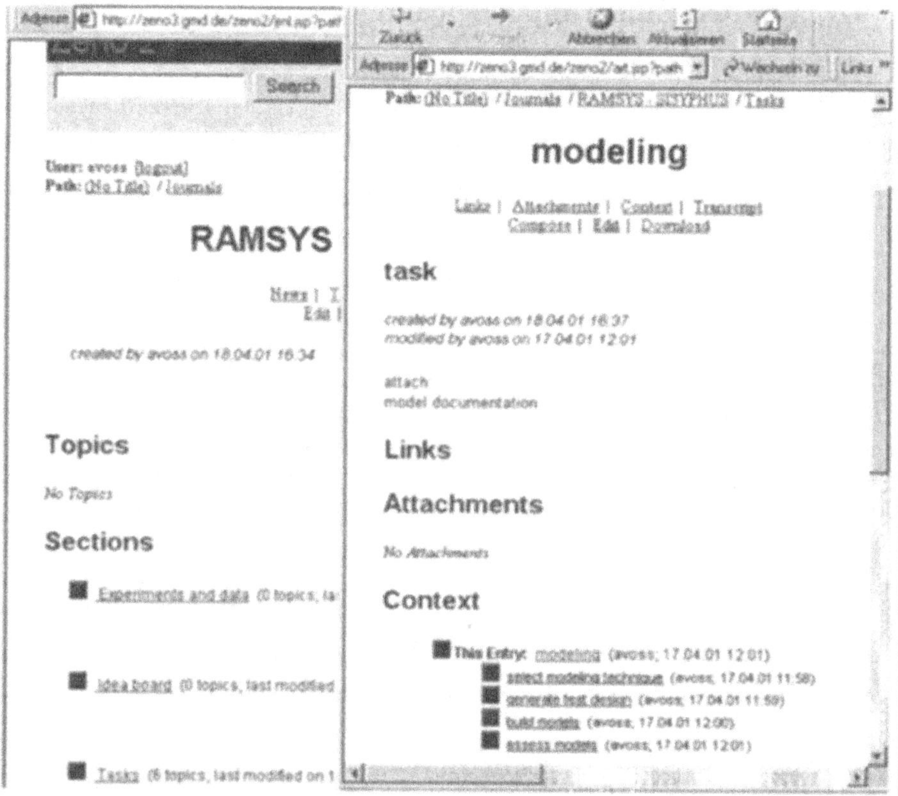

Fig. 3. HTML interface of a RAMSYS project journal and an article representing the modelling task in the Tasks section.

for a news summary, or for editing an article (an example is shown in [13]). For manipulating the content of the idea board in a two-dimensional representation or for sorting lists, users would have to download the Zeno power interface.

4.4 The Address Book for User and Group Administration

RAMSYS data and information must be protected. Zeno gives access only to authorized users and groups. For managing users and groups Zeno has a Web-based interface to an LDAP server. LDAP, the Lightweight Directory Access Protocol [4,12], provides a standard way for Internet clients, applications, and Web servers to access directory listings of thousands of Internet users. Zeno uses OpenLDAP, an open source implementation of LDAP. It is intended that the same LDAP server used by Zeno should also be used by the database applications.

5 Towards Organisational Learning

Up to now, the partners in SolEuNet have solved a range of customer problems in different constellations. They have familiarised with the CRISP-DM methodology and collaborated using the present product version of Zeno 1.9, which provides an address book and shared workspaces with folders, calendars and structured discussion forums [13]. This version, though general purpose, turned out to be useful to the participating data miners in that it supported collaborative work on data mining problems. Thus it was generally felt that the final models produced were of higher quality than would have been achieved by individual groups. In parallel, the idea for RAMSYS was born and elaborated, and project resources are now being shifted to incorporate this unanticipated activity.

In the next phase, the project will build a repository of best solutions from the past customer projects. They aim at a taxonomy of problems and profiles for data mining models and tools. On this basis, the partners are going to develop their competence profiles. Envisaged are yellow pages that describe the partners in terms of the types of problems they can solve, the models, tools and techniques they can apply, and the domains they are familiar with (such as budget distribution). Such a directory represents a valuable asset for a company that considers itself to be a broker of data mining services.

Up to now, it is an open question how such knowledge could systematically be extracted from the experiences as they would be recorded in RAMSYS. This issue is being addressed in the European Project Mining Marts [7]. In particular answers to the following questions would be valuable. How will "best solutions" be described? Will there be more specific templates of RAMSYS journals for specific problem types? Will there be a systematic way to assess RAMSYS-recorded projects? And how will these assessments be added to the records? If the project comes up with very different abstractions for characterising projects, they should somehow influence the presentations of projects in RAMSYS, so that they can improve the work in future data mining projects.

5.1 Beyond Data Mining

Zeno has been designed for flexibility. It would be easy to create journals with different sections and different types of articles, for instance to represent other kinds of tasks, actions or data with different attributes. It will also be easy to implement new classes for articles with other behaviours. Even the user interfaces could easily be adapted using configuration files for the Design Pad interface, and adapting the Java server pages in the HTML interface.

Thus, with moderate effort, we could support new applications that are similar to RAMSYS. Our next candidate is cooperative site planning in the KoGi-Plan project, which is funded by the German government. This application will also use an idea board for discussion, a task structure for archiving results, and an experimentation area with data and action articles. Like data mining, site planning is an explorative activity, but the tools are different (GIS tools, data mining tools, optimization tools and decision support tools). The task structure is simpler (problem identification, data preparation, analysis, result visualization, decision making), but will certainly be elaborated in the course of the project.

Compared to software development, data mining and site planning service-oriented rather than product-oriented, more analytic than synthetic, so that analogies may be less obvious. However, the RAMSYS design may be suitable for the development of innovative software prototypes, or possibly for extreme programming scenarios. In the future, we plan to investigate the use of Zeno for requirements engineering and software process development. In these applications, the subject of communication are not experiments, which are conducted through tools, but pieces of documents (or models). So we expect that we have to replace the experimentation area with a fine-grained document representation and provide close links between parts of the documents and respective annotations and discussions.

References

1. Adriaans, P, and Zantinge, D., *Data Mining*, Addison-Wesley, 1996.
2. P. Chapman, J. Clinton, R. Kerber, T. Khabaza, T. Reinartz, C. Shearer, and R Wirth, *CRISP-DM 1.0: Step-by-step data mining guide.* CRISP-DM consortium, 2000.
3. Fayyad, U., Piatetsky-Shapiro, G., Smyth, P., and Ramasamy, U. (editors), *Advances in Knowledge Discovery and Data Mining*, MIT Press, 1996.
4. D. Flanagan, J. Farley, W. Crawford and K. Magnusson: *Java Enterprise in a Nutshell — A Desktop Quick Reference.* O'Reilly & Associates, Sebastopol, CA 95472, USA, 1999 (Chapter 6 – JNDI).
5. T. F. Gordon, A. Voß, G. Richter, and O. Märker, *Zeno: Groupware for Discourses on the Internet*, KI - Künstliche Intelligenz, Vol. 15, pp. 43 – 45, 2001.
6. A. Jorge, S. Moyle, G. Richter, A. Voß, *Zeno for Rapid Collaboration in Data Mining Projects* - submitted for publication
7. J.-U. Kietz, R. Zücker, and A. Vaduva: *Mining Mart: Combining Case-Based-Reasoning and Multi-Strategy Learning into a Framework for Reusing KDD-Applications*, In: Proc. of the 5th Int. Conf. on Multi-Strategy Learning, Guimarães, Editors Brazdil, P. and Michalski R., University of Porto, 2000.
8. S. Moyle, A. Jorge, and C. Leandro: *RACODAMISYS - a methodology and tool for supporting rapid remote collaborative data mining projects*, LIACC Technical Report, University of Porto, 2000.
9. G. Ruhe, F. Bomarius (eds.): *Learning Software Organization - Methodology and Applications.* Springer-Verlag. Lecture Notes in Computer Science, Volume 1756, 2000.
10. G. Schäfer with R. Hirschheim et al. (editors), *Functional Analysis of Office Requirements: A Multiperspective Approach*, John Wiley & Sons, 1988.
11. SolEuNet: Data Mining and Decision Support for Business Competitiveness: A European Virtual Enterprise. http://soleunet.ijs.si/website/html/euproject.html (as of June 2001).
12. What is LDAP? http://www.gracion.com/server/whatldap.html (as of June 2001).
13. KOMM!forum. http://www.kommforum.de (as of June 2001).
14. WebDAV Resources. http://www.webdav.org/ (as of June 2001).
15. Zeno consensus building. http://zeno.gmd.de/MS/index.html (as of June 2001).

Skills Management as Knowledge Technology in a Software Consultancy Company

Torgeir Dingsøyr[1] and Emil Røyrvik[2]

[1]Department of Computer and Information Science,
Norwegian University of Science and Technology
Currently at: Fraunhofer Institute for Experimental Software Engineering,
Sauerwiesen 6, 7661 Kaiserslautern, Germany
dingsoyr@idi.ntnu.no

[2]SINTEF Industrial Management,
7491 Trondheim, Norway
emil.royrvik@indman.sintef.no

Abstract. This paper presents a skills management system in a medium-sized software consulting company, and how it is used. We found four different types of usage: Searching for competence to solve problems, allocating resources, finding areas for new projects, and to develop competence. Most people in the company seem to regard this tool as useful, both for themselves, and for the company as a whole.

Keywords: Skills Management, Knowledge Management, Software Engineering.

1 Introduction

Software engineering is knowledge work, where it is critical to have employees who know about different technology issues, as well as project planning and customer communication and needs. A major management trend in recent years has been programs to manage the knowledge of the employees better; to record and diffuse, and support the creation of new knowledge in a company. This is often referred to as *knowledge management [1-3]*. Knowledge management has already in some forms and forums acquired the status of a so-called fad. We will not go into that here, just state that we see knowledge management as a potentially fruitful field still in its infancy, emerging at the confluence of organizational learning, the resource bases view of the firm and the new technologies for managing knowledge [4]. We may also add that knowledge management is not a new activity invented lately by organizational theorists, but has taken place at all times within all purposeful collectives such as families, tribes, societies, monasteries, universities and business firms.

We often say that knowledge manifests itself in two types: *tacit* and *explicit*. By tacit knowledge we mean knowledge that a human is unable to express [5], but is

K.-D. Althoff, R.L. Feldmann, and W. Müller (Eds.): LSO 2001, LNCS 2176, pp. 96-103, 2001.

guiding the behavior of the human. For example how to ride a bike is something that is difficult to express, which you have to learn by trial and failure. Another example of tacit knowledge is the struggle of Japanese engineers to make a machine that bakes bread. According to [6], there were several trials to construct such a machine, but the bread simply did not taste as well as bread made by normal bakers. The company NEC decided to send people to a local baker to see how the process of making bread was carried out, to find what went wrong in their attempt. The researchers returned with new insight on the baking process, and later was able to replicate this in their machine. This is an example of tacit knowledge that is difficult to transfer by other means than looking at someone executing the process of baking bread, trying it out yourselves, imitating and experiencing - often referred to as socialization processes. An example from software engineering is the knowledge needed to estimate the size of a module in a software package – this is knowledge that is very difficult to describe.

Explicit knowledge is knowledge that we can explicitly use and represent to ourselves and others through some form of verbal or non-verbal language - represented for example in reports, books, talks, or other communication.

Many computer systems exist for supporting collection and diffusion of explicit knowledge in companies, and many knowledge management programs exist to help people convert tacit knowledge to explicit, in order to make them more transferable to others. But another and cheaper possibility is not to try to represent the knowledge that people have, explicitly, in writing it down, but rather to survey such knowledge and make an index of it, a kind of company-internal "yellow pages". The process of surveying and indexing and making this type of information available, we will refer to as *skills management.*

There exists lots of software tools for managing skills – for example, companies that offer jobs on the Internet usually have some kind of database where you as a job-seeker can store your competence profile (see for example www.stepstone.com). Commercial tools for this purpose are available, like SkillScape[1] and SkillView[2]. The contents of such tools can be: "Knowledge profiles, skill profiles and personal characteristic profiles that define subjective assessments of the knowledge, skills, and personal traits required for the different work-roles within the function" [7].

The purpose of using such tools is mostly to:

- Find staff with the right skills to new projects.
- Find people who know something that you need to know.

In order to have such a working system, the company needs to select a set of skills that they are interested in, have a system for evaluating the employees, and make this information available to different user groups.

Here, we are interested in knowing more about how such systems for managing skills are used in a specific organization. Other interesting issues, such as cost and benefit of such systems, and how they are introduced in companies are beyond the

---

[1] See www.skillscape.com.

[2] See www.skillview.com.

scope of this paper. Also, we do not look at technical implementation of skills management systems, but refer readers with such interests to other literature [8].

We have studied one company using ethnographic methods, and present the different views on - and characteristics of - a skills management tool that is in use. First, we discuss what research method that has been applied, then introduce the company, present findings on the skills management system, and discuss them in section 3, and finally conclude in section 4.

2 Methods

In this study, we have used a research method inspired by ethnography: A method for collecting information for a case study that has been used by anthropologists. It is described as "the art and science of describing a group or culture" [9]. The main element of ethnographic research is the fieldwork: the researcher should get into the environment that she is intending to study, and gradually start to collect data. Another key element in ethnography is to rely on multiple data sources: Participant observation, questionnaires, interviews, projective techniques, videos, pictures, and written material.

The analysis in ethnography is usually concentrated around triangulation – to set different sources of information up against each other, to find patterns of thought or behavior in the community of study. Other methods include drawing organizational charts, making flowcharts of processes that happen, setting up matrices to compare and contrast data, and to use statistics.

Ethnography has been used to some extent within the Computer Science subfield Information Systems, as well as in Software Engineering. Some researchers have used ethnography and discourse analysis to investigate how practitioners apply quality procedures [10]. Others have written about applying ethnographic methods in the construction of information systems and to analyze the development itself [11]. This paper also gives a good introduction to ethnography.

2.1 Collecting Data

The study here is a subpart of a larger study about the use of knowledge management systems in software consulting companies, and also a part of a large four year action research program on several knowledge-intensive business firms (KIBS), where we here have limited the available data to issues related to skills management. We used multiple methods to collect data, and in addition to information gathered in informal settings of participant observation and also in meetings, and have used the following data sources:

- *Interviews* – we used semi-structured interviews with open-ended questions to allow the respondents to speak more freely of issues they felt were important, and to let the interviewer develop the interviews over time. We interviewed a project manager and three people participating in a project, the person responsible for knowledge management, three other management representatives: persons responsible for business consulting, international operations, and the internal competency center. We also interviewed six people who had won an internal prize for sharing their knowledge with others, making it a total of 14 interviews. The interviews were recorded on MiniDisc and then transcribed. The transcripts were sent back to the people who had been interviewed for corrections or further comments. We got feedback from around 50% of the people interviewed, mostly minor corrections. The interviews were done in Norwegian, and the citations that are used in this paper are our translation of what was said.

- *Screenshots* – we gathered screen-shots from different parts of the skills management system.

2.2 Analyzing the Data: "Coding"

From the data we have through analyses seen some patterns emerge, and thus constructed categories on behalf of these patterns.

3 Results and Discussion

First, let us briefly introduce the company that we collected material from: We leave the company anonymous, and refer to it as *Alpha*.

Alpha is a consulting company, which develops knowledge-based systems for a variety of customers. In the annual report for 1999, they state that their vision is to "make knowledge sharing in organizations more effective, and thereby contribute so that knowledge is refined and used to achieve the organization's goal". The company has around 150 employees, and some of them are working in their customer's offices. The company is organized in projects and processes, where knowledge management is considered to be one important process.

When we now go on to discuss the usage of the skills management system, we have on the basis of the patterns that emerged divided the usage into four categories, some with subcategories. From the interviews we see that the system can be used for:

- Searching for competence to solve problems
- Resource allocation
- Finding projects and external marketing
- Competence development

Now, we discuss each of these uses below:

3.1 Searching for Competence to Solve Problems

The developers often need to know something about a topic that they are not very skilled in themselves. We can then divide between two types of usage of the skills management system. First, people use it to find other people in the company that knows something about a specific problem that they have to solve – "short term usage". Second, the people increase their overall insight in what the core competencies in the company are, what we can call more "long term" usage.

Let us look at the short term usage first: One developer says: "it happens [that I use it], if I suddenly have a specific problem in an area that I do not know much about, then it sometimes helps to go in there and find someone who knows about it. I have in fact done that once..." Another developer seems to use it more often: "Of course, when I wonder if there are anyone who can help me with something, I look up in the skills management system to see if anyone has the knowledge that I need". In Fig. 1, we show a screenshot of the skills management system, which gives an overview of skills on object-oriented development. Here, you can also e-mail people who have a required competence in one area. Or you can just print a list of people and ask them yourself, as another developer is usually doing: "Then I find a list, and look at what level they have [...] and then I go around in the house and ask them". Of course, this depends on that people rate themselves in a honest way. One developer used the skills management system to find people, but after asking the believed "experts" found that "I did not get the answers that I needed, so I had to go to someone else. So, it is very dependent on that people update it right. And to describe a level is not that easy, so some overrate themselves and other underrate themselves strongly". Another developer is critical to the categories of competence in the skills management system: "what you can get information about now is if someone knows about web – and that contains quite a lot! ...maybe it is not that general, but not too far off. It is based on the core competency areas of the company, but when it comes to more detailed things, like who that in fact can write a computer program, and who that can find a solution – you do not find that there".

When we look at more long-term usage, we do not find so much material in our interviews. One developer, however, often finds a group that knows something about a subject on the skills management system, and asks them questions by e-mail. But "if it then happens that you have asked questions about SQL to ten guru's, and it is always the same two that answers, then it happens that you start to go to *them* and talk. You learn after a while who it is any use to attempt to get anything out of".

3.2 Resource Allocation

IBM has a worldwide very up-to-date resource allocation management system. At a seminar with David Snowden at IBM's Knowledge Management Institute, it sounded a bit like the system used at Alpha. Every employee updates their skills and competencies and their available time, so that project managers globally can place queries on when and what type of people they need to staff their project. However, Snowden told us how he and all the managers he knew staffed their projects in practice. Snowden called up some of his good friends in the company, people he trusted, and discussed with them who would be the right people for the new project. When they agreed upon the names, they got all the professional details of

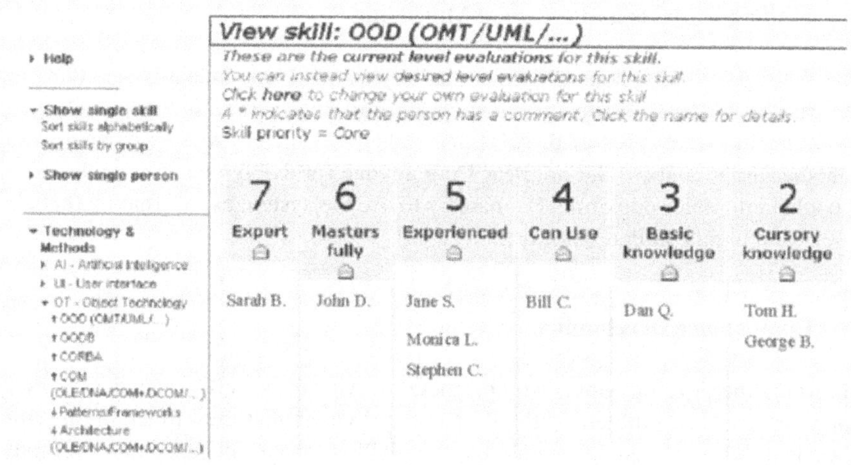

Fig. 1. A part of a Screenshot from a web browser that shows people with different competence levels in Object-Oriented Development. The names of the people have been made up, and company information has been removed. On the left, you have a browsable list of competence categories.

those people and when they had spare time. *Then* they placed a detailed tailored query into the system. Of course, the system chewed out only the names that they already had chosen. And everybody is happy. The managers get the people they want and the system seems to work perfect – and it gets the highest credits on satisfaction ratings! When confronted with this story at Alpha, one of the managers of internal knowledge management said: "This is not the situation at Alpha!"

Let us therefore see how some of the employees comment on this issue. In our empirical material from Alpha, we can see some patterns of the practical uses of the skills management system, in terms of resource allocation.

As one newly employed said: "Contrary to a lot of other companies that uses such a system, here at Alpha we *really use* the system for resource planning." Another comment is on the same track: "I think that the skills manager is a useful tool, but a tool that still has got a lot of potential when it comes to practical use. Those who do the resource-management they already use the tool a lot in the daily resource allocation work."

A third Alpha employee comments on the skill manager as both an important tool for resource allocation, but also for the strategic development of the company:

"The tools I use the most I think is [...] the competence-block-manager [another part of the knowledge management system in the company which is used to organize company-internal courses] and the skills-manager. Definitely! I'm responsible for the content in many databases, and partly the skills-management base. And the skills manager is a tool that is very important both for the resource allocation process [...] Therefore, many employees come up with suggestions to new content, new elements, in the skills database."

3.3 Finding Projects and External Marketing

Another usage of the system is for the sales department. One manager said that "Even sales can use it [the skills management system], to think out new directions to go in". That is, to find what types of projects that suits the company well. We can also think of another usage that we did not hear from anyone (probably because we did not talk to people in the sales department) – namely to use the system as external marketing; as "proof" of a highly skilled workforce.

3.4 Competence Development

Concerning the development of competencies at Alpha, the skills manager also seems to play a part. "The problem with all of our systems is that they function only to the degree that they are used. [Systems] like the Skills Manager depends on everybody to update it often and objectively. That could be solved by work-process support. Skills update could be a natural part of the closing of a project, for example by updating the involved competencies – those that have been in use during the project. You are today allocated to projects on the basis of what you have in the Skills Manager. There we have views devoted to people with free time and the competence required in the project. When you are allocated to a project on the basis of a competence profile, then there is also knowledge in the system about which competencies it is expected to be used in the project, and therefore it would be natural to ask for an update on those competencies when the project is finished."

Another employee sees the Skills manager in light of intellectual capital. "Such tools are very good indicators for accounting intellectual capital. You are able to see in the long term what kind of competencies we will need, evaluate it, and compare it to what competence we already have in the firm, and then say that we have that many man months with C++ competence, or Java, and we see that there is an increase in this compentence, and then we can evaluate that."

In the skills management system at *Alpha*, the employees can use this tool to state what they want to learn about in the future, not only what they know now. In that way, people can develop their competence by working on relevant projects.

4 Conclusions

We have interviewed people in a software consultancy company about how they are using a *skills management* system, which is a part of the company's knowledge management system. We found that the tool is in use for "problem solving" in that people use it to get to know about who knows what in the company. Most people say that they use it to solve problems on a short term, but some also say that the system let them know who to ask the next time. Further, the *skills management* system is in use for resource allocation, to find new projects for the company and to support competency development.

Some are critical to how people rate their competency and to the type of skills that one is able to evaluate oneself in. However, it seems that most people see it as useful both for themselves and for the company as a whole.

Acknowledgement. We are grateful to Reidar Conradi at the Norwegian University of Science and Technology for comments on this paper.

References

[1] Thomas H Davenport and Laurence Prusak, *Working Knowledge: How Organizations Manage What They Know*: Harvard Business School Press, 1998.

[2] K. E. Sveiby, *The New Organizational Wealth: Managing and Measuring Knowledge-Based Assets*: Berret-Koehler Pub, 1997.

[3] Alvesson, *Management of Knowledge-Intensive Companies*. Berlin, New York: Walter de Gruyter, 1995.

[4] A. Carlsen and M. Skaret, "Practicing Knowledge Management in Norway," Working Paper 4/98 1998.

[5] Michael Polanyi, *The Tacit Dimension*, vol. 540. Garden City, New York: Doubleday, 1967.

[6] Ikujiro Nonaka and Hirotaka Takeuchi, *The Knowledge-Creating Company*: Oxford University Press, 1995.

[7] Karl M. Wiig, *Knowledge Management Methods*: Schema Press, 1995.

[8] Irma Becerra-Fernandez, "Facilitating the Online Search of Experts at NASA using Expert Seeker People-Finder," presented at Third International Conference on Practical Aspects of Knowledge Management (PAKM2000), Basel, Switzerland, 2000.

[9] David M. Fetterman, *Ethnography: Step by Step*, vol. 17: Sage Publications, 1998.

[10] Helen Sharp, Mark Woodman, and Hugh Robinson, "Using Etnography and Discouse Analysis to Study Software Engineering Practices," presented at ICSE Workshop: Beg, Borrow or Steal: Using Multidisciplinary Approaches in Empirical Software Engineering, Limerick, Ireland, 2000.

[11] Paul Beynon-Davies, "Etnography and information systems development: Etnography of, for and within IS development," *Information and Software Technology*, vol. 39, pp. 531-540, 1997.

Part 5:

Analysis

Lessons Learned about Structuring and Describing Experience for Three Experience Bases

Mikael Lindvall[1], Michael Frey[2], Patricia Costa[1], and Roseanne Tesoriero[1]

[1] Fraunhofer Center Maryland for Experimental Software Engineering
4321 Hartwick Road, Suite 500
College Park
MD 20740
USA
{mikli, pcosta, rtesoriero}@fc-md.umd.edu

[2] University of Kaiserslautern
AG Software Engineering
Bldg. 57 / 524
PO Box 3049
67653 Kaiserslautern
GERMANY
frey@informatik.uni-kl.de

Abstract. The Experience Factory approach defines a framework for experience management. It has been successfully applied to software development at NASA for more than 25 years and has now been applied to other organizations outside the software development community. The Experience Management System (EMS) developed at Fraunhofer Center Maryland (FC-MD) is a set of tools implemented to support the Experience Factory approach. The Visual Query Interface (VQI), a component of EMS, is used in conjunction with a methodology to help organizations capture, synthesize and reuse experience. To easily add new experience as well as find previous experience packages, the captured experience must be structured and stored in an experience base. This paper describes how we organize and structure experience into packages that can be stored in the experience base. We describe some of the lessons learned from applying EMS to three different organizations.

1 Introduction

The Experience Factory approach [1] defines a framework for experience management. This approach has been successfully applied to software development at NASA for more than 25 years and recently at other organizations [2][4]. The experience factory enables organizational learning and acknowledges the need for a separate support organization that works with the project organization in order to manage and learn from its own experience. The support organization helps the project organization observe itself, collect data about itself, build models and draw conclusions based on the data, package the experience for further reuse, and most importantly, feed the experience back to the project organization. All of this experience is stored in the experience

K.-D. Althoff, R.L. Feldmann, and W. Müller (Eds.): LSO 2001, LNCS 2176, pp. 106-119, 2001.

base, which is utilized by both the project and support organizations. The project organization uses the experience base to search and reuse previous experience. The support organization analyzes and synthesizes experience into new experience packages to facilitate its work with the project organization and to feed synthesized experience back to it.

The Experience Factory approach was initially designed for software organizations and takes into account the software discipline's experimental, evolutionary, and non-repetitive characteristics. In our work with businesses outside the software community, we have found that a tailored version of the experience factory approach is beneficial for creating a learning organization even though its main business is not developing software.

The following are observations on frequently occurring business problems for which we have found the general Experience Factory approach useful. A first observation is that organizations strive to reuse all kinds of documented experience (e.g., proposals and budgets) but that it is not easy to do so in an effective manner. The reuse is rather ad hoc and unplanned and it is often hard to know what to search for or how to find useful documents. The second observation is that the "right" knowledge for solving a problem often exists somewhere within the organization, but the challenge is to take the time to search for it, to identify it, to get access to it and then to learn from it. Due to the fact that experience is represented internally by experts, the major problem is often finding and getting access to the "expert" in order to solve a problem. The third observation pertains to organizations that have the desire to manage experience, for example in terms of lessons learned. In these organizations, structuring and disseminating lessons learned in order to duplicate successes and to avoid known mistakes is a main issue. The fourth observation is that in organizations where raw experience, for instance lessons learned, is managed, the main issue is how to refine, analyze and synthesize the experience, for example by building models based on experience in order to improve business processes.

We have had the opportunity to apply the general Experience Factory approach to several organizations. Aside from the fundamental organizational shift to become a learning organization and adopting such a culture, the main implementation issue has been the experience base: its organization, its content, and its supporting tools. While enabling a culture in which sharing and reusing experience as a natural way of doing business is crucial to success, the implementation of the experience base is what truly can make sharing and reusing happen on a larger scale. Modern information technology makes it possible to build and run an advanced experience management system on top of information servers, but in order to have an accepted and useful system, one has to listen carefully and work closely with potential users and thoroughly analyze the problem at hand. A system developed in such a manner will become a valuable experience base. We have chosen to use a particular structure for packaging experience and a visualization tool for searching and analyzing the packaged experience. In order to understand the implications of our decisions with respect to the experience base, we decided to analyze our own work and share the results with others in the field. The research questions that we tried to answer by this work were:

How do you package and organize experience?
How do you make experience available/searchable?
What kind of experience is worthwhile to package?

In this paper, we start by introducing and describing our implementation of the Experience Factory approach; the Experience Management System (EMS) and its components. Then, we describe how the Visual Query Interface (VQI), a component of the EMS, was applied to three different organizations. The paper focuses on the experience bases of these three implementations by describing how we applied the methodology and the tool to structure the experience of each organization into packages stored in the experience base.

2 The Experience Management System (EMS)

The EMS is composed of content, structure, procedures and tools. The content can be data, information, knowledge or experience, which for simplicity will be called experience from here on. The content is stored as experience packages. The structure is the way the content is organized and is later referred to as the taxonomy or the classification scheme. The content and the structure are often referred to as the experience base. Procedures are instructions on how to manage the experience base on a daily basis, including how to use, package, delete, integrate and update experience. Tools support managing the content and the structure, and carrying out the procedures, as well as helping to capture, store, integrate, analyze, synthesize and retrieve experience. In this paper, we focus on describing the structuring of experience into packages that can be stored in the experience base. In this paper, we describe its connection to the VQI tool.

2.1 Methodology for Implementing an EMS

Different organizations have different needs and cultures, which is the main reason why each EMS implementation needs to be tailored to the target organization. We use a methodology to help us understand and set up an EMS for a specific organization. The methodology helps define the content, structure, procedures and tools that will be part of the EMS. The use of this methodology is very important in guiding the work so that the EMS is successful and accepted by the organization. The following is a description of the steps of the methodology to develop an EMS for a particular organization and domain of experiences. It is based on best practices derived from previous EMS projects and has been and will continue to be continuously improved.

The first step of the methodology is to characterize the organization and to define the current business processes and the existing knowledge. We distinguish between knowledge that is documented, undocumented and unavailable. Many organizations already have procedures in place to manage a subset of the experience but fail to manage all crucial experience. The characterization helps us understand what experience is not covered, and how existing documented experience fits into the new system and how it can be reused. After the characterization of the organization, user roles of the EMS are defined and use cases are developed based on the business processes and the user roles. The user roles are defined based on the culture of the organization and what type of roles different people will perform. Examples of user roles are: *consumer* (anyone who uses the EMS to search for experience), *maintainer* (a person who is responsible for maintenance of the EMS's EB) and *provider* (anyone who contributes experience to the EMS's EB). The user roles can be refined for each main category. An example of this refinement is *topic managers* (anyone who is responsible for maintenance of experiences related to a specific topic). The use cases are defined based on the characterization of the organization, the business processes that are relevant to the EMS and the user roles. The use cases cover procedures that are already in place and add new ones as necessary. The next step is to define a data model (or taxonomy) that is suitable for the organization. The data model is used to classify the experience that will be included in the EMS in order to make it easier for users to find the experience later. In this step, the different types of experience that will be managed are identified and classified. Acceptable values for each component of the data model are also defined. The results of this step are documented into an EMS Requirements Document and a specification for the particular EMS system is created. Based on the EMS Requirements Document and specification, the architecture of the EMS is defined. COTS, glueware, and in-house built components that together fulfill the requirements are used to define the architecture. Applications already in place and used by the organization are considered to be part of the architecture. The architecture is then implemented. Tools that will support the EMS are developed, installed and integrated. After implementation of the architecture, a set of procedures for the regular maintenance of the EMS is created. These procedures are tied to the user roles and are intended to ensure that the system works and that the managed experience is always current. Following the development of the EMS procedures, the EMS's EB is populated with an initial set of experience packages and the EMS is configured and installed. A rollout plan is prepared and executed to train, market and motivate people to use the EMS. After the system is deployed, it is constantly improved based on feedback. Types of feedback considered are formal evaluations, including interviews and tests with users, direct feedback from users, feedback loops embedded in the tools and analysis of usage data of the tools. According to the feedback, the content is constantly updated, new experiences packages are analyzed and synthesized into new experience packages. This step is continuously iterated in order to improve the EMS.

2.2 The Visual Query Interface (VQI)

One important part of the EMS is its supporting tools. Tools are used to support capturing, visualizing, analyzing, storing, and searching for experience. The user interface of the tools is another important aspect to the success of the EMS. It has to be as easy as possible to add and retrieve experience packages. The search and visualization tools that help users find and retrieve experience packages have to be attractive and easy to use [4][6]. We use the Visual Query Interface (VQI), which is based on Shneiderman's work [5], as one way to search for information in the experience base [4][6]; it is also a useful analysis tool (see Fig. 1). The VQI visualizes the content of the experience base graphically using three dimensions: X- and Y-axes, and color. The attributes are used to describe the experience packages and can be used by the user to select how the packages should be visualized. Typical attributes are package id (a number), name (a string) and submitted (a date). Fig. 1, shows the VQI displaying experience pack-

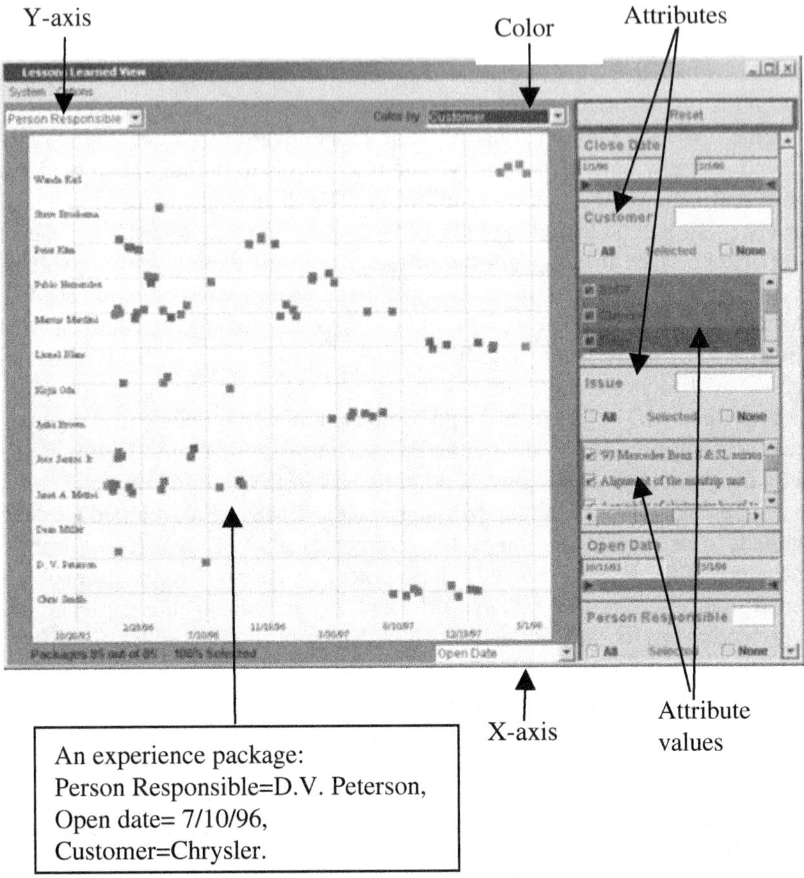

Fig. 1. The Visual Query Interface (VQI)

ages that represent "Lessons Learned" for an organization that designs automobile interiors.[1] The attributes and their values are displayed on the right frame. The X-axis represents the "Open Date," the Y-axis represents the "Person Responsible," and the color represents the "Customer." These dimensions can be changed using the drop down menus. The values of the attributes on the right frame can be enabled or disabled by the user in order to focus the search or visualization. For instance, a user may wish to display only experience packages related to "Alignment of the minitrip unit." In this case, he or she can select this value for the attribute "Issue." If the user wants to see the content of an experience package, he or she can click on the corresponding dot and a window with the description and the actual content of the experience package will be displayed. The definition of the taxonomy for the VQI is one of the main keys to its success and applicability. A well-defined taxonomy will allow experiences to be found more easily and faster and will allow more types of analyses. An understanding of the organization and its processes is crucial for the definition of a useful taxonomy.

[1] A detailed example from this organization is given in Section 3.

2.3 Structure of Experience in the VQI

In the VQI, we structure and organize experience in order to make it easier for users to find later by defining a taxonomy tailored to the individual organization. When defining the taxonomy, different types of experience that will be managed are identified and classified. Experience is described using an experience package that consists of attributes, elements and links. Experience packages are grouped into package types in the taxonomy. In order to capture the experience in a manageable form, we created a data model for the experience package. We use attributes to describe properties of the experience we are trying to capture. These attributes vary depending upon the type of experience being captured. For example, if we were to create a package for this workshop, attributes might include properties such as the workshop date and workshop location. Links refer to related packages within the repository or external references. In the VQI data model, these links are unidirectional. Continuing with the workshop example, links to the experience package for this workshop may include the URL for the workshop web site or links to other packages in the repository related the workshop (such as a package for a related workshop or co-located conference). Elements are the actual files that make up the body of the experience package. In the workshop example, elements of the package might include all of the papers and presentations for the workshop. Experience packages are categorized using package types. The LSO workshop could be an experience package of the type meeting. Other packages in the package type meeting might include other workshops or conferences.

3 Descriptions of the Experience Bases

The methodology, data model and taxonomy described in the previous sections have been applied to create experience bases for three different organizations: Q-Labs, the Fraunhofer Center, Maryland (FC-MD) and Johnson Control, Inc. (JCI). Each organization had different needs and the resulting experience bases have varying structures that gave us insights into using the data model and taxonomy.

3.1 Q-Labs EMS

Q-Labs is an internationally distributed software engineering consulting company. With offices in Europe as well as in the United States, Q-Labs needed an infrastructure to share experience between employees no matter where they are located. Q-Labs calls this infrastructure the "virtual office", and it is supposed to be used by all Q-Labs employees. The main problem Q-Labs faced was employees "reinventing the wheel" over and over again. Often, a consultant developed a document from scratch without knowing that another consultant at Q-Labs (possibly in another office) had already done similar work. Using an existing document as a basis for a new task saves consultants' time and thus money for the company. This kind of reuse can also improve the quality of a document, because consultants can take advantage of work that has already been done and concentrate on follow-up work and improvements instead of spending time on the basics.

We addressed these problems by creating a Q-Labs EMS, which stores documents and their descriptions in the experience base. The descriptions consist of attribute-value pairs and enables users to search for documents within the Q-Labs virtual office. The search, performed using the VQI, enables users to modify search queries online and receive immediate feedback about the results. Experience packages in the context of the Q-Labs EMS contain single computer documents, including text, slides, graphs, scanned images, and numeric data. Although the VQI is able to handle packages that consist of multiple files, Q-Labs identifies a package as one single computer file. Content-wise the objects are lessons learned, templates, and artifacts from previous projects or earlier phases of a currently executing project. In addition to the actual files, a package stores data about the context in which it was developed. The package includes information on the employee who is responsible for it. This person can be the "owner" or "creator" of the package or someone who took over responsibility after the original creator left the project or the organization. Furthermore, a package provides links to externally stored information such as web pages. The size of the Q-Labs EMS prototype contains approximately 150 packages, distributed over three package types: consultants, documents, and projects. Most of these packages (about 65%) were stored in the documents area of the VQI. More information on the Q-Labs experience base can be found in [4] and [6].

3.2 FC-MD EMS

The Fraunhofer Center for Experimental Software Engineering, Maryland is a subsidiary of the European Fraunhofer Gesellschaft that supports applied research in several fields. The main objectives of EMS at the FC-MD are sharing business procedures and processes among employees and also supporting new employees without spending a lot of experts' time for training. The users of this instance of EMS are primarily scientists, but also managers and project managers working at the FC-MD. The FC-MD faces the problem that new employees need a lot of training and thus requires a considerable amount of experts' time before becoming productive. Since the FC-MD is a rapidly growing organization, this constitutes a major problem. Another problem is that employees, whether they are new to the organization or not, develop documents from scratch without being aware that similar documents might have been developed by other employees. Knowing about these documents and where to find them could reduce development costs since the employee could save development time. This kind of reuse can also improve the quality of documents because scientists can build on existing expertise and improve the work instead of starting all over again.

The FC-MD EMS prototype, which is based on the VQI, provides attribute-based search and retrieval functionality for documents that remain in their original location within the organizational computer network. It also provides the means to find information about employees, procedures, and policies. Thus, new employees are enabled to find answers to their questions without taking experts' time. Furthermore, all employees can search for experience packages in order to find reusable or useful documents or guidelines for their ongoing projects. They can also search for other employees who are experienced in a certain field. In contrast to the Q-Labs EMS, experience packages in the context of the FC-MD EMS are collections of computer files instead of a single file. Thus an, experience package in the FC-MD EMS is a rather large entity. Experience packages at the FC-MD provide information about:

Corporate documents: papers, proposals, presentations, books, and journals.
People: including their expertise, research interests, CVs, and links to home pages
Projects: including partners, corresponding proposals, funding, and deliverables.
Business processes: submitting conference papers, visas processing, Fraunhofer policies, how is hiring done, what should you know about writing a proposal.

Since the FC-MD EMS is in a prototype phase, the number of packages is low.

3.3 JCI EMS

Johnson Control, Inc. (JCI) is a manufacturer of automobile interiors like dashboards, seats, and visors for many automotive companies. The actual users within JCI are designers of auto interiors who primarily work at CAD workstations. Following their internal guidelines, JCI employees have been collecting lessons learned for years. Hundreds of lessons learned are stored in several MS Word™ documents across the company, which renders them less valuable since finding all lessons learned related to a specific topic (for example overhead reading lights) was virtually impossible.
JCI also faced the problem of losing experience when employees leave the company. Similar to all knowledge intensive organizations, they are dependent on their employees. Furthermore, sharing knowledge among employees is time-consuming for experts who are already very busy. Another problem is bringing new employees up to speed so they become productive sooner. By analyzing, characterizing, and packaging lessons learned, we demonstrated that it was possible to populate an experience base to search and retrieve relevant lessons utilizing the VQI interface of EMS. Appropriate attributes and their values for the characterization were developed during discussions involving FC-MD and JCI employees. In contrast to the Q-Labs EMS and the FC-MD EMS, the JCI EMS prototype supports and improves the actual process of developing automobile interiors. An employee, working on the design of a car seat can, for instance, use JCI EMS to learn how to avoid known pitfalls in this process. Another distinguishing criteria between the JCI EMS and both of the previously mentioned systems is that the JCI system consists of only one package type called *lessons learned*, which means that the JCI EMS is a specialized experience base, exclusively for lessons learned. These lessons were learned in previous projects or earlier steps of a current project, and are limited to a few paragraphs of text, so the granularity is small compared to the granularity of the Q-Labs EMS and FC-MD EMS. The prototype system consists of 85 packages; all of them are stored in the *lessons learned* package type. This project indicated that even a very specialized experience base that is only designed to handle lessons learned could be very useful and improve the way a company is doing business.

3.4 An Example

The experience base developed for lessons learned is illustrated by this example. The problem to be solved by the system was to make captured lessons learned available to a larger group of people enabling the organization to learn from its own experience. The approach we used was based on the methodology described previously. It focused on defining use-cases encapsulating how future users would use the experience base. We then analyzed a set of existing lessons learned and created a taxonomy that would simplify searching and retrieving lessons learned in the context of the use-cases. The taxonomy was based on a set of attributes and the definition of valid values of these attributes. Examples of attributes are:

Product area: Values are Door Panels, Instrument Panels, Seats, and Overhead
Product item: Examples of acceptable values are Sunroof, Console, and Compass.
Open Date: The date the lessons learned was identified.
Person responsible
Problem
Solution

Each lesson learned was turned into an experience package of the experience base by first categorizing it according to the taxonomy by assigning attribute values. Second, by linking it to a related lesson learned. Third, by linking the lesson learned to the text describing it (stored as a file).

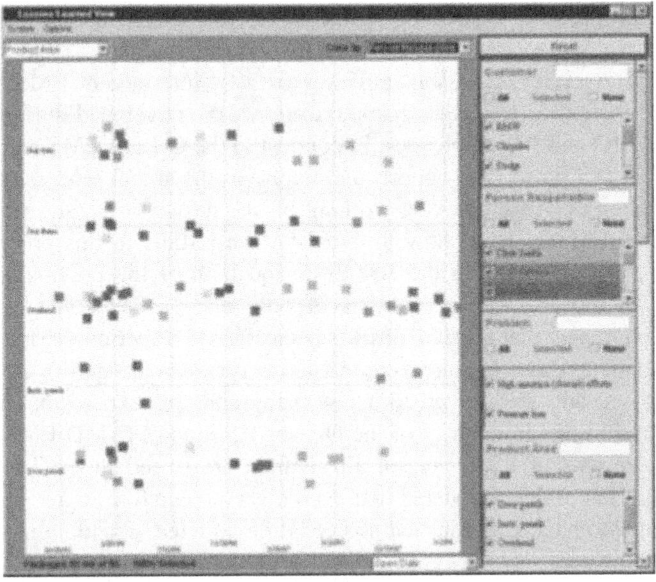

Fig. 2. VQI applied to Lessons Learned. Each dot represents a Lesson Learned. Dots are colored by the person responsible for the Lesson Learned. There are 85 Lessons Learned in total.

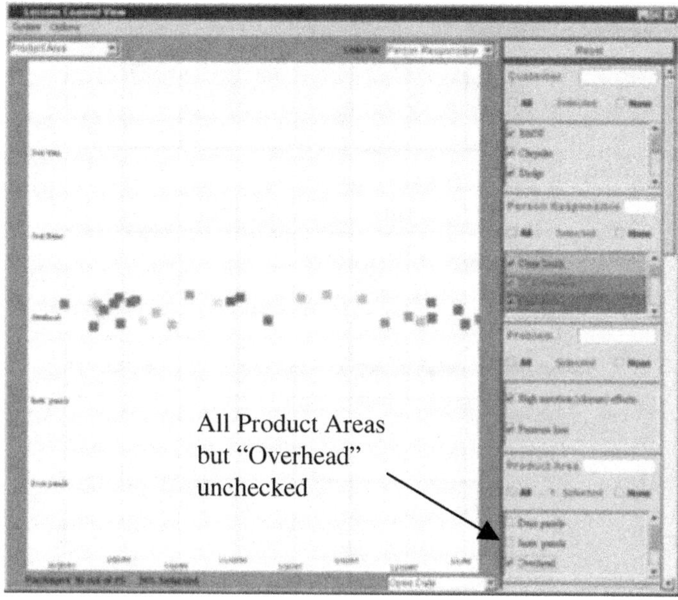

Fig. 3. All product areas but "Overhead" are filtered out reducing the number of Lessons Learned (dots) to 30.

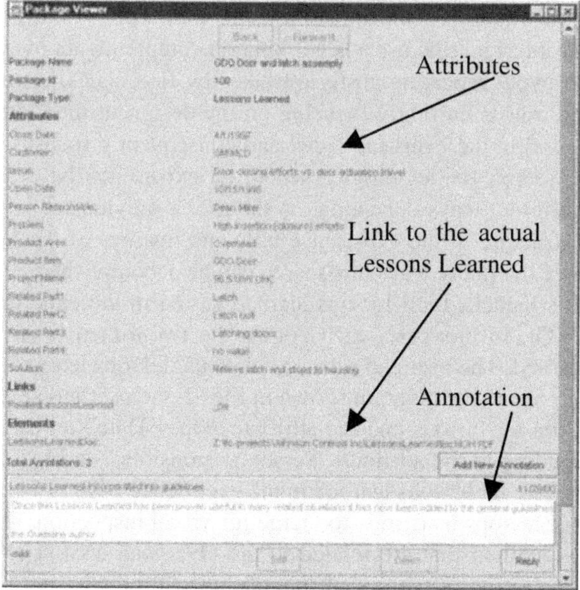

Fig. 4. The package viewer shows the values of all attributes of this package including links to other packages and html-pages as well as links to files. The annotation part at the bottom of the package viewer enables users to feed data back to the system.

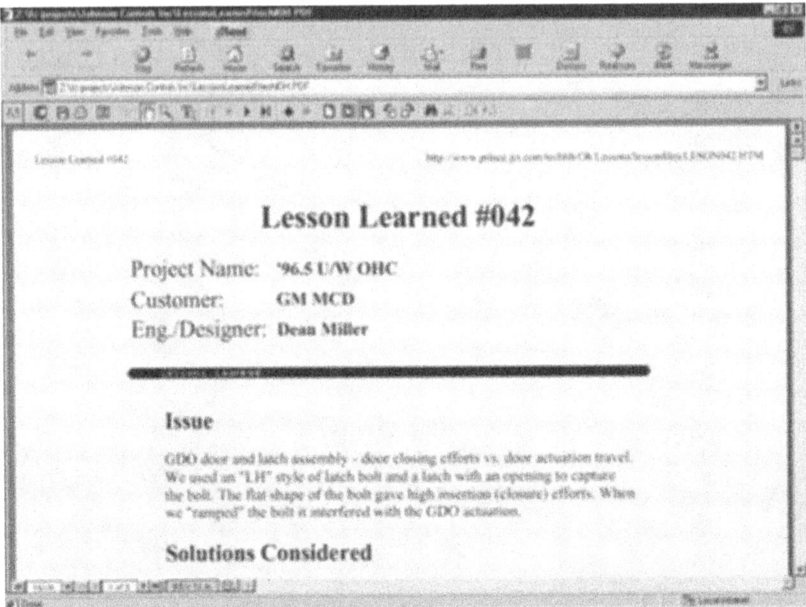

Fig. 5. When the user clicks on the link to the lessons learned, the system displays the actual Lessons Learned document.

The use-case we will use to demonstrate how the prototype system works assumes that a designer of car interiors (the user) is working on completing an overhead design. The user's goal is to avoid repeating costly mistakes by first checking for lessons learned in this area. The user is currently focusing on the design of the Garage Door Opener Door (GDO Doors) in the overhead panel and consequently focuses the search on the same area. The search for lessons learned in an experience base using VQI can be done in many different ways depending on the user's previous experience and knowledge about the structure of the experience base and features of the VQI. The example shows only one of the many ways this search can be accomplished.

When the VQI is launched, all lessons learned stored in the experience base are displayed by the VQI. In this case, each dot on the two-dimensional grid represents a single lesson learned. The user can select to view the lessons learned in many different ways. In order to create the diagram shown in Fig. 2, the user has selected the attribute "Product Area" on the Y-axis and the attribute "Open Date" on the X-axis. The dots are colored according to the attribute "Person responsible." In Fig. 2, the VQI reports that in total there are 85 lessons learned in the experience base.

As the number of lessons learned is too large for visual inspection, the user focuses on only the lessons learned that are related to the Overhead area. The user reduces the result set by deselecting all values of the attribute "Product Area", but "Overhead." (See Fig. 3.)

The result, 30 lessons learned, is still not focused enough and the search needs to be refined further. As a last refinement, the user instructs the system to display the set of lessons learned related to "closure efforts," which is the focus of the design of the

GDO Door. As a result of the refinement one lesson learned remains. Fig. 4 shows the panel that is displayed when the user clicks on this remaining lesson learned. Fig. 4 also shows the feedback feature, the annotation at the bottom of the picture, which enables users to document their experiences with the system in general and this experience package in particular. The annotation in Fig. 4 indicates that this lesson learned has been proven useful and has been further analyzed and synthesized, and incorporated into the corporate guidelines. To open up the lesson learned, the user clicks on the link in Fig. 4. (See Fig. 5.)

4 Lessons Learned and New Directions

Having described how we experimented with three different prototype EMS systems based on the VQI at different organizations, we will now discuss our own lessons learned related to our questions stated above. The questions were:

How do you package and organize experience?
How do you make experience available/searchable?
What kind of experience is worthwhile to package?

We have experimented with different forms of experience packaging. In the FC-MD EMS, an experience package is considered to be a collection of files. This definition makes the granularity of the FC-MD experience package much coarser than, for example, the experience packages for Q-Labs EMS and JCI EMS. We experienced that this coarse granularity caused several problems:

Whenever people are talking about experience packages, they still think in terms of files, which seem to be more intuitive for most people. In addition to this, putting together a complex package is a very time-consuming activity. Some packages in the FC-MD EMS took several weeks, some even longer, to create. This problem is one reason why there are only a limited number of packages in this instance of FC-MD EMS so far. This has implications for the selection of search and retrieve tool, in this case the VQI, which graphically displays the contents of the experience base. A question that arose in this context is: "If we only have so few packages, why do we need a state-of-the-art visualization tool or sophisticated search and retrieval capabilities?" For this reason, we are working on populating FC-MD EMS to make the system as useful as possible for our coworkers. This touches on another issue that we are currently experimenting with: How do you make the experience base useful even though it is not fully populated? If experience packages were less complex, we would be able to create more experience packages over a shorter period of time, thus addressing the problem of populating the experience base. A less complex experience package would also better support the notion of organic growth, which in essence means that the experience base should ideally grow in directions where there is demand for experience.

The question on packaging ties to the VQI tool itself and how users of the system perceived it. VQI was a central part of these systems and was the front end to the experience base. Although people generally like the VQI and the way it visualizes the content of the experience base, helping the user find experience packages and revealing patterns of the experience base [SMBK99], it was perceived that one single front end doesn't cover all possible usage scenarios. There are many potential uses of an experience base, so being limited to the VQI as the only interface to the experience base was considered to be too restrictive. For that reason, we are working on a set of different tools to complement the VQI.

We noticed that the VQI proved to be very flexible and easy to tailor for new applications. This is due to the fact that it automatically generates the search interface based on a number of standardized query devices. It also automatically generates all data entry forms, which are used for populating the experience base with new packages as well as the presentation of all components of the package in the package viewer. This flexibility makes it easy to quickly set up a visualization demo or a prototype for a new area.

The drawbacks with using a two-dimensional visualization tool as the front-end to an experience base are, for example, that multi-value attributes are hard to represent. Normally attributes have one value. The document attribute "number of pages" could have the value 5. However, to best describe the type of experience that was covered by the systems in this paper, multi-value attributes were needed. An example of a multi-value attribute is author. The attribute author could have many values, for example, "Hans", "Sean", and "Tamika" are all authors of the same document. The representation of multi-value attribute using database technology is trivial, but it is a non-trivial task to modify the package-display in the grid pattern of the VQI to represent multi-value attributes. In addition, supporting multi-value attributes has severe implications on the query-input. We are, nevertheless, working on a solution to provide this feature in a future version of EMS and the VQI.

We have experimented with different kinds of experience, from regular office information to lessons learned. Our own lessons learned related to the question "which experience is worthwhile packaging?" are that no experience is too simple to collect, as long as users find it useful. Researchers may find it interesting to collect experience related to complex tasks that are highly creative and therefore hard to describe, while users of the system ask for support to remember daily activities that occurred at the work place. Our experience is that it is most important to support the work force where they most need the support, independently of how advanced or simple this support may be. Our experience is that only when it has been proven that experience management works where it is most needed can it be extended to other areas, which might be more complex.

5 Conclusions

The best way to learn and improve is to analyze previous experience and draw conclusions for future direction based on them. It is even better when such experiences can be shared within a larger community of people working in the same area.

We analyzed three experience bases in order to better understand how to improve our Experience Management System. The three experience bases are all based on the same concepts, the experience factory as a general framework for organizational learning, and the VQI as the Experience Management System, which implements the experience factory approach. The three experience bases have much in common, but there are also differences.

An example of such similarities and differences regarding the taxonomies is that the three experience bases are all based on the same concepts of package types and packages. Differences are that the taxonomy of the Q-Labs experience base is narrow, but each package type has many packages. The FC-MD experience base is broader and has more package types, but there is fewer packages for each package type. The JCI experience base is, on the other hand, extremely narrow and its only package type is Lessons Learned, but there are many packages of that package type.

In our own lessons learned, we mentioned both strengths and weaknesses with the current approach and we identified areas for improvements as well as new research questions.

One such an improvement is integrating the VQI with an information server such as Hyperwave™, which would provide a robust back-end for the EMS, whereas the VQI would play the role as one of many interfaces to experience base. The VQI would also act as an analysis tool for analyzing the content in the experience base as well as for analyzing how the experience is used.

We are also addressing the problem of how to get people to use our systems and are, for example, experimenting with what we call "knowledge dust". Knowledge dust is that day-to-day knowledge that everybody needs in order to perform at work, but to which no one attributes any value. We are experimenting with collecting such knowledge dust, which we will bring together to a critical mass and feed it back to the organization in a useful form. Early results indicate that this approach will be a great complement to the more complex experience package approach and that experience bases based on knowledge dust can grow rapidly and provide much value to the organization.

References

1. Victor R. Basili, Gianluigi Caldiera, H. Dieter Rombach. The Experience Factory. Encyclopedia of Software Engineering. 2 Volume Set, pp 469-476, Copyright by John Wiley & Sons, Inc., 1994.
2. Peter Brössler. Knowledge Management at a Software House: An Experience Report. Workshop on Learning Software Organizations: Methodology and Applications. Kaiserslautern, Germany, June 1999.
3. Frank Houdek, Kurt Schneider, Evo Wieser. Establishing Experience Factories at Daimler-Benz: An Experience Report. International Conference in Software Engineering (ICSE) 1998, pages 443-447.
4. Manoel Mendonca, Carolyn Seaman, Victor R. Basili, Yong-Mi Kim. A Prototype Experience Management System for a Software Consulting Organization. Conference on Software Engineering and Knowledge Engineering (SEKE) 2001.
5. N. Jog, B. Shneiderman. Starfield Information Visualization with Interactive Smooth Zooming. CS-TR-3286, CAR-TR-714, ISR-TR-94-46. IFIP 2.6 Visual Databases Systems Proceedings, pp 1-10, Lausanne, Switzerland. March 27-29,1995.
6. Carolyn Seaman, Manoel Mendonca, Victor R. Basili, Yong-Mi Kim. An Experience Management System for a Software Consulting Organization. Software Engineering Workshop, NASA Goddard Software Engineering Laboratory, Greenbelt, MD, December 1999.

Knowledge Elicitation through Web-Based Data Mining Services*

Shonali Krishnaswamy[1], Seng Wai Loke[2], and Arkady Zaslavsky[1]

[1]School of Computer Science and Software Engineering
900 Dandenong Road, Monash University, Caulfield East, Victoria –3145, Australia.
{shonali.krishnaswamy, arkady.zaslavsky}@csse.monash.edu.au
[2]School of Computer Science and Information Technology
RMIT University, GPO Box 2476V, Melbourne, Victoria-3001, Australia.
swloke@cs.rmit.edu.au

Abstract. Knowledge is a vital component for organisational growth and data mining provides the technological basis for automated knowledge elicitation from data sources. The emergence of Application Service Providers hosting Internet-based data mining services is being seen as a viable alternative for organisations that value their knowledge resources but are constrained by the high cost of data mining software. In this paper, we present two alternative models of organisation for data mining service providers. We use the interaction protocols between organisations requiring data mining services and the service providers to motivate the need for specification of data mining task requests that adequately represent the requirements and constraints of the clients and also illustrate the importance of description mechanisms for data mining systems and services in order to support Internet delivery of such services. We present an XML-based approach for describing both, data mining task requests and the functionality and services of data mining service providers.

1 Introduction

A "Learning Organisation" is characterised by [8] in terms of four constructs: knowledge acquisition, information distribution, information interpretation, and organisational memory. It is one that focuses on continuous learning and adaptive behaviour for its survival and growth. It proactively supports the processes that improve its ability to learn. The principal advantage of emphasising organisational learning is that - like all other forms of learning - it results in *knowledge*, which is increasingly seen as a key to providing a competitive edge and supporting the strategic decision making process within an organisation. In an organisational context, knowledge can be acquired by learning from several sources, including data and human resources. Data mining is an important technology for "business intelligence"

---

* The work reported in this paper has been funded in part by the co-operative Research Centre Program through the Department of Industry, Science and Tourism of the Commonwealth Government of Australia.

K.-D. Althoff, R.L. Feldmann, and W. Müller (Eds.): LSO 2001, LNCS 2176, pp. 120-134, 2001.

and supports the organisational knowledge acquisition from data resources by automating this process. However, data mining is an expensive activity and establishing a data mining infrastructure within an organisation is a stumbling block for many small to medium scale companies. The recent trend of the Application Service Provider (ASP) paradigm is leading to the emergence of Internet-based data mining service providers such as Digimine [2]. This is becoming an important and viable alternative for fostering certain aspects of organisational learning (through knowledge acquisition from data sources) in companies that were previously constrained by the high cost of data mining software. By facilitating access to technology that supports learning from data sources without having to incur the costs associated with buying, setting-up and training, Internet-based data mining services provide a means to increase organisational learning levels. The focus of this technology is on facilitating learning from data, which we recognise is only one aspect of organisational learning. However, we believe, that this is one step forward for companies to evolve into learning organisations. In this paper, we present a multiple service provider model for Internet-based data mining services as an improvement over the currently pre-dominant single-service provider approach.

Application Service Providers underline the commercial viability of "renting" software out [1]. Thus, instead of buying an expensive software package and installing it, organisations logon to an application service provider (either through the Internet or dedicated communication channels) and use the packages provided by the ASP and pay for this usage. Data mining has several characteristics, which allow it to fit intuitively into the ASP model. The features that lend themselves suitable for hosting data mining services are as follows:

Diverse requirements: Business intelligence needs within organisations can be diverse and vary from customer profiling and fraud detection to market-basket analysis. Such diversity requires data mining systems that can support a wide variety of algorithms and techniques. The continuous growth and evolution of data mining systems from stand-alone systems characterised by single algorithms with little support for the knowledge discovery process to integrated systems incorporating several mining algorithms, multiple users, various data formats and distributed data sources notwithstanding, the current state of the art in data mining systems makes it unlikely for any one system to be able to support the wide and varied organisational business intelligence needs. Application Service Providers can alleviate this problem by hosting a variety of data mining systems that can meet the diverse needs of users.

Increased demand for business intelligence. Technologies like e-commerce provide an opportunity for small and medium range companies to compete in global markets, which were previously the domain of large organisations and multi-nationals. These companies are hitherto looking towards business intelligence tools to provide them with a competitive edge, by maximising the gain obtained from their information resources and supporting their strategic decision-making process. The high cost of data mining software can be prohibitive for small to medium range organisations. In such cases, the application service providers are a viable and intuitive solution.

Need for immediate benefits. The benefits gained by implementing data mining infrastructure within an organisation tend to be in the long term. One of the reasons for this is the significant learning curve associated with the usage of data mining software. Organisations requiring immediate benefits can use ASP's, which have all the infrastructure and expertise in place.

Specialised Tasks. Organisations may sometimes require a specialised, once-off data mining task to be performed (e.g. mining data that is in a special format or is of a complex type). In such a scenario, an ASP that hosts a data mining system that can perform the required task can provide a simple, cost-efficient solution.

There are two aspects to delivering web-based data mining services. The first approach focuses on the provision of data mining facilities and access to this infrastructure as a web-based service [9][10]. The second concept involves providing data mining *models* as services on the Internet [14]. The currently predominant modus operandi is for organisations that require data mining services to send their data to the service provider (with whom the company typically has a long term service level agreement (SLA)) and access the results through a web interface. However, there are situations where this model is not adequate. Consider the following scenarios and the questions they raise.

Case 1. An organisation requires a specialised data -mining task to be processed, for example, it has acquired a data set that is of a complex data type and needs this to be mined for patterns. The company's data mining service provider does not have the ability to process this task.

1. What are the mechanisms for location of appropriate service providers?
2. How is the most cost-effective and efficient service provider determined? What are the performance metrics that are available?
3. What languages for task description such as DMQL (Data Mining Query Language) [7] and the Microsoft OLE DB standard for data mining [12] does the service provider support?

In the context of ASP hosted services, what are the parameters required to specify a data mining task in addition to the traditional specifications such as the type of output required, the data set, the background knowledge, qualitative and quantitative measures [7]. For instance, in the above case, how is it specified that the requirement is mining spatial data?

Case 2. An organisation is unwilling to ship its sensitive data across to the service provider.

1. Does the service provider have the infrastructure to provide on-site mining? What are the mechanisms that can make this possible?

Case 3. An organisation is particular about having an increased level of control over the data mining process.

1. How would they be able to specify requirements such as the mining algorithm to be used or the need for comparative results from different mining techniques?

It is evident that the concept of providing Internet-based data mining services is still in its early stages and there are several open issues – some of which are generic to ASP's - such as:

Lack of performance metrics for the quality of service.

Lack of well-defined models for costing and billing of data mining services.

Data mining standards such as Microsoft's OLE DB [12] initiative are still emerging and PMML (Predictive Model Markup Language) [6][13] focuses on describing predictive models generated by the data mining process, rather than data mining services.

Need for mechanisms to describe data mining task requests and services.

In this paper, we present two models of organisation for data mining service providers. We use the interaction protocols between clients and the service providers to motivate the need for specification of data mining task requests that adequately represent the requirements and constraints of the clients and also illustrate the importance of description mechanisms for data mining systems and services in order to support Internet delivery of such services. We present XML document type definitions for describing data mining task requests and the functionality and services of data mining service providers. The paper is organized as follows: section 2 presents the models of organisation for data mining service providers and the respective interaction protocols, section 3 presents the information exchange process for the different models of organisation, section 4 presents the document type definitions for the different XML messages that are exchanged between clients and data mining service providers, section 5 compares our work with related research and section 6 summarises and concludes the paper.

2 Models of Operation for Data Mining Service Providers

Prior to discussing the description language for data mining services, this section presents alternative models of structuring for data mining service providers. These models illustrate the context of interaction and communication between "clients" and data mining service providers. There are two models that are discussed. They are:

1. Single service provider hosting several DDM systems.
2. Multiple service providers, where each supports multiple DDM systems.

2.1 Single Service Provider Model

This has simpler operational semantics of the two models and is the currently predominant approach to providing Internet-based data mining services. A client organisation has a single service provider who meets all the data mining needs of the client. The client is well aware of the capabilities of the service provider and there are predefined agreements regarding quality of service, cost and protocols for requesting services. The service provider hosts one or more distributed data mining systems, which support a specified number of mining algorithms. The service provider is aware of the architectural model, specialisations, features and required computational resources for the operation of the distributed data mining system. The interaction protocol for this model is as follows:

1. Client requests a service using a well-defined instruction set from the service provider.
2. The service provider maps the request to the functionality of the different DDM systems that are hosted to determine the most appropriate one.
3. The "suitable" DDM system processes the task and the results are given to the client in a previously arranged format.

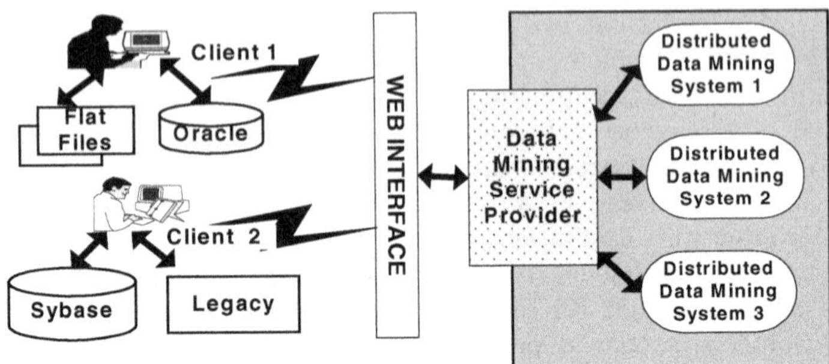

Fig. 1. Single Service Provider Model

The implication of having to map task requests to an appropriate DDM system is that it necessitates a structured means of specifying the functionality of each individual DDM system in terms of the algorithms and data types it supports and its architecture (i.e. whether it performs distributed mining in client-server mode, uses mobile agents or a hybrid approach). Additional information that is required might be performance metrics such as the time taken to perform a given task by a system, the computational resources provided for the system and details such as the format in which a data-mining task is specified and specifying the output produced. The key to automated mapping of requests to appropriate DDM systems is a specification language for describing data mining task requests and the services, architectures and functionality of data mining systems that are hosted by ASP's. While such a language is not paramount for the functioning of this model, it is definitely advantageous. The primary characteristics of the single service provider approach for hosting data mining services are:

It satisfies the basic motivations for providing data mining services and allows organisations to avail the benefits of business intelligence without having to incur the costs associated with buying software, maintenance and training.

The cost for the service, metrics for performance and quality of service are negotiated on a long-term basis as opposed to a task-by-task basis. For example, the number of tasks requested per month by the client and their urgency may form the basis for monthly payments to the service provider.

However, the model has limitations such as the inability to meet the needs of the scenarios outlined in section 1. It implicitly lacks the notions of competition and that of an "open market place" which gives clients the highest benefit in terms of diversity of service at the best price. In summary, this model falls short of allowing the Internet to be an electronic market place of "services" (as it is becoming for goods).

2.2 Multiple Service Providers, Multiple DDM Systems

This model, as illustrated in figure 2, is characterised by clients being able to request data mining services from several service providers who host one or more DDM systems. It represents the culmination in the incremental development of models of operation of data mining service providers. This approach provides the highest level of flexibility for the client and represents the establishment of an open, virtual market place of data mining service providers.

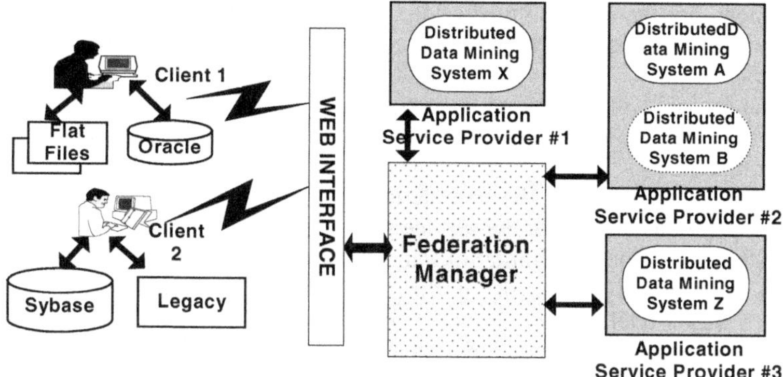

Fig. 2. Multiple Service Provider Model

The multiple service provider model operates in the form of a "federation" [10]. The "federation manager" is a co-ordinating component in the system that manages the interactions between the client and the data mining service providers. The interaction protocol for this model is as follows:

1. The client requests a service by providing a task specification to the federation manager. It must be noted that the parameters for specifying the task must be well defined and must facilitate the requests to be made at the level of granularity that the client deems appropriate.
2. The federation manager broadcasts this to the data mining service providers that are registered with it. The federation manager maintains information about each data mining service provider such as the name, address, contact information, DDM systems hosted, algorithms, architectures and functionality supported by those systems and the computational resources that the service provider has.
3. The data mining service providers evaluate the requested task against the capabilities and functionality of the DDM systems that they host.
4. If they can meet the needs of the requested task, the data mining service providers respond by presenting an estimate of the cost, possible time frame for completion of the task and liabilities for not meeting the targeted response time. This information is presented to the federation manager in a specific, structured format.
5. The federation manager presents the responses it receives along with the information that it already maintains about the respective service providers to the client.
6. The client decides which service provider it deems most appropriate and informs the federation manager and the chosen service provider.
7. The service provider gives the client a legal document/contract, which makes the commitment to maintain the confidentiality of the data that is mined and the consequent knowledge that is produced.
8. The client is then required to provide a security deposit in the form of a credit card number to the federation manager. The actual is payment is made on completion of the task and provision of results to the client.

9. The client and the data mining service provider exchange information regarding the transfer of data, passwords to access systems and the mode of transfer of results.
10. The data mining service provider processes the task, provides the results to the client (in the agreed format and method) and informs the federation manager of task completion.
11. The client acknowledges the completion of the task to the federation manager and the payment is made to the service provider.

This model overcomes the limitations and restrictions imposed by the two previous approaches in meeting the needs of the requirements outlined in section 1. The operation of this model centres around two concepts. Firstly, there is a need for a well-defined and structured mode for exchange of information between the clients and the service providers. The issues that arise in this context are:

What are the parameters that need to be specified at the various stages of the interaction protocol?

What is an appropriate format and medium for the information exchange?

Secondly, there is a need for a co-ordinating entity such as the "federation manager". The principal role of the federation manager is to maintain a registry of data mining service providers and their basic capabilities. It also acts as an intermediary in the interactions between the clients and data mining service providers. The federation manager must provide the infrastructure for the following basic operations:

Allowing data mining service providers to register and de-register themselves with the federation.

Maintaining information that reflects the current capabilities of the data mining service providers that are registered.

Co-ordinate the interactions between the clients and service providers.

As opposed to the previous approaches, the multiple- service-provider model involves a short-term contractual arrangement between client and the service provider. This necessitates the determination of service costs and quality of service levels (such as response time) on a task-by-task basis. This also requires contracts of confidentiality for the data and the knowledge that is produced to be drawn for every service that is required. In summary, this model provides a wider choice of data mining services for clients and caters for selection of the most appropriate and cost-efficient service provider by the implicit competition in the approach. The Internet provides the infrastructure to facilitate an on-line market place for electronic goods; the multiple-service-provider model presented above, is a step towards establishing an on-line market place for data mining services.

3 Information Exchange Process

The previous section illustrated the variation in the interaction protocols and the information exchanges between the clients and the data mining service providers based on the different models of service provider organisation. At a high level of abstraction the information exchanged can be classified into five categories as shown in table 1.

Table 1. Summary of Information Exchanged

Information	Description	Provider
Data Mining Task Request	General description of the task and the preferences of the client	Client
Service Provider Description	General description of the service provider capabilities	Service Provider
Data Mining Task Description	Detailed specification of the mining task (e.g. condition, decision attributes etc.)	Client
Client Access	Specification of how to access the client for either transferring data or to mine the data locally	Client
Service Provider Access	Specification of how to access the results on completion of the task	Service Provider

However, there is a significant difference in the manner in which the information exchange takes place between the models involving a single service-provider and the multiple service provider approach. The principal difference, as illustrated in figure 3, is that information such as access information for the client and description and access information for the service provider needs to be exchanged only once in the single service provider model. This does not hold for the multiple-service-provider model, where the contractual agreement between the service provider and the client is relatively short-term (and typically limited to a single task). This in turn necessitates exchanging information all the information on a per-task basis. Further, in the multiple service provider model, the data mining task description, client access information and service provider access information (indicated in figure 3 as stages (3) and (4)) take place only after the appropriate service provider is selected by the client on the basis of the descriptions provided (as indicated by stage (2)). After selecting the service provider the information exchange occurs directly between the client and the service provider by passing the intermediary.

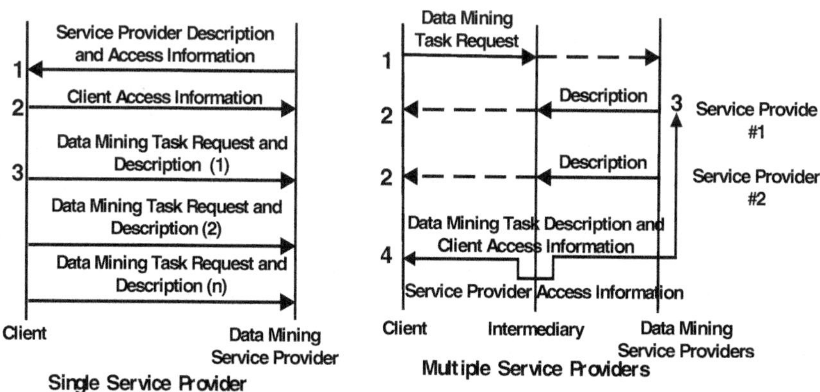

Fig. 3. Comparison of the Information Exchange Process

Based on the above exchanges, we now specify the information content that is passed between clients and data mining service providers at each stage of the interaction. We use XML documents to manage the exchange of information. XML is widely used in metadata standards for data content representation and is suitable for standardised information interchange in many domain specific contexts [5]. Moreover, it is now the defacto approach for exchanging information in e-services environments. The following section presents the structure and content of XML Document Type Definitions (DTD) for the documents/messages that are exchanged.

4 Document Type Definitions

As discussed in section 3, there are five types of documents that are exchanged in the interaction between clients and data mining service providers. They are:

Data mining task request
Service provider description
Data mining task description
Client access information
Service provider access information

In this section, we present the structure and content of the XML DTD's for the above documents. It must be noted that due to constraints of space, we present a description of the information that is contained in the documents, rather than the DTD's in XML notation. For a complete specification readers are referred to [11].

4.1 Data Mining Task Request

A data mining task request is initiated by the client and is a general description of the type of service required and the client's preferences and constraints for the task. It does not contain a detailed specification of the data mining task. This separation of the client's task request and the actual task specification is to facilitate the short-term interaction model where the client might not wish to broadcast sensitive/confidential information about their data. The specification of the task description has been developed to accommodate clients who might wish to include detailed requirements such as format of the results and the type of algorithms to be used and those who might not have such fine grained knowledge about the data mining process and might wish to describe their requirements at a higher, more general level of abstraction. The information contained in this DTD is as follows:

Task Descriptor. The task descriptor indicates the basic type of data mining task that is required such as market basket analysis, customer profiling, fraud detection.

Algorithm Preference. This indicates the preference or requirement for a specified data mining algorithm to be used. This is optional and can be left unspecified when the client has no preference.

Output Format. This specifies the preferred or required output format for the results (e.g. association rules, classification rules, visual/graphical output).

Comparative Results. This allows the client to specify that they require the dataset to be mined using two or more mining techniques and a comparative analysis of results to be presented.

Data Type. This indicates the type of data that has to be mined (e.g. text, ascii, temporal, relational etc.).

Data Format. Additionally, if the data is in a standardised format it can be specified.

Dataset Size. This information is provided so as to allow the service provider to form an accurate estimate of the response time.

Location. This indicates the preferred or required location for the mine to occur. Thus, the client can specify this option as either "local" (to indicate that the data cannot be shipped and must be mined on site), "remote" (to indicate that the data can be mined remotely) and "anywhere" (to indicate no preference). In case "local" or "anywhere" is specified, the computational resources that are available for the data mining process must also be declared. This allows service providers to estimate the response time for the task (in the context of the local resources).

Response Time. This indicates the required response time for completion of tasks and can be specified as a range.

Cost. This can be used to optionally indicate the cost that the client is willing to bear for the service.

4.2 Service Provider Descriptor

The service provider descriptor contains information about the service provider and the data mining systems hosted by the service provider. In [10] we presented Distributed Data Mining Systems – Markup Language [DDMS-ML], an XML DTD that allows data mining systems to specify their architectures and functionality. The service provider descriptor principally contains a modified version of DDMS-ML documents to represent and describe each data mining system that is hosted. The information contained in this document is as follows:

Service Provider Details. This includes information such as the name of the service provider, address, business registration details and contact details (phone, fax, email and web address).

Computational Resources. This component includes information about the computational resources that the service provider supports. A service provider can have several servers. A server is either a stand-alone system or a parallel server or a cluster. A server may or may not be dedicated for distributed data mining (depending on whether the service provider hosts a variety of applications). A server's physical configuration such as the operating system, the CPU, the memory and the number of nodes (if the server is a cluster) is recorded. This information allows the client to understand the infrastructure of the service provider.

Task Specific Details. This includes details that are specific to a particular task. Depending on the nature and longevity of the relationship between the clients and the service provider, this information may or may not be exchanged. Further, in the multiple service provider this information is provided after the task request has been made. The information specified in this component are details such as the estimated response time for the task, the cost of the task (depending on where it is deployed and what architectural model is requested by the client) and the liabilities in terms of constraints and the respective cost-reductions (e.g. the inability to meet the estimated response time, the cost of the task reduces by x dollars per hour of delay).

Data Mining Systems. This includes details about the different data mining systems that are hosted by the service provider. A data mining system is described in terms of its functionality and architecture as follows:

Meta Information. This part of the document contains information about the DM system such as its name, version, date of development, organisation and developer. We impose the constraint that within each service provider descriptor DM system must have a unique name.

Architectural Model. This component states whether the DM system uses the client-server approach, the mobile agent paradigm or a hybrid model (integration of both client server and mobile agents) for distributed data mining. This information is important in situations where a client requires a particular architectural model. For instance, a situation where the data to be mined is sensitive and the client does not want the data to be transported to the service provider will warrant that a DM system that uses mobile agents be used. It is also possible then that the mobile agent performs its task and is destroyed and not allowed to leave the site to provide further protection to the client. Further, if the system supports the mobile agent model and/or a hybrid approach, the agent environment/toolkit required needs to be specified, to enable the client to have the requisite agent server in place for the data to be mined at their site.

Data Types. This part of the document states the data types that can be mined using a given DM system. The following options have been specified: text, relational, spatial, temporal, image, video, multimedia, object-oriented and hypertext. However to cater for flexibility and extensibility, the DTD allows specifying other data formats apart from the ones listed above.

Specialisations and Features. This section of the document allows DM systems to describe their distinguishing functions and special services. Similar to the data types, the DTD has some pre-specified options such as support for parallel algorithms, optimisation, cost-efficiency, pre-processing, mobile users and visualisation. However, it also allows a DM system to present any other special features that it may possess. This component also includes information about support for "knowledge integration" which is the process of integrating results obtained from distributed data sets.

Algorithms. This component specifies the mining algorithms that are supported by the DM system. The specification includes details such as the algorithm's name and optionally the version. This is followed by details regarding the structure of the input file for the algorithm and the type of output model produced. The current version only allows the specification of a text input file. Specifying the structure of complex data files is a non-trivial task and is not part of our current focus. For such input data, the DTD only allows specifying the data type and the respective file extension required. This component of the document allows the presentation of details about algorithm usage to clients who might wish to use a particular system.

4.3 Client Access Information

This document contains information that the client provides to the service provider so that the data can be accessed or transferred (depending on whether the client wishes the mine to be performed on-site or at the location of the service provider). This information is released after the contractual agreement of maintaining the confidentiality of the data is finalised. The information contained in this document is as follows:

Data Transfer Mode. This indicates how the data is transferred for it to be mined in a remote location. The options include:

Client transfers data to a specified location of the service provider.

Service provider transfers data from specified locations of the client. In this case, access to the data must be specified in terms of hosts, ports, user names, passwords and directories where the data is located.

Local Data Access . This indicates the access mode when the mine has to be performed locally at the client's site. This is typically achieved by the service provider dispatching mobile agents to the client's site. In this case, the client needs to specify the location where the mobile agent server is running (in terms of the host and port) and where the data is located. In some instances the client might require the agent toolkit/environment to be provided by the service provider to enable local deployment. This requirement should also be specified in this document/message.

4.4 Data Mining Task Descriptor

There are on-going initiatives and standardisation efforts to specify the parameters that needed for a data mining process such as Microsoft's OLE DB for data mining [12] and data mining query languages such as DMQL [7]. We do not wish to propose a parallel scheme for describing/ specifying a data mining task. Typical parameters that need to be specified include attributes to be considered in the mining process, the condition and decision attributes, data types and distribution of the values of the attributes. Given such a specification, the service provider should feed this in to the mining algorithms/systems that are hosted to process the task.

4.5 Service Provider Access Information

This document specifies how the client can access the service provider to deposit the data if they choose to and how to access task status information and the results. The information contained in this document is as follows:

Access. This specifies the host, port, user name, password and directory for the client to submit the data to be mined.

Security. This specifies the encryption to be performed on the data prior to transfer.

Task Status. This specifies the URL of the site from where clients can obtain status reports of their tasks. It also specifies the user name and password to access this site.

Results. This specifies the URL of the site from which the results can be downloaded/viewed along with the user name and password to access this site.

In this section, we have presented the content of the XML DTD's to support the interactions between clients and Internet-based data mining service providers through a structured exchange of information. The interactions are driven by the need to first identify service provider(s) that can best meet the preferences and requirements of the clients and then support the Internet-based processing of the data mining task by exchanging information at a finer level of granularity.

In [11] we have presented a matching scheme algorithm based on XPath expressions to establish the correspondence between the DTD's, which allows the explicit mapping of the preferences and needs of clients to the functionality provided by different service providers. This is important as it proves that the design/structure of the DTD's is consistent with their stated objectives of facilitating the identification of appropriate service providers. It is often possible that a single service provider will not be able to meet all the requirements specified by the client and that there will be several service providers who may be able to satisfy different combination of preferences. Therefore the issues of ranking service providers and automated negotiation of e-services are important research questions in the multiple service provider model. We are currently investigating ranking measures for service providers.

5 Related Work

We now present a brief overview of related research. To the best of our knowledge there is no other work that focuses on describing the interactions and exchange of information to support the Internet delivery of data mining services in a multiple service provider domain. However, there are two data mining/business intelligence related XML initiatives – namely Predictive Model Markup Language (PMML) [6] and OLE DB for Data Mining [12]. PMML is an XML-based approach for describing the predictive models that are generated as the output of data mining processes. PMML is primarily used for knowledge integration of results obtained by mining distributed data sets. Microsoft's OLE DB for data mining is a description of a data mining task in terms of the data sets that are being mined and allows specification of the attributes to be mined, the attributes to be predicted and the type and format of the attributes. It incorporates a version of PMML and is primarily intended to allow "plug and play" of data mining algorithms. As discussed in the previous section, this specification (as it evolves into a standard) can easily be used in conjunction with our work, which focuses on specifying user preferences for data mining tasks that are processed by application service providers.

We now discuss our work in the context of the following developing standards and systems that support services on the Internet:

E-Speak is an e-services infrastructure developed by Hewlett Packard [4]. It provides the underlying technology to support registration of services by service providers and location of services by clients. A service provider registers a service by providing a description using a "vocabulary". The service provider descriptor presented in this paper is a possible vocabulary for data mining service providers using e-speak. However, whether e-speak allows for the type of interaction required by data mining tasks (given the implicitly confidential nature of the process) needs to be examined.

Web Services Description Language (WSDL) is an XML format developed by Microsoft to support the communication and network details to support exchanging messages over the web [16]. Elements in a WSDL document include information such as the port, the port type, the network bindings and the actual message that is being exchanged. It facilitates web services at the lower level of data communication and is not intended for describing the semantics of services.

Universal Description, Discovery and Integration (UDDI), is a standard developed and supported by Ariba, IBM and Microsoft [15]. UDDI is a universal registry that allows global registration and description of web services to facilitate the location of services by clients and the interaction to enable usage of the service. In the context of our work, UDDI provides the supporting infrastructure / functionality of the federation manager. However, the actual description of the services is the responsibility of the service providers. Therefore, the XML DTD's presented in this paper provide the basis for data mining service providers using UDDI to describe themselves.

E-Business-XML (eb-XML) is an initiative supported by United Nations and OASIS [3]. The stated objective of eb-XML is to support open and interoperable e-business. The eb-XML architecture provides mechanisms to define business processes and their associated messages and the registration and discovery of business process sequences with the related message exchanges. Therefore, eb-XML can be used to implement the multiple service provider model for hosting data mining services. The information exchange process that we have developed for data mining services and the XML messages that we have specified can be easily incorporated for use in an eb-XML environment.

In summary, it can be seen that there are several emerging standards and infrastructures to support Internet delivered services. The distinct contribution of our research is to identify the processes required to support the delivery of data mining services and specify the information content that needs to be exchanged between organisation requiring data mining services and data mining service providers.

6 Conclusions

The emergence of Internet-based data mining service providers is proving to be a viable means for satisfying the business intelligence needs of knowledge-centric organisations. We see this as an enabling technology for fostering organisational learning from data – especially for companies that were constrained by the high cost of data mining software. We have presented the structure and contents of XML documents/messages to support knowledge elicitation from web-based data mining services. These documents have been specified to cater for the incorporation of organisational constraints and requirements that arise when data mining services are outsourced using the Internet. The current model of operation for web-based data mining service providers is the "single service-provider" approach. However, it can be seen that the multiple service provider model has relative advantages in providing a wider choice of services and the option of getting the most appropriate service for the most acceptable price. The potential benefits of this model along with the emergence of platforms and standards to support e-services are significant factors that impact positively on the realization of this model. The contribution of this paper is the development of interaction protocols and specification of the information exchanged between organisations that outsource their data mining processes to application service providers. This is one step towards the creation of a virtual market place for data mining services.

References

1. Clark-Dickson,P., (1999), "Flag-fall for Application Rental", Systems, (August), pp.23-31.
2. digiMine – URL: http://www.digiMine.com
3. e-Business XML (eb-XML). URL: http://www.ebxml.org
4. e-Speak. URL: http://www.e-speak.hp.com
5. Goldfarb,C,F., and Prescod,P., (1998), "The XML Handbook", Prentice-Hall PTR, New Jersey, USA.
6. Grossman,R,L., Bailey,S., Ramu,A., Malhi,B., Hallstrom,P., Pulleyn,I., and Oin,X., (1999), "The Management and Mining of Multiple Predictive Models Using the Predictive Modeling Markup Language (PMML)", Information and Software Technology, Volume 41, pp. 589-595.
7. Han,J., Fu,Y., Wang,W., Koperski,K., and Zaiane,O., (1996), "DMQL: A Data Mining Query Language for Relational Databases", Workshop on Research Issues on Data Mining and Knowledge Discovery (DMKD'96), Montreal, Canada, June.
8. Huber,G,P., (1991). "Organisational Learning: The Contributing Processes and Literatures", Organisation Science, Vol. 2, No. 1, February, pp. 88-115.
9. Krishnaswamy,S., Zaslavsky,A., and Loke,S,W., (2000), "An Architecture to Support Distributed Data Mining Services in E-Commerce Environments", Proceedings of the Second International Workshop on Advanced Issues in E-Commerce and Web-Based Information Systems, San Jose, Californinia, June 8-9, pp.238-246.
10. Krishnaswamy,S., Zaslavsky,A., and Loke,S,W., (2001), "Federated Data Mining Services and a Supporting XML Markup Language", Proceedings of the 34th Annual Hawaii International Conference on System Sciences (HICSS-34), Hawaii, USA, January, In the "e-Services: Models and Methods for Design, Implementation and Delivery" mini-track of the "Decision Technologies for Management" track.
11. Krishnaswamy,S., Zaslavsky,A., and Loke,S,W., (2001), "Towards Data Mining Services on the Internet with a Multiple Service Provider Model – An XML Approach", Submitted to the Journal of Electronic Commerce Research – Special Issue on E-Services and Operations.
12. Microsoft OLE DB for Data Mining, URL: http://www.microsoft.com/data/oledb/dm.htm, March, 2000.
13. Ramu,A,T., (1998), "Incorporating Transportable Software Agents into a Wide Area High Performance Distributed Data Mining Systems", Masters Thesis, University of Illinois, Chicago, USA.
14. Sarawagi,S., and Nagaralu,S,H., (2000), "Data Mining Models as Services on the Internet", SIGKDD Explorations, Vol. 2, Issue. 1, http://www.acm.org/sigkdd/explorations/ , accessed 01 April, 2001.
15. Universal Description, Discovery and Integration (UDDI). URL:http://www.uddi.org
16. Web Services Description Language. http://msdn.microsoft.com/xml/general/wsdl.asp

A Model for Analyzing Measurement Based Feedback Loops in Software Development Projects

Claus Lewerentz, Heinrich Rust, and Frank Simon

Software and Systems Engineering Research Group
BTU Cottbus P.O. Box 10 13 44, D-03013 Cottbus, Germany
Tel. +49 (355) 69 3881, Fax 3810
{lewerentz,rust,simon}@informatik.tu-cottbus.de

Abstract. Measurements can be used as feedback instrument for improving software development. Much previous work considers technical preconditions; additionally we examine some psychological and social conditions that have to be analyzed and understood. Since these conditions depend a lot on the specific organizational environment of software development, we applied Argyris' and Schön's concept of 'organizational learning'. We get a two-level feedback system for learning in software developing organizations by metrics based analysis. We identified three dimensions which can guide the analysis of measurement activities and which help to detect a strategy to increase the learning capabilities. As examples we analyzed the personal software process, experiences of applying a metrics tool, and extreme programming with respect to these dimensions.

1 Introduction

How can software measurements be used to help software developing organizations to learn, or more exactly, optimize their work processes?.

Feedback mechanisms in software development projects are being considered as underrepresented in today's software development technique collections (c.f. [7]). The use of measurements is one technique to organize feedback and learning in software development. Properties of both the work process and of the resulting products are measured. The results of these measurements might provide important insight about what is going on in a project. But it is not trivial to decide how measurements are used in a project. Who performs which measurements, and when? Who gets access to the measurement results? Whose interpretation of the results is relevant? And who is allowed to draw consequences?

We use three areas of experiences to demonstrate the necessity of embedding measuring activities into a larger context: (1) Humphrey's Personal Software Process (PSP) uses measurements as an important vehicle for learning; (2) members of our research group applied a locally developed metrics tool to the products of software development projects; and (3) the Extreme Programming (XP) approach to software project organization embeds measurements into the organizational structure. We shortly describe these three areas of experience.

K.-D. Althoff, R.L. Feldmann, and W. Müller (Eds.): LSO 2001, LNCS 2176, pp. 135-149, 2001.

1.1 Area 1: PSP Experiences

One of these areas are experiences with Watts Humphrey's Personal Software Process (PSP, cf. [5]) in a course situation. Humphrey describes a way of organizing individually one's work process as a software developer. The way to work is specified in great detail, different properties of the working process and the products are measured, and from time to time, these data are evaluated to change the definition of the process followed in the work. In the course proposed by Humphrey in his book, all this is done by each course participant in isolation, and elaborated metrics-based statistical methods are used in the process for evaluating the measurement results. In the course situation, this approach works nicely for the students, most of them see progress in the efficiency of their work and the quality of their work products, and they become accustomed to reflection on their working process. But if asked if they expect that they will use the PSP techniques in practice, the course participants give two reasons why they expect this to be improbable: The first is that they feel that the overhead for measurement and reflection in the PSP approach is larger than necessary. The second is that, based on the results of measurements, they are frustrated by being forced to correct their often too positive self-image.

The third problem with the PSP is that it does not deal systematically with the organizational context in which the individual software developer works. Because of this, neither the problems nor the opportunities of practical use of the PSP in an organizational real-world situation are systematically reflected in the PSP. One specific problem arising from this is that measurement data are very sensitive because they are easily misused for other goals than what the PSP uses them for, and this is not systematically dealt with in the PSP.

1.2 Area 2: Software Product Measurement Experiences

The other area of experience was a pattern of reactions from members of real software development projects while using a metrics approach for product quality assessments [8].

In cooperation with several companies developing large object oriented software systems, the approach was tried out. For this, quality models on top of product metrics were used which were partly constructed ad-hoc, partly derived from descriptions in literature. After measuring the software systems, a report was produced. The report included the measurement results with an identification of those classes of the software system which the chosen measures identified as somehow strange, e.g., very strongly coupled with other classes.

Such reports were presented to and discussed with developers and their managers. We repeatedly experienced that managers were generally highly interested in the results; developers were partly skeptical, partly interested. Not infrequently, they became quite defensive about their software. This reaction is not implausible, because of the following reasons:

- The quality models used in the assessments had not been validated independently; thus, it was easy for the developers to discount the relevance of our findings for the "true" quality of their software.
- Developers saw their work subjected to checks with quality criteria they had no chance to influence or discuss, and worse, which they did not even know about beforehand; thus, it was quite understandable that they felt being treated unfair, especially since features of their work results were made accessible to colleagues and management which they had never expected to be made explicit.
- Managers saw an opportunity for reliable and cheap control of important quality aspects of developers' work.

In spite of the problems, fruitful discussions arose about different measured quantities. Components which were known to be especially problematic to the developers were also identified by the tool, but the tool identified some components as critical which the developers saw as not needing changes, because the strange measured values were somehow justified.

These sessions led to a concept of using measures in the software development process in which neither the set of measures used nor their interpretation is accepted as fixed. The main idea is that the results of the application of a measurement tool are used to focus a peer review[6].

1.3 Area 3: Extreme Programming and Pair Programming

"Extreme Programming" (XP) [3] is an approach to organize software development projects with a low organizational overhead, which stresses communication and rapid feedback between developers and customers and between the developers themselves. In contrast to the PSP, the social situation of software development is used explicitly. For example, developers work in pairs. This "pair programming" seems to help them to adhere to the design standards and coding standards they agreed upon earlier, and it seems to imply a low-overhead and automatic review process. Additionally, it is more fun than software development in isolation, and if the pairs recombine from time to time, it helps to share experiences, i.e. it helps the developers to learn.

Another aspect of XP is the combined development of code and tests and the frequent execution of the tests. This gives rapid feedback about the effect of a change to some code. Additionally, system tests are supplied by the customers (at least their design is), which means that the customer can control the quality of the result by designing sufficiently specific test cases.

For project tracking, a simple reporting scheme based on four measurable variables is used: resources, time, quality and scope.

First experiences with the XP approach of organizing software development work are promising. In the measurement context dealt with here, the approach is relevant because each execution of the regression tests, i.e. of both the unit tests or the system test, is a measurement of the quality of the current configuration, and much stress is laid on making such measurements easy to perform, their results accessible to the developers, and meaningful to interpret.

1.4 Organizational Structures for Learning

The experiences sketched above led us to investigate more deeply the conditions for appropriately applying software measurements in software development processes. Is there some theory which can explain the reactions of the students learning to use the PSP, of the managers and developers of the projects whose source code we measured, and of the sometimes enthusiastic users of XP? Or more generally: What conditions must be fulfilled in order that measurements can be applied productively in a software development project?

We came to the conclusion that an answer to these questions would have to deal with two phenomena: (1) each software development project takes place in a specific organizational setting, and (2) measurements are a vehicle for learning in this organization. Because of this, we looked for theories of learning in organizations, in order to specialize them for software developing organizations.

One theory which has been proposed to conceptualize organizational learning and to define conditions for this is the one of Argyris and Schön, an outline of which is presented in section 2. We propose to use this theory in order to conceptualize the software development project as a learning organization. This supplies a framework into which measurements are integrated as a way to make experiences explicit.

Argyris' and Schön's theory rests on a metaphor from cybernetics: Learning in the sense understood here only takes place if some kind of feedback takes place. The work results of a software development project are abstracted from by the measuring operation, this abstraction is fed back to the project members somehow, and this should have an impact on the working process in order to fulfill some given goals. In this framework, the following questions are important: Which are the relevant variables in the cybernetic system, how do these variables influence each other, and how can the feedback paths be designed in order to ensure appropriate adaptation of the software developing organization to changing environment conditions?

These variables influence directly and indirectly the individual action strategies. These lead directly to a specific software development process and its results, in the form of products. Some of the properties of these processes and products are measured, and the measurement results are fed back to the project team. The important questions are then: How often does this feedback occur? Who controls when and what is measured? Who will interpret the results? Which consequences are taken?

2 Organizational Learning

A software developing organization can be seen as a *learning organization* in the sense of Argyris and Schön (cf. 2, 5]). We think that the stress that this conceptualization puts on the necessity for continuous learning is adequate in the software industry.

Argyris' and Schön's concept of 'organizational learning' can be characterized in the following way.

Organizational learning is a kind of *practical*, in contrast to purely theoretical, learning. It deals with effective *action*, i.e. with being able to act so as to reach an expected outcome of an action, it does not deal primarily with accumulation of theoretical knowledge.

Organizational learning starts when some surprising *mismatch* is experienced between an expected and the actual outcome of an action. Thus, learning presupposes that expectations are formed, that actions are performed, and that a feedback loop exists.

The learning process includes both *thinking* and further (experimental) *action*, with the goal of harmonizing actual outcomes and expectations. It is no coincidence that these two types of activities, theory and practice, are also important in scientific approaches to learning, stressing the building of theories and their testing by experiments. Argyris and Schön transfer this technique of scientific inquiry into organizations in general, to help them structure their learning process.

Organizations learn by *individuals* learning as their *representatives*. Two aspects have to be stressed: (a) The acting of a member of an organization in the context of this organization is influenced by (partly implicit, partly explicitly formulated) organizational norms which are common to the members of the organization. Thus, these norms can be seen as a kind of organizational memory which regulates the actions of the organization's members. (b) Changes of organizational norms can happen intentionally or non-intentionally, and they take effect by individuals changing their conceptions of the organizational norms. If several organization members change their conception about these norms in accordance with each other, it is more probable that the change becomes relevant for the organization as a whole.

For the learning to become organizational, the individual learning must be transported into *organizational patterns*. To these belong the images which the individuals have of their organization as well as (implicit) common action strategies by members of the organization, but also explicitly described rules and procedures.

2.1 Main Dimensions in Argyris' and Schön's Model

Three dimensions are given which are especially important in the approach of Argyris and Schön. One is the dimension "governing value vs. action strategy", one is "individual vs. organizational level", and the last is "used in practice vs. espoused".

2.1.1 Governing Values vs. Action Strategies

Argyris and Schön distinguish between single-loop learning and double-loop learning. The difference between the two has to do with action strategies and their governing values. Governing values directly influence action strategies, but there is no direct influence the other way round. Single-loop learning deals with optimizing the action strategies with respect to fixed governing values, whereas double-loop learning also changes governing values. As long as the governing values match the requirements of the environment, only single-loop learning is necessary. In quickly changing environments, however, governing values have to be adapted, and this means that double-loop learning is necessary.

See Fig. 1 for a model of an organization allowing both single-loop and double-loop learning. The lower rectangle represents single-loop feedback. Action strategies influence both development and the product and process analysis. Development leads to product and process data. Product and process data are feed into analysis, and this analysis changes the action strategies. The second feedback loop is concerned with the governing values which influence the action strategies chosen. These can be changed by a reflection process which takes the whole lower-level feedback loop into consideration.

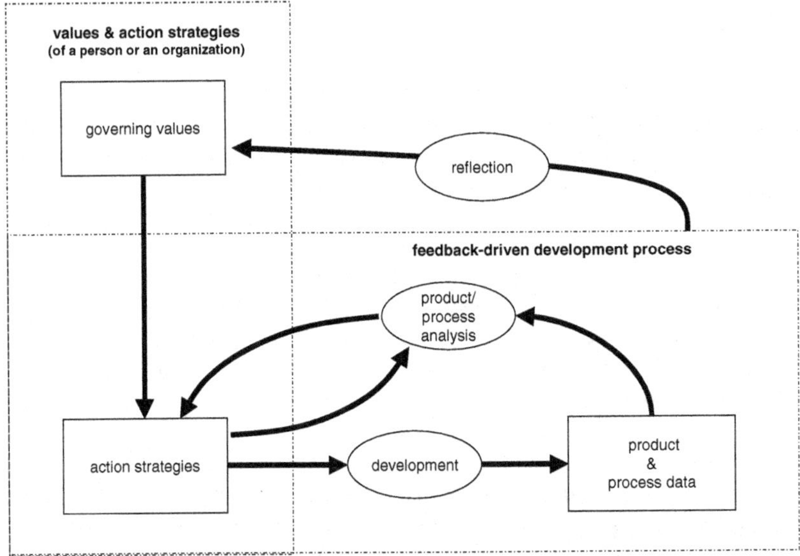

Fig. 1. A two-level feedback system

2.1.2 Espoused Theory of Effective Action and Theory-in-Use

Argyris and Schön describe two kinds of theories of effective action. The actions with which they deal take place in organizations, and they contain a considerable social component. Both kinds of theories are concerned with appropriate governing values which should be assumed to reach some goals, and with the action strategies which are to be used to pursue the goals. The two kinds of theories differ with respect to their practical relevance. One kind is called *'espoused theory'*. This is the theory which some persons say that they believe in when they are asked which are the right goals to pursue, and which are the right strategies to use to pursue these goals. The other kind of theory is called *'theory-in-use'*. This is the theory individuals really seem to follow in their actions. It can be considerably different from the espoused theory thus yielding some tensions between them.

2.1.3 Individual and Organizational Level

The last important dimension in Argyris' and Schön's model we deal with here is the tension between the individual and the organizational level. All governing values, action strategies, espoused theories and theories-in-use exist both on the organizational and on the individual level. For example, effectively used action strategies of a single person can be stabilized by officially espoused organizational action strategies, or they might be destabilized by generally accepted governing values which are in conflict with the individual action strategies.

We have to distinguish two influence mechanisms between the individual and the organizational level: The organization can, by espousing a set of values, try to induce the individuals to use matching values and action strategies; and, by implicit acceptance, the values which most individuals seem to follow in their work will be accepted at least as an unofficial but nevertheless organizational standard, even if these values contradict the espoused values. The organizational features are the common component of many individual features, at least as far as effective (in contrast to only espoused) features are concerned.

3 Learning in Software Development Organizations

3.1 The Relevance of Argyris' and Schön's Framework for Software Development

Argyris' and Schön's framework for organizational learning is highly relevant for software developing organizations because of several of its properties.

Reflection on working conditions. Reflection on one's practice is an important ingredient of Argyris' and Schön's framework. Learning does not only mean to reach one's goals more effectively, but also to get to know oneself better. One's practice and one's conception of one's practice are contrasted, and discrepancies are reflected upon. This reflective character is appropriate also in software development. It opens up opportunities to reflect one's working conditions and on ways of improving them.

Focus on practice. We do not only want to understand what happens in software development projects, we also want to help development teams solve their problems, i.e. we want a practice oriented approach. The approach of Argyris and Schön is practice oriented. In contrast to theories of learning which have a primarily theoretical focus and only want to explain, organizational learning has both a theoretical and a practical component, and also proposes a strategy for intervention. Discrepancies between one's theoretical conceptions about adequate behavior and one's factual behavior are pointed out, and the learners strive for a better correspondence between their (espoused) theory and their practice.

The emphasis of the interaction between individual and organizational learning. Software development occurs in teams, in organizations, and the organization context in which software development work takes place is an important influence on the capabilities of teams. In Argyris' and Schön's model, the individual and the organizations levels both have their relevance. Approaches which only stress the individual side of learning can not account for organizational traits which enhance or diminish the capabilities of individual learning, or for the results that individual learning can have for an organizational learning system. Approaches which only stress the organizational side can not point out in which way individuals can start learning in an organization, and how they can change the learning system of the organization. Since interventions have to start at the individual level, a practical approach to learning must conceptualize the role of the individual.

Double-loop learning necessary in a turbulent environment. The approach emphasizes double-loop learning as a necessary capability of organizations in quickly changing environments. Since the environment of software developing organizations often is turbulently changing, this focus on not only optimizing the action strategies for fixed individual and organizational goals, but on checking the adequateness also of the goals from time to time and systematically changing them, is relevant.

The function of surprise. Argyris and Schön stress the function of surprise, resulting from a discrepancy between expectation and factual result of an action, as the main mover in organizational learning. In software development, expectations are often rather imprecise. Often, it is expected by the developers that a project will not finish in the time planned for it by a manager, and this expectation is too imprecise to allow for a surprise. Surprises need detailed expectations, or in this case: realistic plans.

A strategy for organizational learning. The strategy proposed by Argyris and Schön for changing the behavioral repertory of the members of an organization can also be relevant for the members of software development teams. Like in any organization, also in software development organizations there are norms about the proper behavior. This includes not only explicitly fixed procedures, e.g. the software processes to be followed in projects in an organization, but also informal rules which regulate when it is appropriate to talk about some problems with whom. These rules and procedures form an organizational learning system.

3.2 A Specialization of Argyris' and Schön's Theory of Organizational Learning to Software Development

This section presents a specialization of the theory of organizational learning by Argyris and Schön which is usable for analysis of measurement use in software developing organizations. We illustrate this specialization with Fig. 2. The following features are important:

- The lower rectangle encompasses a single feedback loop: Action strategies for software development lead to a specific way of doing software development. The software development activities lead to products and process protocols, which are used in analysis activities, in our case metrics based. These analysis activities, like the software development, are driven by action strategies, but their goal is to generate feedback which might change the action strategies, thus there is also an influence back to the action strategies.
- The large scale structure of the model is a double feedback loop. From time to time, reflection should take place to check if the governing values are acceptable. This reflection takes the whole lower feedback loop into account, and the effect might be changes in the governing values, which influence the action strategies.

Governing values, action strategies, the products and process data and even the whole first-level feedback loop are not monolithic. One dimension for their differentiation is the difference between espoused and effective governing values rsp. action strategies. Analysis activities and the reflection process must consider the danger to consider only espoused action strategies and only change espoused values. Instead they should strive to get data about effective values and strategies.

The other dimension for the internal differentiation of governing values, action strategies, and products and process data is the difference between an individual and an organizational level. Particular individuals and particular (sub)organizations might have different features in these respects. We already dealt with the interaction between individual and organizational values and strategies. It is important to be sensitive for these differences in order to install effective feedback processes on both levels.

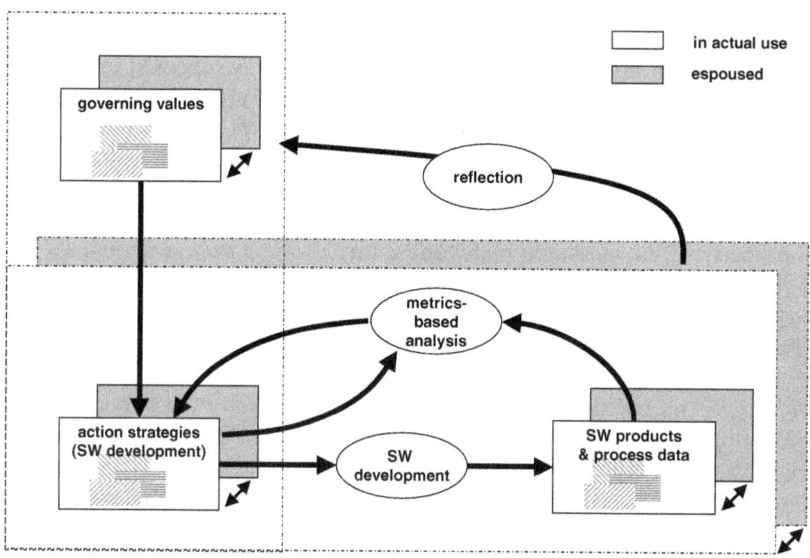

Fig. 2. The two-level feedback system for learning software development organizations

In the primary feedback loop, software metrics play an important role in our adaptation of Argyris' and Schön's framework. Specific uses of metrics in organizational learning are discussed in the next section.

4 Software Measures and Organizational Learning

4.1 Software Measures

A Definition of 'Measurement'. Measurement activities in software development are becoming increasingly popular. What does 'measurement' mean? Fenton's and

Pfleeger's definition is ([4] p. 5): **Measurement** *is the process by which numbers or symbols are assigned to attributes of entities in the real world in such a way as to describe them according to clearly defined rules.* This definition does not deal with the reasons for doing the descriptions. It stresses that a measurement is an abstraction, and it does this in three ways:

by dealing just with *some* attributes of a real-world entity, and

by defining the goal of the measurements the *description* of something, and

by contrasting *concrete* attributes of real-world entities with *abstract* entities like symbols or numbers.

Additionally, the abstraction is to be done *according to clearly defined rules*. This often is a social criterion, since a set of rules is clearly defined if their interpretations by the relevant people are equal, but there might also be a mathematical exactness principle involved.

Operationalizations. In the social sciences, the relation between an intuitive (and often abstract) concept and a concrete procedure which is supposed to measure some real-world entities with respect to this concept has a special name: The concrete procedure is an *operationalization* of the intuitive concept. A well-known (if problematical) example is the measurement of human intelligence with an IQ test.

The relation between operationalizations and measurements is the following: A measurement together with an associated claim that the result expresses some high-level property of the measured real-world entity is an *operationalization* of the high-level property.

Three requirements are often given for operationalizations: They are objectivity, reliability and validity. We consider the three requirements separately.

Objectivity means that the identity of the investigator does not influence the measuring results. The phrase *according to clearly defined rules* in the definition above can be interpreted as implying objectivity.

Repeatability means that if the same persons perform the same measurement on the same real-life entities at different times, they will get the same results. Of course, it is difficult to check reliability of an operationalization if the measured values are meant to be time dependent, but in general, the phrase in the definition above which has been interpreted as ensuring objectivity also can be interpreted as ensuring reliability.

Validity means that the measurement results are meaningful for the goals one wants to use them for.

Process Measurements and Product Measurements. Measurements can be classified in different respects (cf. [5, p. 208] or [4, p. 74]). In this paper, the difference between process measurements and product measurements is relevant. *Process measures* are concerned directly with properties of the work process. Typical examples for process measures are the times it takes to complete some task or work phase, or event counts like the number of program faults encountered during some time. *Product measures* are concerned with properties of the entities which are produced in the course of a work process. Typical examples are 'average answering time' or 'lines of code'.

Product Measures for a Process Focus. In this paper, we focus on situations in which process properties are in the focus; thus, we deal with questions like "How long does it take to complete this task?" or "How many defects are detected by this technique in which time?" or "How long does it take to change this software?" This focus suggests the use of process measurements. But there are two problems with this.

The first problem with process measurements is that it takes some effort to collect these data from the side of the developers, while product measures can be performed by a quality assurance group on their own. Most convenient are product measures which are valid for process properties, since their use requires the least knowledge about the context. Process measures are more attractive if they can be based on data which is reliably collected automatically. Some kinds of process data can be collected automatically if appropriate tools are used (e.g. configuration management systems, cost accounting system, problem reporting and tracking system). Unfortunately, in many cases such process data are not easily accessible, and thus, it becomes interesting to find some product measures which allow implications for properties of the process.

4.2 The Role of Software Measures in Organizational Learning

Software measures can play several specific roles in our framework of organizational learning in software developing organizations (cf. Fig. 2).

Features of espoused action strategies can be formulated and compared to those effectively in use. According to Argyris and Schön, a precondition for learning is a surprising mismatch between expectations and factual outcome of some action. Thus, to learn in some area in this sense, one has to develop an expectation. Expected values of software measures are a possibility to describe these expectations exactly. For process measures, these expectations typically are formed before the process has been run through, i.e. they take the form of *projections*.

During the run of the process, data are collected which are summarized at the end of the process. A baseline can be established with which expectations and later developments can be compared.

Preparations for activity specific effort measurements make features of the working style explicit. Process measurements in which the efforts spent for different types of activities are a common example in the software process movement. One necessary preparation for this type of measurement is the classification of one's activities. Already this classification and orderly writing down which amount of time is spent on which type of activity opens up opportunities to reflect on one's working style. Users of Humphrey's PSP can experience this. For software engineers who are accustomed to having clearly cut categories for the application field with which they have to deal, it can be an enlightening experience to try designing clearly cut categories for their own activities. They might find out that, in spite of the fact that some activities can not be categorized as clearly as could be wished, nevertheless they are able to learn from the time protocols.

Goals can be set, and feedback can be given if one is approaching them or not. There is a difference between setting a goal and formulating an expectation. An expectation should be realistic, which can be ensured by basing it on prior experience. A goal may be unrealistic, given the current state of the practice, but if learning opportunities are provided, it means to strive for a change of the practice, i.e. for a learning, such as to make the goal realistic.

The setting of concrete quantitative goals can give the learning process a good focus. It is a common technique investigated in work psychology, but it normally works only if the actors get feedback about their performance with respect to the goal.

Organizational norms can be fixed. Argyris and Schön differentiate between the organizational and the individual level, where norms established at the organizational level influence those at the individual level and are influenced by them. The establishment of organizational norms in software development can be supported by making them specific via specifying measurement values. If some product property has been deemed important it might be formulated as an explicit organization norm that all delivered software modules have to pass a measure-based acceptance test. In this way, the result of some organizational learning process can be fixed very concretely as an organizational norm.

Discussions get a focus. In software development, more quite abstract features of the work process must be used for analyzing the work process, since, in difference to the typical situation analyzed by Argyris and Schön, it is not direct communicative behavior which is in the focus of the analysis. In this case, measurements can present indisputable facts. Of course, these facts have to be interpreted to acquire a meaning. The objectivity of the measurement is an opportunity to dig deeper, to make explicit what is not encompassed in the measurement. A measured number can be the fixed point in a discussion at which the communication partners have to become explicit about their differing interpretations of the same set of numbers. As an element in the learning process of a group, it has the function of focusing a discussion, of forcing out differing conceptions.

5 Analysis of the Three Areas of Experiences

We now discuss the three experience areas presented in the introduction in the context of our adaptation of the conceptual framework of Argyris and Schön (Sec. 3.2, Fig. 2). This helps to systematize and thus partly explain the different experiences in the three areas.

5.1 Area 1: PSP

Why is it expected that the PSP measurement activities are difficult to uphold in practice? One point is that the differences between espoused behavioral patterns and those effectively in use can be frustrating for the PSP users. Perhaps it is this what makes keeping detailed time protocols so unattractive for many software developers. But they might fear disillusion by looking at the times they need for debugging, for rebooting their machines, for installing software etc. In order to help the developers deal with this frustration, an organizational context, e.g. with appropriate organization norms, would be sensible.

Another point is that the collection of data and their analysis incurs some overhead. This is only accepted as long as it is not too large. In the PSP the overhead is felt as being too large. This means that the first level feedback loop (cf. the lower rectangle of Fig. 2) might already be broken: The data collection or data analysis already does not take place.

Another problem with the PSP is that it is too much focused on the individual: the difference between individual and the organizational goals is not explicitly dealt with. This means that the process data is always in danger of being misused for external assessment, e.g. by management, of single developers, instead for assessment of the learning potential of the organization, and it means that there is no constructive way given how the experiences and measurement results of PSP users can be used to establish organizational learning, i.e. of making the collected knowledge accessible to other members of the team.

5.2 Area 2: Use of Measurement Tool

In order for the measurement data to be of value for developers, (a) data collection and analysis must really take place, (b) the measurement results must reach the developers, and (c) they must be meaningful for them in the sense that they have to be able to change their software development strategies, which means in particular (d) that measurement results must reach the developers quickly enough, so that the measurements data are relevant for what the developers are doing when they learn about them. Our second area of experience illustrates some problems in these respects:

If the results of the applications of a measurement tool are mainly discussed with managers, this can have different negative consequences: For example, it may incite defensive behavior from the side of the developers. Such a use of measures might well be counterproductive instead of helpful, since it stops learning. At least, developers will not be able to learn from the measurement results if these are not intensively discussed with them. This situation can be described in our model as a broken feedback loop: The feedback results do not travel back to the developers. Additionally, there might be conflicts between the management's action strategies and the developers' governing values and action strategies.

Such a management-centered view of measuring can have other harmful effects: For example, if the measurements are performed by a separate quality assurance group (QA group), the measures used might be just inappropriate, if the QA group does not intensively discuss with the developers what measures are really relevant for their work.

Even misunderstandings might result, which might lead to developers taking the wrong consequences. The QA group which performs the analysis might have governing values different from those of the developers, which may lead to analysis strategies which are inconsistent with the strategies of the developers.

5.3 Area 3: Extreme Programming

The third area of experience described in the introduction is the Extreme Programming (XP) way of organizing software development work. Why might this be successful? One reason is that very simple measures are used with very clear validity for the work of the developers: The percentage of successful unit tests and of successful system tests are obviously measures of high validity for project progress; the way these measures are collected and analyzed incur only very small overhead. Communication friendly techniques incurring minimal overhead for describing requirements, prioritizing tasks, checking design ideas, and implementing the designs provide quick and low-overhead feedback loops for different kinds of project-relevant information. Both data collection and analysis are done in a simple and efficient way. This means that at least the first level feedback loop (cf. lower rectangle of Fig. 2) will probably work.

Feedback about the percentage of successful systems tests represent the team's success in the project, which helps to relate the individual and the organizational level. The same is true for the reporting scheme for project tracking. The simple structure makes it easy to interpret and it ensures that all project participants have a common view of the project.

Differences between espoused and practically used behavioral patterns can quickly be made explicit in this way, since the social situation adopted for many development tasks, especially the pair programming, helps to confront the participants quickly with differences between what they think how they act and how they really act.

Another important feature of XP is that the governing values (explicitly, simplicity, communication and testing) and their relation to action strategies are dealt with explicitly. They make clear for all project participants where the project is heading to, they allow a common vision for the team to be formed, discussed and headed to. This explicitness of governing values is a first step to installing a reflection process which checks if the governing values are adequate in a given project.

Altogether, we see most dimensions of the framework are dealt with in some productive way in the XP approach.

6 Conclusion

Barriers to learning exist on organizational and individual levels. The organizational learning framework of Argyris and Schön presents a context in which both technical and organizational problems can be analyzed and with which a strategy to increase the learning capabilities of software development organizations can be implemented. We used three main dimensions of their framework for analyzing the context of measurements activities in software development organizations.

We see our approach as guiding the analysis of measurement activities in software development projects by emphasizing six areas: (a) the difference between single-loop and double-loop learning, including the difference between governing values and action strategies; (b) the difference between espoused theories of effective action and theories-in-use; (c) the difference between the individual and the organizational level;

(d) the question where the information feedback loops which the measurement activity is part of might be broken; and (e) the question of the overhead incurred by measurement and analysis activities might be too high for these activities to be accepted as worthwhile, and (f) the question if a reflection process from time to time checks if the governing values have to be adjusted.

The analysis of these areas might lead to intervention recommendations, i.e. to recommendations for changes to the organization of measurement activities in a software development project. Our first experiences suggest that we identified six key areas for successful embedding of measurements activities in software development projects; more empirical analyses of different kinds of measure uses would be helpful.

References

1. Chris Argyris. *On Organizational Learning*. Blackwell, Oxford, 1992.
2. Chris Argyris and Donald A. Schön. *Organizational Learning II: Theory, Method, and Practice*. Addison Wesley, Reading/ Massachusetts, 1996.
3. Kent Beck. *Extreme Programming Explained: Embrace Change*. Addison Wesley Longman, Reading/Massachusetts, 1999.
4. Norman E. Fenton and Shari Lawrence Pfleeger. *Software Metrics: A Rigorous and Practical Approach*. International Thomson Computer Press, London et al., 2 1996.
5. Watts S. Humphrey. *A Discipline for Software Engineering*. AddisonWesley, Reading/Massachusetts, 1995.
6. Gerd Köhler, Heinrich Rust, and Frank Simon. An assement of large object oriented software systems. In *Proceedings of the Workshop "ObjectOriented Product Metrics for Software Quality Assessment", 12th ECOOP*, pages 16–22, Brüssel, July 1998.
7. M. M. Lehman. Feedback, evolution and software technology – the human dimension. In *ICSE 20 Workshop: Human Dimensions in Successful Software Development*, 1998.
8. Frank Simon and Claus Lewerentz. A product metrics tool integrated into a software development environment. In *Proceedings of the European Software Measurement Conference (FESMA 98)*, Antwerp, Belgium, 1998.

Part 6:

Learning

Process-Integrated Learning: The ADVISOR Approach for Corporate Development

Philipp Starkloff [1] and Katja Pook [2]

[1] b-educated! GmbH Business Education Solutions, Kaiserstr.94,
D-69115 Heidelberg, Germany
starkloff@b-educated.com
www.b-educated.com
[2] University of Heidelberg, Institute of Psychology, Hauptstr. 47-51,
D-69117 Heidelberg
katja.pook@uni-hd.de
http://paeps.psi.uni-heidelberg.de

Abstract. This paper highlights ideas and experiences of the ADVISOR approach to increase process awareness among employees. *ADV*anced *I*nstruction Technologies for *S*ervices *OR*ganisations aim to look at learning and training from a process point of view. Whereas training is often somewhat detached from daily business here knowledge and skill acquisition within the business processes is emphasised. A front-end information system was built with a business process management software toolkit by adapting the toolkit to the needs of e-learning and knowledge management. Employees are presented customised views on process chains which are enriched with target specific information and learning objects. It is argued that ADVISOR can substantially support the introduction of new software and other change projects in an organisation.

1 Introduction

Activities to implement and optimise business processes are still playing a crucial role in corporate development, due to global mergers, implementation of enterprise-resource-planning (ERP) systems and other technological changes. Organisational experts and consultants use specialised tools which help them to analyse and re-design processes. However, many different parties are involved and many different tools are being applied, when it comes to the communication of process changes and the training of processes. This often leads to a lack of co-ordination, which prevents fast and flexible corporate development.

In the recently finished EU co-funded research and development project ADVISOR, three European insurance companies, together with software and consulting houses, aimed to overcome such fragmentation. The basic idea of ADVISOR was to extend the functionality of a business process management toolkit in order to create a corporate environment for process oriented e-learning, information and knowledge management. The ADONIS®-ADVISOR solution allows to enrich process models with target group specific content and to produce a multi-media learning environment for process knowledge.

K.-D. Althoff, R.L. Feldmann, and W. Müller (Eds.): LSO 2001, LNCS 2176, pp. 152-162, 2001.

Based on the trial experiences and the evaluation results in the project, this article describes ways to bring learning activities in line with core business processes. The software and the methods are outlined, experiences are reported and future applications are being discussed.

1.1 The Importance of Business Process Management in the Face of Technological Change

Today's businesses face a variety of organisational and technological changes [1]. Generally, business changes can be described on three inter-related dimensions: goals, technology, and processes. Whenever new business goals are defined, they result in process changes. The same applies to the introduction of new technology: technological change implies process changes. Hence, processes play a key role in any organisational change. Even if there are no changes in goals or technology, process optimisation can lead to improved business performance. Examples for the importance of business processes for corporate flexibility can be found in [2].

If organisational changes do not show the expected outcomes, often the 'human factor' is blamed for the failure. Although, it is mostly left open what exactly must be understood under the term 'human factor', the role of human (social) behaviour is thought to be essential in change management. Even in technology dominated businesses, people act and decide in critical domains. And only people are able to change and to contribute to changes by adapting to and creatively designing new ways of doing things, namely by learning and by transferring knowledge. A major challenge is to integrate as many people as possible in business changes. We regard process-integrated learning as an often uncared for, but important, method for successful change management.

1.2 The Role of a Process View on Learning and Training

As a matter of fact, learning and training is often detached from the actual business. In standard face-to-face seminars, computer-based-training (CBT) or web-based-training (WBT) programmes, it is hard to take specific features of individual work places into account. More so, learning is often left with the individuals in an auto-didactic, trial-and-error fashion and educational measures only happen occasionally. Both - learning by structured training and individual learning "by chance" – rarely meet current business needs.

Today's standard corporate training is very much product oriented: People need to be qualified in Microsoft Office, SAP R/3, Lotus Notes, and the like. They learn many things about the products they will never apply, but fail to relate important issues to their own work. Examples and exercises, which try to cover the application of products, are mainly very general. Transfer of knowledge is left to the individual. This is problematic, because transfer is the most critical success factor for corporate training measures. And if there is no (measurable) business impact, management will cut down training costs. Taking business processes as an anchor helps to direct learning activities towards the core interests of business without disregarding individual perspectives. If people are explained how to apply products in order to get to results they need to perform their actual job, they will learn quicker and they will be motivated to try out what they have learned.

2 ADVISOR: A Process-Integrated Learning and Training Framework

In ADVISOR, software and methods have been developed to enable employees of three European insurance companies to learn more about their business processes and to relate the idea of process orientation to their own work. ADVISOR integrates training and business process modelling to avoid a fragmentation of conceptualisation and understanding of corporate objectives and tasks, and to treat process optimisation and learning as one coherent developing system.

Usually, information about the organisation and its processes is captured to allow for reengineering, rationalisation, quality-management and application-development. However, existing process documentations are hardly usable for employees in their daily job, because they are not adapted to the needs and language of employees in operational business. ADVISOR tries to overcome this by providing employees with an intranet information resource that can be used for learning and training as well as for performance support. The resource is easily adaptable to changes and therefore provides up-to-date information.

The approach focuses on transforming individual learning into corporate learning by:

1. Relating learning activities to business processes;
2. Making process orientation a salient corporate value;
3. Delivering mission critical knowledge to every single employee;
4. Providing information in a meaningful context;
5. Enabling people to identify the information that is relevant for their own personal contribution to the process chains;
6. Allowing the identification of qualification requirements based on process models;
7. Avoiding unnecessary disturbance of operational business by providing on the job learning and training.

2.1 The ADVISOR Software

Technical basis for ADVISOR is the business-process-management software-toolkit ADONIS® from BOC [3]. ADONIS provides a database connected flow-charting modeller with components to analyse, simulate and evaluate meta-models. Furthermore, it offers a wide range of data export and exchange functionality, including Lotus Notes and Office compatible formats, HTML and XML. Data-exchange through interfaces is possible for example with ERP systems (i.e. SAP HR), case and workflow tools.

The core domain of these tools is the mapping and description of business processes and business objects. Object oriented application development is supported with UML model types (use case and activity diagrams) [4]. A number of generic methods and reference models are available, but the tools should also be open for the definition of new and customised methods that include specific types of meta-data and meta-models. At first sight, management of meta-models appears as an overhead activity. The more organisations are faced with complex systems and pressure to change, the more likely they care about a management on a meta-level and engage, for example, in standardisation activities. Tools like ADONIS manage meta-knowledge and allow a better translation of strategies and concepts into operational business, i.e. workflow and e-business applications.

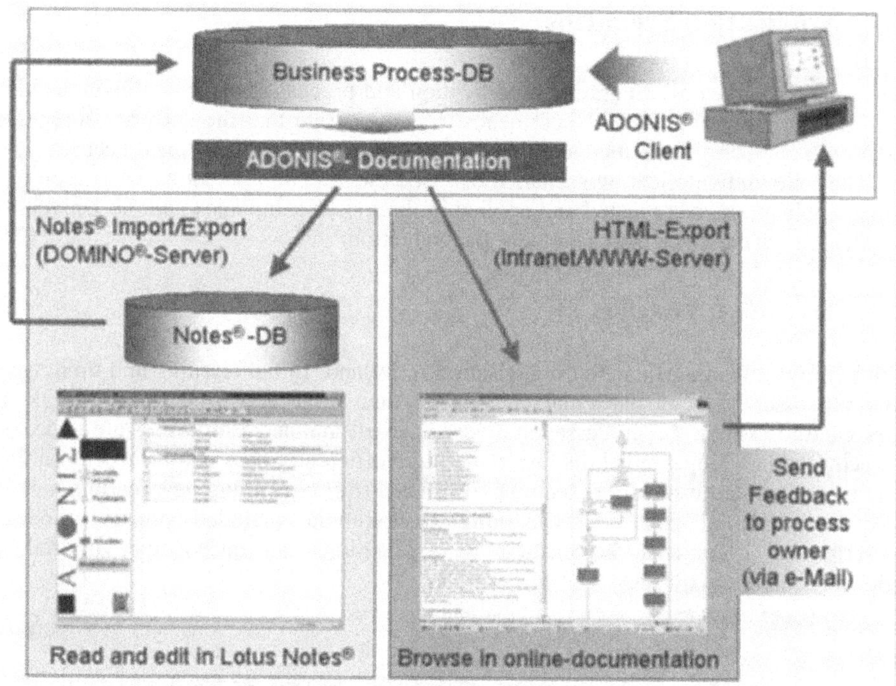

Fig. 1. The ADVISOR architecture

With the growing education market and extending software support, many corporate universities need to re-define their role and need to develop new business models. The planning and evaluation of systems and services around learning activities can be supported with ADONIS-ADVISOR. This is done in the core module. The end-user (learner) accesses the information through a web-front-end with a standard browser, without the need to use the ADONIS client. The (enriched) process documentation can be exported to RTF, HTML or Lotus Notes. The export is comfortable and can be adapted to different information needs. Filters can be applied that hide selected information which are confidential or that would confuse users. It is also possible to export into different language versions. A feedback loop helps to keep the database up to date and user-centred.

Using the described architecture, ADVISOR aims to create a process-oriented perspective in all employees by providing a framework for information transmission and for mental knowledge representation. By organising all information around business processes, it fosters the process idea to guide individual knowledge acquisition.

This, as well, facilitates communication since all employees can refer to a common ontological perspective and the according terminology. This last aspect refers to what Nonaka & Takeuchi [5] call socialisation. But not only the exchange of implicit knowledge is supported, but also the transformation of implicit into explicit knowledge (externalisation) and vice versa (internalisation). Common perspective and language are essential for making an information system a valuable source of knowledge on an individual, group and organisational level.

3 Application Scenarios

Given that the idea of integrating qualification and process management is innovative and useful, the ADVISOR project needs to demonstrate that the software supported approach can be implemented and that it offers solutions to real business needs.

The following application scenarios describe the system's potential. During project time, applications were tested and applied in three user companies and the University of Heidelberg executed a social-scientific evaluation.

3.1 Scenario 1: Training

Irish Life is a leading financial organisation in Ireland. Initial learning and training of the processes was of particular interest in their trial department. ADVISOR is designed to explain the processes in a very detailed manner. Employees are expected to acquire knowledge and skills faster and more efficiently than before, when training in this department basically relied on experienced staff explaining new recruits how to do the particular jobs. The learning environment included process models, descriptions, comments, screenshots of applications, an introductory tutorial, a glossary and a few quizzes.

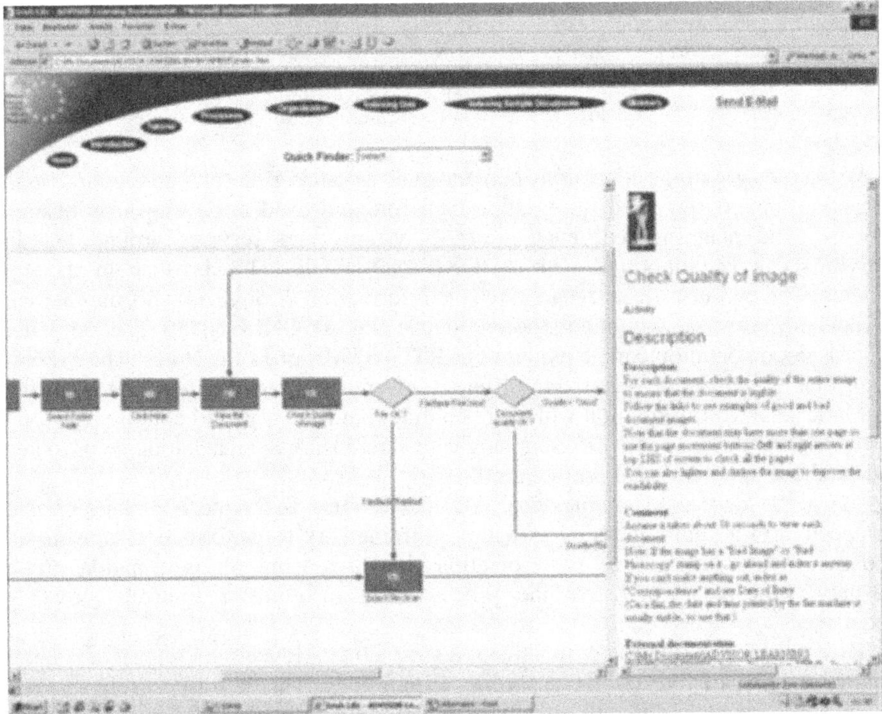

Fig. 2. Screenshot of an ADVISOR prototype (HTML)

Before the actual training is initiated, business processes are documented (as-is) and re-designed (should-be) or optimised if necessary. Relevant process data are included. Then a learner perspective is taken: Potential problems are anticipated and necessary knowledge for the execution of the tasks is identified. This process is similar to a cognitive walkthrough [6], with the exception that the subject is not necessarily a software application but can be any work process. Graphical models, task descriptions and denominations are adapted to the needs of the target group(s). Depending on the necessity to deliver alternative perspectives and levels of detail, relevant information is added, too. Some processes might need to be mapped in detail to illustrate all activities involved. External documentation (Word, PDF, HTML,...) can be linked to the process elements. Additionally, instructionally prepared material can also be referenced: URLs, Screen-cam pictures and animations, learning objects, tutorials (CBT/WBT), audio and video files, etc. Information about face-to-face courses and printed books can be provided, too. If an LMS is available, both systems can be integrated in that courseware from an LMS can be referenced. ADVISOR is not designed to replace LMS, but to provide different perspectives on the content and to structure the database accordingly.

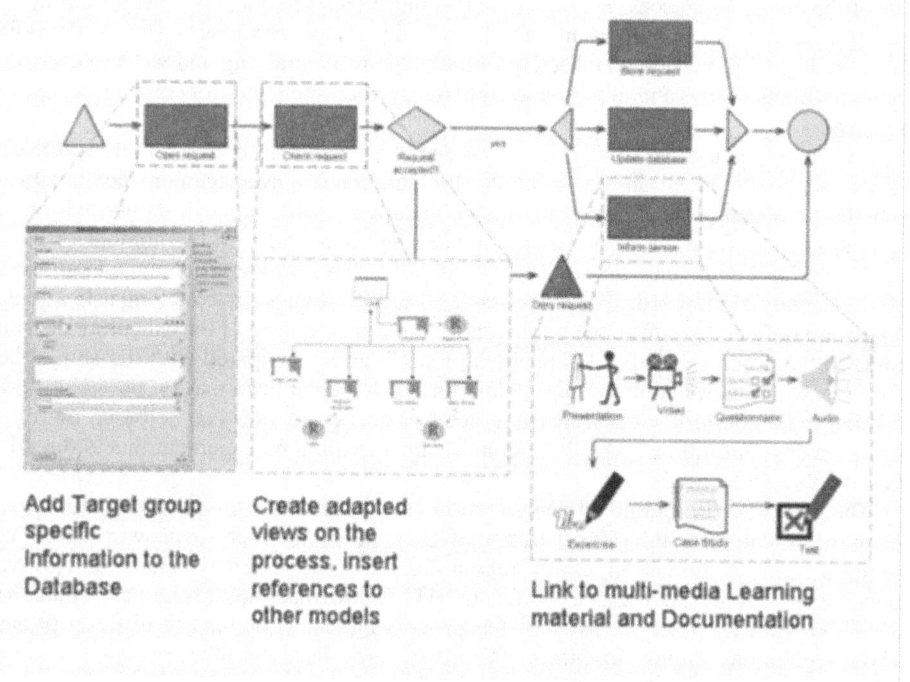

Fig. 3. Steps in the design of an ADVISOR online learning environment

Evaluation results show that ADVISOR did well on providing a tool to support the training of a cohort of new recruits. They integrated much quicker in the area than staff in former years. The introductory training could be reduced from approximately three months to the same number of weeks. ADVISOR seems especially helpful in the creation of a mental representation of the interdependent jobs in the department. Trainees appreciate the transparency of work processes. The time people spent with browsing in ADVISOR was as little as two to five hours, indicating that no extensive training was needed. Nevertheless, much of peoples' knowledge was still acquired from on-the-job-learning.

The overall improvement may be based on the fact that the communication between new recruits and experienced staff had improved because of a common background provided by the ADVISOR documentation. Results indicate that by using a coherent structure for knowledge acquisition and transfer, and by adopting the same process-oriented perspective onto business aspects, a common background is established. The project delivered good results with respect to an efficient combination of personal support and self-guided learning.

3.2 Scenario 2: Performance Support

The German based Gothaer SchadenService Center (GSC) is a call-centre where customers can report claims and where minor claims are regulated immediately. Not all of the employees necessarily have an insurance background. They need training in different domains, an important of which is insurance processes. The ADVISOR handbook should provide an effective online-support for training and work execution. Search functionality and a keyword glossary were included for fast information retrieval.

ADONIS was used to model the processes in the call-centre and in current release offers adapted simulation functionality for call-centres. Management can analyse whether the centre is capable to answer peoples' calls in peak hours within a maximum time frame. Resources can be allocated depending on the number of calls and work schedules can be adapted in advance. For the identification of learning requirements, skill profiles describe each role according to relevant qualifications. Skills are defined by considering the qualification that is needed for executing certain tasks in the process chain. As-is profiles of staff can be compared with the should-be profiles and qualification requirements for each person can easily be identified. Similar to the identification of learning needs, selection of staff can be based on roles or on process definitions. ADONIS supports qualification management that is directly based on business needs.

The ADVISOR online documentation is distributed to peoples' desktops. Employees can look-up information that they need in order to answer customer requests and to initiate a claim regulation. A large external handbook (Word document) was indexed and exported to HTML, so that the subchapters could be accessed from the relevant parts of the process charts. Additionally to descriptions about regulations, forms, templates, checklists, to-do lists and other resources can be added that are needed in a work context. It is also possible to launch other applications.

The evaluation revealed a critical factor: If the information is incomplete, out-dated or not applicable, people lose trust in the system. In consequence, adequate amount of manpower needs to be invested in a continuous maintenance of the information database. Process owners need to be defined and an up-date process needs to be established. Ideally, domain experts and team leaders are actively involved, giving feedback and providing content.

3.3 Scenario 3: Customer Relationship

Cesce is a Spanish insurance company for trade risks. They offer products that need to be adapted individually to the customer and their trade business. The process, until the customer gets coverage, is complex and involves the customer's bank also. In order to increase customer satisfaction, process models are integrated in the corporate web presentation, giving customers the opportunity to get information from the Internet. This is expected to take some workload off the employees, because the communication between employees and customers should be facilitated.

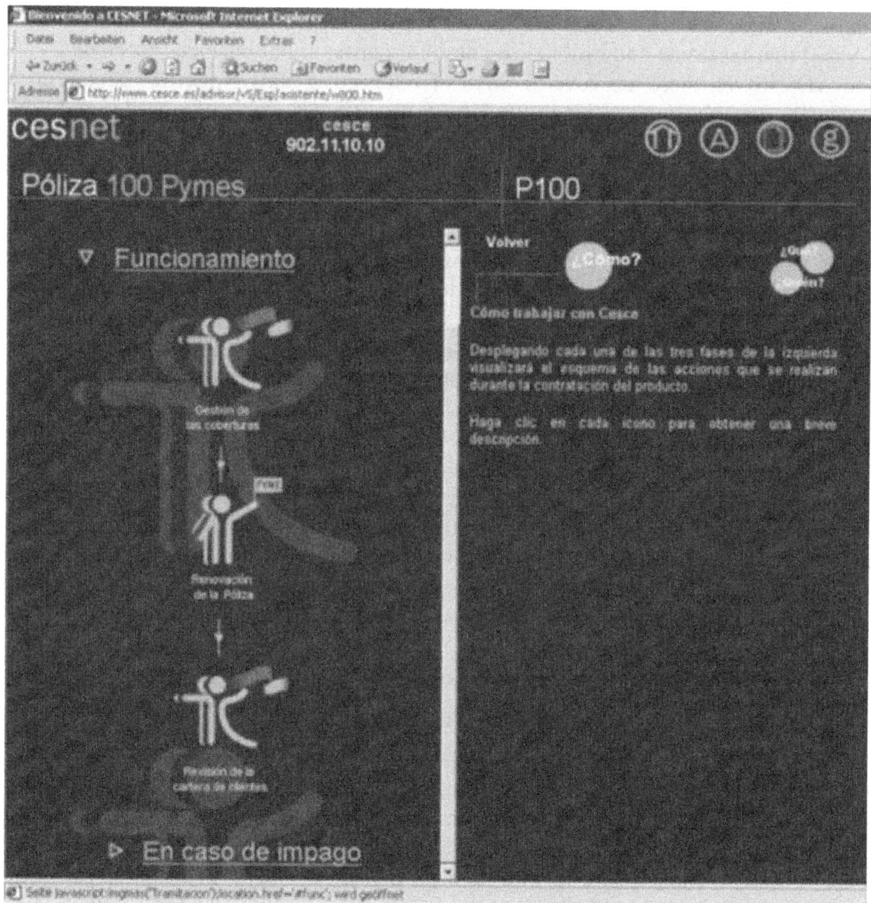

Fig. 4. An ADVISOR-based web interface for customers (here: business-to-business) [7]

ADONIS was used to design and maintain the database, so that the information is always consistent with the ISO900x documentation, which is also maintained in ADONIS. The presentation of the data for the customer is simplified and modified to the corporate design of Cesce. This application demonstrates that the information repository can be used for third parties, which makes it a useful approach for supply chains and customer relationship management.

3.4 Scenario 4: Continuous Process Optimisation

The success of reengineering measures largely depends on the ability of people to accept the changes and to work accordingly. First, they need to understand the changes, which is supported with a well-designed documentation. Second, employees need to be able to give their feedback and contribute to the documentation and maybe to the design of optimised processes. If the importance of the human factor is valued, process-management can be improved by integrating peoples' expertise in the cycle of optimising business-processes [8]. This requires adequate organisational as well as technical concepts. Organisational aspects largely depend on existing organisational structures and ways of communication. Technological mechanisms need to be provided that facilitate and rationalise communication about business processes.

In ADVISOR, there are several ways of integrating staff expertise, depending on the distribution platform. With Lotus Notes, user access rights can be defined which allow a direct modification of parts of the Notes database. In an HTML-based solution, E-mails can be sent to the process owner. If domain experts are requested to contribute content, e.g. a description of an activity, they can also use Excel spreadsheets that are generated by ADONIS. Another method of directly involving staff is workshops that are usually held in the beginning of a reengineering project. With a laptop and a beamer, process models can be projected, discussed and directly adapted in the system.

Operational IT systems can feed back data to ADONIS. The closer the data are to reality, the more valid are simulation results and the richer is the captured knowledge about the processes, the organisation and the (IT-) systems in use. An optimisation of processes is most effective when feedback from multiple sources (IT and people) is collected and processed on a regular base.

From the employees point of view, the integration of all people's knowledge into corporate planning, steering and organization implies one core aspect: Each individual employee is considered as an expert of his/her own daily work. It is made transparent that knowledge in operational business is regarded valuable for corporate development. People get involved and participate in continuous optimisation.

4 Outlooks and Further Development

In the educational sector, process thinking has only recently caught attention. ADVISOR fosters the integration of human and corporate development by helping HR professionals to think in processes and to structure learning and training in a process context. The application can be used in various ways. It opens up the source of process knowledge to all employees by providing a platform for acquisition and exchange of expertise. Highly valuable information that is normally used only for BPM in central departments is exploited to train employees and to integrate them in continuous optimisation of business practices.

Further on, it is a management toolkit that can model training processes, i.e. instructional methods. IT systems (i.e. LMS) and human resources (i.e. trainers) can be mapped. Educational business processes can be designed: How does the organisation purchase and produce content (supply chain)? How does the organisation deliver the content (e-business)? How does the organisation recruit staff (personnel selection)?

In large HR departments, corporate universities and training organisations, a systematic approach for qualification processes is necessary to ensure the quality of the services, especially if a certification is targeted [9]. Documented qualification processes also help to intertwine the supporting function of training with the core business of the enterprise. Training is expensive and a return on investment can hardly be calculated. People will only buy training if they are convinced of the quality of the service and the benefit for their own business.

The documentation functionality of ADVISOR can quickly generate complex hyper-linked learning environments for the scenarios described above. This makes the approach also attractive for non-training experts, who can build a system that responds to common information needs of employees and management.

There is definitely a big potential for process management in educational settings. The experiences are quite limited so far, so that future application areas can only be anticipated. With a growing popularity of standards like AICC [10], IMS [11] or SCORM [12], meta-data for learning content are getting more important. XML offers a technical solution to exchange information between platforms and applications [13]. Tools like ADVISOR are well prepared to manage these meta-data and integrate them in meta-models.

5 Summary and Conclusion

Companies are constantly faced with the need to optimise their technological support systems. Often employees are expected to learn quickly how to handle a new system without disturbing the running operational business. Training and learning activities are required that are well integrated in job execution and that support central business interests. Any corporate changes have effects in the business processes. With the ADVISOR approach, learning and training is organised around the process chains, and a front-end online handbook reduces the time of initial training substantially. This results in higher acceptance and effectiveness of new systems or practices, because they are understood in the context for what they are designed for: supporting business. An integration of feedback mechanisms can lead to an effective process optimisation, where staff is actively involved. A major advantage of ADVISOR is the provision of target group specific views on processes, which makes it also capable for educating third parties (i.e. in supply chains).

ADONIS-ADVISOR is a technical solution that allows many different ways of addressing process-integrated learning. Individual learning is directed towards personal qualification as well as towards mission critical process knowledge for the company's business. We see current challenges for e-learning in the integration with concepts of the 'learning organisation' and knowledge management, focussing on how to implement new ways of learning in existing environments. Learning, and e-learning in particular, are regarded as supporting the core business. There must be an obvious link between learning goals and business objectives in order to engage in learning activities. The evaluation of ADVISOR has shown that the solution fosters a communication about processes. This is vital for the development of a culture of learning and change.

References

1. Zucchermaglio, C., S. Bagnara, et al., (eds.): Organizational Learning and Technological Change. NATO ASI Series F. Springer-Verlag, Berlin Heidelberg New York (1995)
2. Heisig, P.: Business Oriented Knowledge Management - Methode zur Verknüpfung von Wissensmanagement und Geschäftsprozessgestaltung. WM 2001. Electronic publication, Baden-Baden, Germany (2001)
3. Junginger, S., Kühn, H., Strobl, R., Karagiannis, D.: Ein Geschäftsprozess-management-Werkzeug der nächsten Generation - ADONIS: Konzeption und Anwendungen. Wirtschaftsinformatik, 42 (2000) 5, 392-401.
4. Nonaka, I. & Takeuchi, H.: The Knowledge creating company. Oxford University Press, Oxford. (1995)
5. Müller-Ettrich, G.: Objektorientierte Prozessmodelle: UML einsetzen mit OOTC, V-Modell, Objectory. Addison Wesley Longman, Bonn Reading, MA (1999)
6. Wharton, C., J. Riemann, et al.: The Cognitive Walkthrough Method: A practicioner's guide. In: J. Nielsen and R. L. Mack (eds.): Usability inspection methods. John Wiley & Sons, New York (1994) 105-140
7. http://www.cesce.es/advisor/v5/Esp/portal.htm
8. Zangwill, W. I. and P. B. Kantor: Toward a Theory of Continuous Improvement and the Learning Curve. Management Science, 44 (1998) 7, 910-920
9. Ruessmann-Stoehr, C., Herrmann, D., Glaubitz, G., Klug, A., Seibt, H., Wienkamp, H. (eds.): Seminare auf dem Prüfstand: Ein Qualitaetsmanagement-System für wirtschafts-psychologische Trainings (einschliesslich zertifiziertem Beispiel-Handbuch nach ISO-9001). In: Pabst, Lengerich, (eds.): Sektion Arbeits-, Betriebs- und Organisations-psychologie im Berufsverband Deutscher Psychologinnen und Psychologen. (2000)
10. http://www.aicc.org/
11. http://www.imsproject.org
12. http://www.adlnet.org/Scorm/scorm_index.cfm
13. Süß, C., Freitag, B., Brössler, P.: Metamodeling for Web-Based Teachware Management. In: P.P Chen, D.W. Embley, J. Kouloumdijan, S.W. Liddle and J.F. Roddick: Proc. Intl. WWWCM`99, Paris. Springer-Verlag, Berlin Heidelberg New York (1999)

Task-Specific Knowledge Management in a Process-Centred SEE

Harald Holz[1], Arne Könnecker[2], and Frank Maurer[3]

[1] University of Kaiserslautern, Department of Computer Science,
D-67653 Kaiserslautern, Germany
holz@informatik.uni-kl.de

[2] Vignette Deutschland GmbH, Heinrich-Heine-Allee 53,
D-40213 Düsseldorf, Germany
arne.koennecker@vignette.com

[3] University of Calgary, Department of Computer Science,
Calgary, Alberta, Canada, T2N 1N4
maurer@cpsc.ucalgary.ca

Abstract. This paper discusses how a process-centered knowledge management and coordination support approach can be used to create learning software organizations. We describe our extensions to the software engineering environment MILOS that allow us to model and interpret information needs that occur during project planning and enactment; this enables MILOS to automatically provide users with task-specific information. In order to capture actual information needs, we propose an extended feedback loop to update the process model stored in an experience base. The result is a knowledge management approach that is process-oriented and supports continuous process improvement.

Keywords: process-oriented knowledge management, process support environments

1 Introduction

Creating effective knowledge management structures is one of the key factors in software process improvement initiatives (like the Capability Maturity Model, Spice, Trillium, etc.). Most often, the knowledge management needs are only mentioned implicitly. Specific organizational structures (e. g. a software process group) are developed for the purpose of managing and distributing knowledge about software development. These structures are costly to maintain, and improving the efficiency of their members by a dedicated tool infrastructure would be very useful.

In general, two mainstreams concerning tool infrastructure can be distinguished: first, process-centred software engineering environments (PSEE) [10] are acknowledged tools to help in planning, managing and executing today's software projects. Their support is mainly focused on the coordination of the different activities within a project following a defined development process, i.e. focused on project coordination. That is why the support for the individual participating agent in per

K.-D. Althoff, R.L. Feldmann, and W. Müller (Eds.): LSO 2001, LNCS 2176, pp. 163-177, 2001.

forming tasks is mainly restricted to provide access to input products for a task and to tools to create defined output products.

Secondly, tools that aim at supporting the Experience Factory proposed by Basili et.al. [4] are being developed (see e.g. [1]). They encompass mechanisms which help to capture and make information and knowledge accessible and (re)usable. The main concept here is to document and store any kind of information (e.g., knowledge, experience) and to access it via provided interfaces in a structured way. The common information retrieval based on statistic document analysis techniques mainly used in document management systems (DMS) is extended by, e.g., similarity-based or ontology-based retrieval, to better find relevant information items and to extract new information facts by the combination of two or more existing items.

The MILOS[1] project of the University of Calgary and the University of Kaiserslautern aims at providing an infrastructure that integrates these two mainstreams. Its primary goals are

- to provide access to relevant task-related knowledge when a task is planned or executed
- to integrate knowledge management with project planning and process coordination
- to create a feedback loop from process execution to knowledge management resulting in support for learning software organizations
- to develop tool support (the MILOS system) for this closed-loop approach

Section 2 describes our process-centered knowledge management approach. In Section 3, we sketch the feedback loop for updating the process models. An example for our approach is given in Section 4. The last two sections discuss related work and compare it to our approach.

2 Process-Centred Knowledge Management

As a PSEE, MILOS provides means to define generic process models and to set up concrete project plans based on these models. Furthermore, MILOS' web-based workflow engine supports the enactment of project plans, providing team members with individual to-do lists and relevant documents. During plan enactment, MILOS allows on-the-fly plan changes, notifying team members affected by those changes and updating the workflow engine accordingly [13].

Whereas MILOS supports project planning, coordination and enactment on the project level, so far there has been little or no support for the individual project member when confronted with a specific task. Rather, it is assumed that he already is equipped with all the information relevant to perform the task that has been assigned to him, or that he at least knows how to retrieve that information. However, studies show that people often are not aware of information that might be relevant to them, even though this information has been explicitly stored in the company's organizational memory [14].

---

[1] Minimally Invasive Long-term Organizational Support

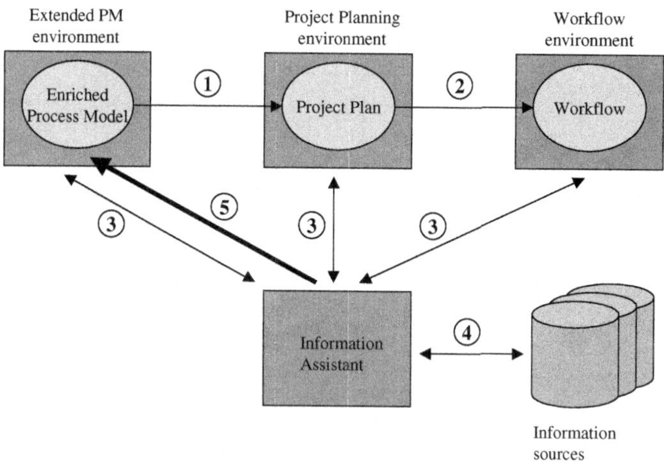

Fig. 1. An abstract view of the knowledge delivery concept within PSEEs: process models (PMs) with associated information need objects (INOs) can be created in an extended PM environment. These enriched PMs can be used as templates for a project plan (1), which is interpreted (2) by a workflow engine using the added scheduling information. Users carrying out activities in the planning or workflow environment are supported by the Information Assistant with information (3), based on available INOs from the PM. The IA queries (4) information sources on demand to retrieve information and deliver it (3) to a user. From within the IA, a user can post questions that are added to the appropriate process model element (5) as part of the feedback loop (see Section 3).

Therefore, we extended MILOS by an "Information Assistant" (IA), an explicit information delivery concept. The concept is based on an explicit modeling of information needs that might arise during specific tasks, together with an automatic query to the appropriate information source from which the answers can be retrieved; Fig. 1 gives an overview on this extension.

Generic Process Models are reusable workflow descriptions of software development processes. Primarily, these models describe different tasks[2], ways how to solve tasks (called *methods*), conditions describing when a task can be started, criteria its results must fulfill, required qualifications for tasks, and the document flow between tasks. For a more detailed description see [17].

In order to provide task-specific knowledge delivery, we have extended our representation of process models by *information need objects* (INOs; see Fig. 2). INOs represent potential information needs that might arise during planning or enactment of specific processes; they are characterized by the following attributes:

representation: a textual representation that describes the information need, e.g. "What bugs have been reported for component <componentName> ?". The represention can contain variables (delimited by '<' and '>') that correspond to attributes defined in the process model. During planning or enactment, they will be substituted by their current values.

[2] In the following, task and process are used synonymously.

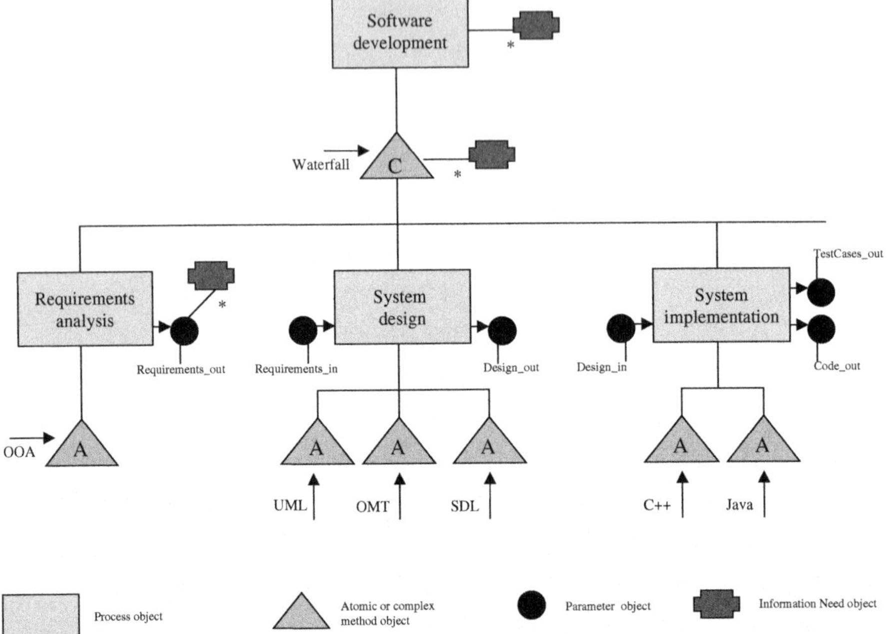

Fig. 2. A part of an example process model, where INOs have been attached to different model elements, e.g. to processes, complex methods (i.e. process decomposition), atomic methods i.e. process specialization) and parameters. The "*" denotes that several INOs can be associated with a model element.

information source: specifies which resource can be used to retrieve information that might be helpful to satisfy the defined information need. Sources can be e.g. bug tracking systems, information agents, databases, or document management systems. A number of typical interfaces (eg. SQL, CGI, HTTP) have been predefined within MILOS to allow access to different types of information sources.

Query representation: specifies a query in the syntax required by the given information source, `e.g.: "?bug_status=NEW&product=<component Name>"`. The query will be executed automatically to retrieve potentially helpful information items from the information source.

Supported roles: specifies one or more roles to which the retrieved information will be relevant. For example, that way we can distinguish between information needs typical for planners or enactors.

Information category: specifies one or more categories under which the INO will be organized; examples of predefined categories for the role `planner` are: "`agent assignment`", "`project scheduling`" etc.

Precondition: a Boolean expression that specifies when the information need normally occurs and the query can be launched, e.g.: "`componentName.hasValue()`"

Thus, a process model not only serves as a means to store knowledge about best practices, but also maintains generic links to knowledge items that have been found useful in the past when planning or enacting specific processes.

Project Plans are set up by the planner by tailoring generic process models to the needs of a concrete project. This includes:

- selecting processes and methods from the generic process model that should become part of the project plan. For example, the generic process model contains a process "System Design" with methods "UML", "OMT" and "SDL". The project manager can add an instance of the process " System Design" to the project plan and then select "UML" from the set of alternatives as his method of choice.
- standard project planning: Assigning tasks to responsible agents, scheduling tasks, cost estimation etc. These activities are commonly supported by COTS tools like MS Project.

In order to support planners in these knowledge intensive activities, we want to enable our PSEE to provide them with situation-specific information that helps them in their decision-making.

Since project plans are tailored process models, plan elements inherit the generic INOs associated with the corresponding process model elements. In the context of the current project, variables referenced in the INO definitions can now be substituted by their values (e.g. the variable <assignedAgent> is substituted by the team member to which the task under consideration is currently assigned to). As a consequence, INOs that are intended to reflect a planner's information needs can now be presented to him by the Information Assistant, in order to signal available access to potentially useful information.

Using a flexible **workflow engine**, project plans are interpreted in order to actively guide human users in their work. It manages the state of the processes contained in the plan, to-do lists for individual users, the products created during process enactment, and traceability relationships between process entities [19]. In addition, the INOs associated with plan entities are presented to those team members on whose to-do lists the entities appear; thus, they are given situation-specific access to potentially relevant information.

Before we illustrate the functionality with an example scenario in Section 4, we briefly sketch the proposed feedback loop in the following section.

3 Creating a Feedback Loop for Continuous Learning

To support an organizational learning process, our approach links process-centered knowledge management with project planning, enactment support and experience packaging. We follow a four-step process (see Fig 3).

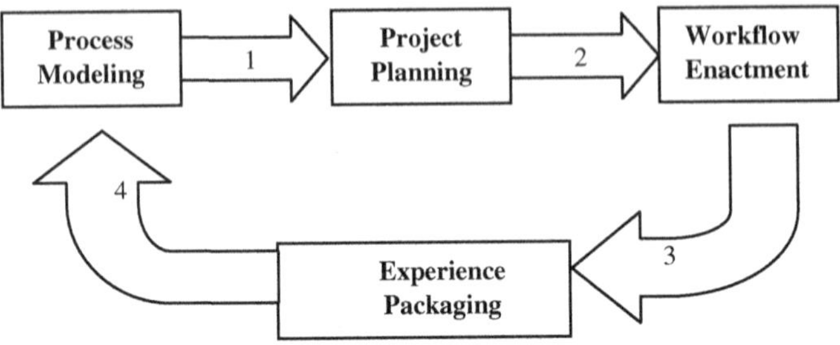

Fig. 3. Knowledge Utilization Cycle

The process model library contains descriptions of best practices in software development for a given company. In step 1, the project manager selects processes and methods from the library to create an initial project plan. This plan includes references to background knowledge (generic queries, modeled as INOs) that were stored in the process model. However, the planning process is incremental: we can change the plan at any time during process execution. The current project plan is the basis for enactment supported by our workflow engine (2). Using a standard Web browser, a user is able to connect to the workflow engine, access her to-do list, accept/reject/restart a task, access task inputs, and edit task outputs. After completing a task, the outputs are accessible as input for the successor tasks.

The next step is to extract reusable process knowledge from the current project plan (3). A user can select parts of the project plan (e.g. a method for a specific task or the newly added information resources) and upload/integrate them into the generic process model library (4).

During planning and enactment, the Information Assistant allows users to formulate new information needs in the form of questions. These information needs are associated with the task in the context of which they occurred. Thus, members of the software process group are alerted to existing information needs during experience packaging, and can try to complete the partially specified INO. That way, next time the respective process occurs in a project, users can be provided directly with the requested information.

4 Examples

In the following, we illustrate how we set up the Information Assistant within MILOS for use in our environment. First, we give examples of information needs that we intend to be able to satisfy, and for which we set up (or are currently in the process of setting up) appropriate information sources. Second, we illustrate our system's functionality with the help of an example scenario motivated by our own project's software development process.

Table 1. Typical information needs of planners

Category	Information need
Anticipating difficulties	What problems occurred in similar tasks? How were they solved? What relevant problems/shortcomings/bugs with the tools used in the current task are known?
Agent assignment	Which agents match the skills required for the task? Which agents have performed a similar task before? Which agents are available at the time period in question?
Effort estimation	What quality models exist for the task? What was the time effort of similar task?
Task refinement	What standard refinements exist for the task? How were similar tasks performed in the past?

4.1 Modeling Information Needs

Both planners and plan enactors are confronted with a set of standard problems that occur for every task, e.g. anticipating potential difficulties, finding a skilled team member with free capacities, estimating the time effort, and, depending on the task's granularity and the team member's expertise, developing an outline of how to perform the task. Table 1 lists examples of typical planning information needs related to these problems.

In order to enable the Information Assistant to satisfy these information needs, we require the availability of appropriate information sources from which the desired information can be obtained, e.g.: (i) the organization's resource pool, including skill information for each agent, (ii) a calendar database providing schedule dates for agents, (iii) bug and issue tracking systems, project and task case-bases, (iv) an experience base storing process and quality models, (v) a DMS holding general documents, etc.

Table 2. Example of a generic INO that is associated with every task

INO attributes	Value
Representation	"Who has performed similar tasks before?"
Query	retrieve_similar_tasks(<currentTask>)
Information source	Task case-base
Precondition	Task case-base available
Information category	agent assignment, task execution
Supported roles	planner, enactor

As mentioned above, information needs are represented as INOs that reference an information source; Tab. 2 shows an example INO that references a task case-base. In order to launch the query execution, the IA must be able to access the task case-base via a predefined interface. In accordance to this interface, it must also replace the variable <currentTask> with the appropriate representation of the task for which the INO's query execution is requested. In the example of our task case-base, this means replacing the variable with the current task's string representation; this representation becomes part of a parameter string for a CGI-script that performs the similarity-based search.

In addition to information needs that typically occur for all tasks, we capture information needs that only occur for certain tasks. Processes in the process model are enriched with INOs as depicted in Fig. 4, where we define an INO that reflects a coder's information need to view the list of bugs that have been reported for the component he is currently implementing.

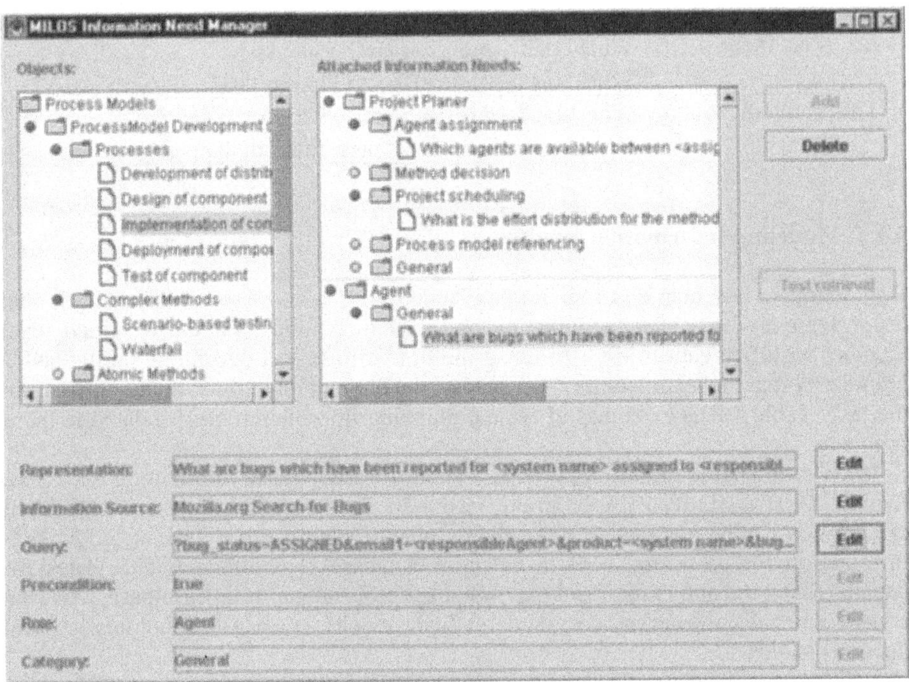

Fig. 4. The MILOS INO editor: from the tree in the upper-left part of the window, the user has selected the process object 'Implementation of component' from a process model. The tree in the upper-right part displays the associated INOs, using the role and information category attributes for structuring. The attribute values of the selected INO are shown in the lower part of the window

4.2 Example Scenario

In our example, the project planer starts the MILOS PSEE to set up a new project, i.e. to define a project plan. For his current project he provides a characterization by specifying the project name ('Distributed workflow management system'), the system architecture type ('Distributed'), and the estimated duration ('2 years'). Before creating a new project plan, he tries to remember similar projects conducted in the past that might help him in his planning. Since the Information Assistant (integrated into the MILOS PSEE) signals possible support in the current context, he starts the Assistant from the project planer UI and executes the information retrieval that is associated with the presented question "Which similar projects exist?". The retrieval results are presented to him in a browser, showing MILOS project plans which have been stored in a project plan database using case-based reasoning technology (see e.g. [Althoff98]).

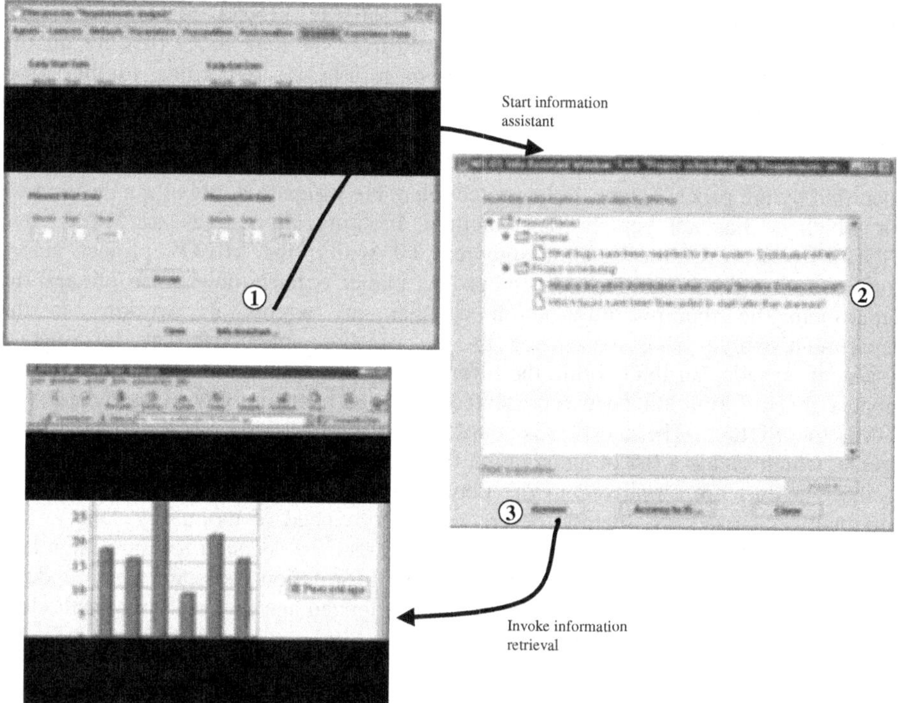

Fig. 5. The project planer starts the Information Assistant from the scheduling tab within the MILOS project planer via the enabled button (1) to get support in his scheduling task. The IA presents him the current relevant and available INOs and he selects the question "What is the effort distribution for the process model 'Development of distributed systems'?" (2). After he pressed the "Answer" button (3) in the IA, the browser in the lower left picture opens and present him an effort distribution diagram.

Inspecting the most similar project plan, he can see that this plan used the process model 'Development of distributed systems' from the MILOS PM library. Hence, he browses the process model library and selects this process model as a basis for his project plan. As a result, the processes from the process model now define tasks within the project plan. Besides the specification of these processes, their parameters, and the possible methods, the corresponding instances in the project plan include the INOs that are attached to the process model objects.

The chosen process model maintains knowledge about the development method 'Iterative enhancement' which the project planer thinks is appropriate especially because of the long project duration and the component-oriented architecture. Next, the planner wants to make a rough estimation of the time effort required for the task 'Requirements analysis'. This can be done by consulting a quality model that describes the effort distribution with respect to process steps in the chosen process model. Using the Information Assistant (see Fig. 5), he accesses the information associated with the question "What is the effort distribution when using Iterative Enhancement?" which is listed in the information category 'Project scheduling'. The questions that relate to this information category are available within the Information Assistant because the current work context of the project planer is 'project scheduling'. A corresponding diagram retrieved from the experience base for quality models is displayed in a window as shown in Fig. 5. According to the effort distribution and the estimated total time of 2 years for his project, he can now provide rough estimates for all tasks.

Furthermore the planer has to assign responsible agents to each of the tasks specified by the process steps in the project plan. He wants to do this for a design task for which he has not yet chosen a method. Existing alternatives are 'UML' and 'SDL'. He accesses the agent assignment UI within the MILOS project planer component for the design task. As the project planer is fairly new in his job and the department, he requires information whether any agents are working in the department which have experience in one of these methods. The Information Assistant provides an INO within the information category 'agent assignment' which models this information need represented as "Which agents have experience with 'UML' or 'SDL'?". The question is coupled with the retrieval on a skill database for agents, which yields a list of agents with the required skills. He can see that for both methods agents are employed in the department. He decides to use 'UML' as he personally has used this method before and is convinced of its quality. Due to this decision, his current work context changes as the method decision for the design task gets the value 'UML'. This is propagated to the Information Assistant which updates his list of INOs. The general question about experienced agents for all two methods is not longer required as a decision has been made.

Since he has already provided start and end dates for the design task, he is now interested in agents which have experience with 'UML' and are available in the given time frame. Thus he uses an according question from the Information Assistant to query the schedule database for available agents, checking only those agents that have been retrieved as agents with UML skills.

The project planer knows from formerly planned projects that another method for design is 'OMT'. Besides the planning for the current project he is interested if any agents in the new department have experience with this method. As 'OMT' is not a defined method in the process model he has received from the PM experience base, the Information Assistant does not offer support for this question. But as the retrieval for 'UML' and 'SDL' has been done on a skill database, he uses the Assistant to access the query engine interface of this information source. Now he defines his own query to search for agents with 'OMT' experience and launches it. As he thinks this information need might occur again in the future (maybe even the 'OMT' method can be modeled as additional method in the process model) he starts the INO Manager within MILOS and adds a corresponding INO to the INO list of the 'Design' process into the information category 'Agent assignment'. From now on, this INO appears whenever someone uses the support concept while doing agent assignment for the 'Design' task.

Likewise, as with the agent assignment for the 'Design' task, the project planner proceeds with the remaining tasks in the project plan.

Agents that participate in the project can access individual workspaces provided by the MILOS workflow engine. The project planer has assigned a task 'Implement WFE component' during project planning to the agent 'Alice' and, accordingly, this task appears in her to-do list (see Fig. 6 for an illustration of the to-do list UI).

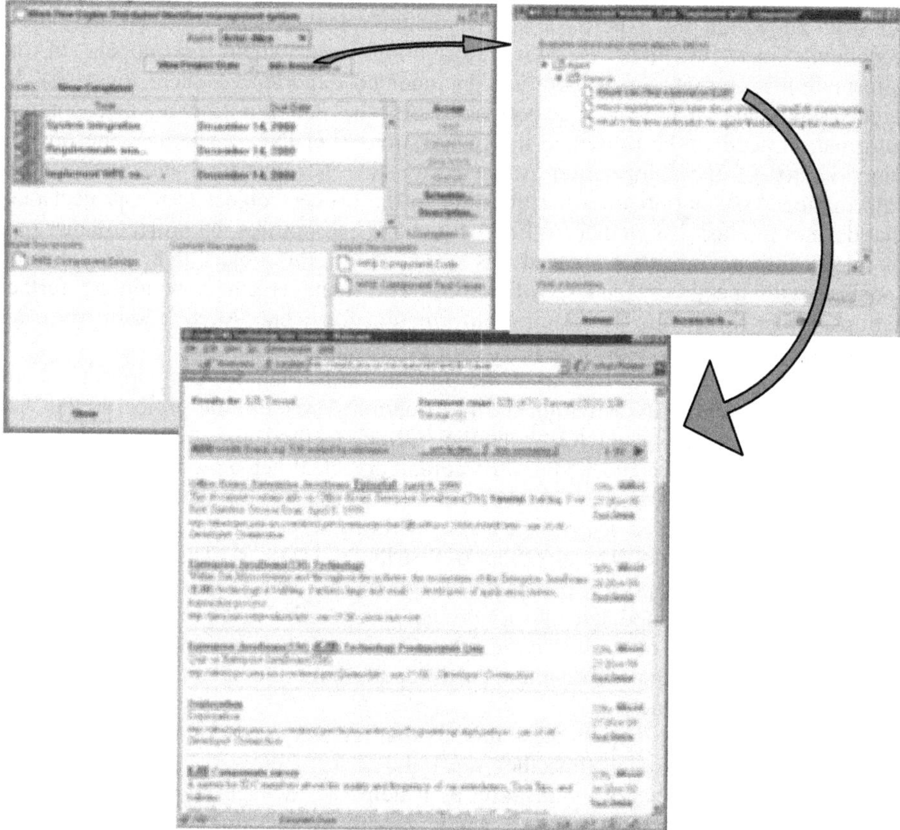

Fig. 6. INO execution to find an EJB tutorial: agent "Alice" has selected the question "Where can I find a tutorial on EJB?" in the Information Assistant (left picture). After she has pressed the 'Answer' button at the bottom, a browser opens and presents her a list of links which have been retrieved from the Javasoft homepage to the topic "EJB Tutorial". She can now refer to the hyperlinks to access the information items

The workspace allows her to browse the information associated with each task, e.g., scheduling information or the input and output products that have been specified in the project plan and are listed in the lower part of the window when she selects a task.

When she starts working on the task 'Implement WFE component' she runs into a problem while trying to implement an EJB. She remembers that this once has been explained to her in a tutorial. She launches the Information Assistant again and identifies her question "Where can I find a tutorial on EJB?" in the presented list, which is exactly what she is looking for. She selects the INO and executes the retrieval (as shown in Fig. 6) to receive a list of items found on the Javasoft homepage which has been known as a good source by the one who modeled the INO. She follows the hyperlink to the EJB tutorial, in order to refresh her knowledge while following the tutorial steps.

A further look in the Information Assistant window guides her to the question "Which experience has been documented for Java/EJB implementation?". She does not even know that any experience is documented related to that, but seemingly these documents exist as otherwise this information need would not appear in the Information Assistant. Since there are documented experiences, there must also be agents who have made these experiences. As she can not find a corresponding information need in the presented list of questions (i.e. INOs), she uses the posting functionality of the Information Assistant to state her question and post it. The Information Assistant attaches the question to the process object in the project plan that defines the task 'Implement WFE component' and notifies the project planer (i.e. manager) that an information need has occurred for this object that has not been satisfied with the given INO specifications. The manager can now initiate further actions, either to provide the required information for agent 'Alice' and/or to model this information need as a persistent INO for future support.

In summary, besides having used the provided information need support via the execution of modeled INOs within the Information Assistant, the project planer has modeled at least one new INO about the 'OMT' method and Alice has posted a question which has been attached to project plan object. When a project is finished the process model can be written back into the MILOS library. Using this technique the newly modeled INOs and the posted questions become persistent in the PM library, here in the process model 'Development of distributed systems'. They are available in the future every time a project planer reuses this model for a project plan. The posted questions need to be modeled into a completely specified INO (e.g. coupled to an information source) to be usable in the future. Before that, they serve as a marker for an INO modeler that an information need occurred for the specific process model object to which it is attached.

Using this feedback loop, process models that are frequently used and maintained provide better support each time they are tailored for a project. The approach thus creates a learning software organisation as it helps to package required information and to provide it at the right time (i.e. while planning or enacting a particular task) to the right agent.

5 Related Work

Related work comes mainly from two areas: Software Process Improvement and Knowledge Management. We first discuss software process improvement and we analyze some KM approaches.

Most process improvement approaches, e.g. capability maturity model, require describing the development processes more or less formally. Within the framework of software process modeling, several languages were developed that allow for describing software development activities formally ([15], [6], [2])

Software process models represent knowledge about software development. They describe activities to be carried out in software development as well as the products to be created and the resources & tools used. These models can be a basis for continuous organizational learning as well as the actual basis for the coordination and the management of the software engineering activities.

Software process modeling and enactment is one of the main areas in software engineering research. Several frameworks have been developed (e.g. procedural [15], rule-based ([11],[16]), Petri net based [3], object-oriented [5].

Managing software process knowledge is also the goal of the experience factory approach [4]. They distinguish between the organizational structure to manage the software knowledge (the experience factory department) and the activities that have to be carried out to build an experience factory.

Knowledge management and organizational memory is currently a hot topic in research (for example, see ([7], [18]). The use of case-based reasoning technology for experience management in software engineering is discussed in [1]. Their approach is not directly linked to project execution support and therefore fails in providing an operational feedback loop between project execution and organizational learning. Their approach could be easily integrated with MILOS by pointing our CBR queries to their system.

The expert system group at the German DFKI is also following a process-centered approach to knowledge management. Their tool is based on a business process modeling approach and is, compared to MILOS, fairly inflexible at enactment time: changing the process by simply replanning the project with a COTS tool is not supported. On the other hand, their approach is based on domain ontologies [12] that allow for a semantic-oriented information retrieval.

Ontology-based retrieval is also investigated by [8]. Ontology-based KM approaches are not providing a process-centered approach and therefore require the user to specify queries for a given task (whereas MILOS can provide users with predefined queries for tasks). A similar argument holds for hypertext-based approaches (e.g. [9]): they do not provide task-oriented access to knowledge but force the user to navigate to it.

6 Conclusion

In this paper we described our approach for supporting learning software organizations. The MILOS system is an Internet-based process-centered knowledge management environment that structures knowledge around development processes.

Linked to a process, the user can find methods (describing ways how to perform the process to reach its goals), products (input and outputs to the process), knowledge about the qualifications needed to perform the process and knowledge about typical information needs, together with ways to satisfy them.

The process-centered structure of the system has the following advantages:

Processes are “natural“ entities for managers and team members: they are well used to thinking in processes (e.g. for project planning).

For their daily work, people don’t need knowledge per-se but knowledge for performing specific tasks. A process-centered knowledge management system associates explicitly the task with the knowledge needed for it.

By linking relevant information sources and generic queries to task, the "lost in hyperspace" problem is reduced because the user is actively guided to available knowledge needed instead of being forced to somehow find relevant information on his own.

The feedback cycle creates a learning software organization: our approach allows to package "good" elements of successful project plans into reusable process models and, hence, supports the implementation of a continuous process improvement strategy for software companies.

In Section 1, we mentioned that we are aiming at an improved efficiency of an organization's process group. Whereas undoubtedly the introduction of new tools at first results in an increased workload, we argue that, in the long run, the proposed Information Assistant will relief the process group from answering standard questions in the same way as help-desk applications already have proven to do in other domains (e.g. trouble-shooting for technical devices). We expect he Information Assistant to provide answers to the users' standard questions (especially to those of new employees), so that the human experts in the process group need only be consulted for new, more difficult problems.

In order to collect first experiences with the approach presented here, we intend to apply it within our own software development projects (e.g. master theses). Whereas the coordination aspect often can be neglected in these personal processes, a lot of knowledge about the MILOS implementation, its design and concepts (both past and future) is typically required, making it very difficult for new students to get started with their work.

Acknowledgements. The work on MILOS was supported by the DFG (as part of SFB 501: "Development of large systems with generic methods"), NSERC, The University Of Calgary, and Nortel with several research grants. We would like to thank Sigrid Goldmann and Martin Schaaf for their valuable input, and tec:inno - empolis knowledge management division[3] for providing us with their CBR middleware 'Orenge'.

References

1 Althoff, K.-D. & Bomarius, F. & Tautz, C. (1998). Using Case-Based Reasoning Technology to Build Learning Software Organizations. In Proceedings of the 1st Interdisciplinary Workshop on Building, Maintaining, and Using Organizational Memories (OM-98), 13th European Conference on AI (ECAI'98), Brighton, http:// SunSITE.Informatik.RWTH-Aachen.DE/Publications/CEUR-WS/Vol-14/

2. Armitage, J., and Kellner, M. (1994). A conceptual schema for process definitions and models. In D. E. Perry, editor, Proc. of the Third Int. Conf. on the Software Process, IEEE Computer Society Press.
3. Bandinelli, S., Fuggetta, A., and Grigolli, S. (1993). Process Modeling-in-the-large with SLANG. In IEEE Proceedings of the 2nd Int. Conf. on the Software Process, Berlin (Germany).
4. Basili, V. R., Caldiera, G., and Rombach, H. D. (1994). Experience Factory. In Encyclopedia of Software Engineering (J. J. Marciniak, ed.), vol. 1, John Wiley Sons.

[3] www.tecinno.de

5. Conradi, R., Hagaseth, M., Larsen, J. O., Nguyen, M., Munch, G., Westby, P., and Zhu, W. (1994). EPOS: Object-Oriented and Cooperative Process Modeling. In PROMOTER book: Anthony Finkelstein, Jeff Kramer and Bashar A. Nuseibeh (Eds.): Software Process Modeling and Technology, 1994. Advanced Software Development Series, Research Studies Press Ltd. (John Wiley).
6. Curtis, B., Kellner, M., and Over, J. (1992). Process modeling. Comm. of the ACM, 35(9): 75–90.
7. Davenport, T.H. & Jarvenpaa, S.L. & Beers, M.C. (1997). Sloan Management Review, 37 (4):53-65, Improving Knowledge Work Processes,1997.
8. Decker, S., Erdmann, M., Fensel, D., and Studer, R.(1999). Ontobroker: Ontology Based Access to Distributed and Semi-Structured Information. In R. Meersman et al. (eds.), Semantic Issues in Multimedia Systems, Kluwer Academic Publisher, Boston.
9. Euzenat, J. (1996). Corporate Memory through Cooperative Creation of Knowledge Bases and Hyper-documents. In Proceedings of the 10th Knowledge Acquisition, Modeling and Management for Knowledge-based Systems Workshop (KAW'96), Banff.
10. P.K. Garg, M. Jazayeri: *"Process-centered Software Engineering Environments"*. IEEE Cumputer Society Press, 1996.
11. Kaiser, G. E., Feiler, P. H., and Popovich, S. S. (1988). Intelligent Assistance for Software Development and Maintenance, IEEE Software.
12. Kühn, O. & Abecker, A. (1997). Corporate Memories for Knowledge Management in Industrial Practice: Prospects and Challenges. In Journal of Universal Computer Science 3, 8, Special Issue on Information Technology for Knowledge Management, Springer Science Online. URL: http://www.iicm.edu/jucs_3_8/ corporate_memories_for_knowledge.
13. Maurer, F., Dellen, B, Bendeck, F., Goldmann, S., Holz, H., Kötting, B., Schaaf, M.: *"Merging Project Planning and Web-Enabled Dynamic Workflow Technologies"*. IEEE Internet Computing May/June 2000, pp. 65-74.
14. Mahe, S. and Rieu, C.; Towards a Pull-Approach of KM for Improving Enterprise Flexibility Responsiveness: A Necessary First Step for Introducing Knowledge Management in Small and Medium Enterprises. In: Proceedings of the International Symposium on Management of Industrial and Corporate Knowledge (ISMICK '97), Compiegne, 1997.
15. Osterweil, L. (1987). Software Processes are Software Too. In: Proc. of the Ninth Int. Conf. of Software Engineering, Monterey CA, pp. 2-13.
16. Peuschel, P., Schäfer, W., and Wolf, S. (1992). A Knowledge-based Software Development Environment Supporting Cooperative Work. In: Int. Journal on Software Engineering and Knowledge Engineering, 2(1).
17. Verlage, M., Dellen, B., Maurer, F., and Münch, J. (1996). A synthesis of two software process support approaches. In Proceedings 8th Software & Engineering and Knowledge Engineering (SEKE-96), USA.
18. Wielinga ,B.J. & Sandberg, J. & Schreiber, G. (1997). Methods and Techniques for Knowledge Management: What has Knowledge Engineering to Offer, Expert Systems with Applications 13, 1, 73-84.
19. Dellen, B., Kohler, K., and Maurer, F. (1996). Integrating Software Process Models and Design Rationales. In: Proc. of Knowledge-Based Software Engineering Conference (KBSE-96), IEEE press.

Computer-Supported Reuse of Project Management Experience with an Experience Base

Matthias Brandt[1] and Markus Nick[2]

[1]Universität Leipzig, Wirtschaftswissenschaftliche Fakultät, Institut für Wirtschaftsinformatik, Marschner Strasse 31, D-04229 Leipzig, Germany
brandt@wifa.uni-leipzig.de

[2] Fraunhofer IESE, Department of Systematic Learning and Improvement (SLI), Sauerwiesen 6, D-67661 Kaiserslautern, Germany
nick@iese.fhg.de

Abstract. Numerous studies show that the deficit of IT employees with project management (PM) skills will increase in the next few years. As a countermeasure, companies have to make the knowledge of their experts in PM explicit in order to support a continuous organizational learning process and to reuse the experiences of these experts. In this paper, we present the newly designed approach COPER for computer-supported reuse of project management experiences, which considers aspects of systematically recording, structuring, and distributing such experiences. COPER is based on tailoring the DISER methodology for the development of experience management systems in software engineering to the PM domain. We realize this adaptation on the basis of the PMBOK® Guide to the Project Management Body of Knowledge developed at PMI, which is internationally accepted as IEEE standard (1490-1998). The result is a methodology for the acquisition, modeling, and reuse of project experiences customized to the PM domain.

Keywords: reuse of project management experiences, experience-repository-based organizational learning, experience factory, case-based reasoning

1 Introduction

There is a general agreement today that increasing individualization of business performance and business processes is the reason for the assimilation of routine-oriented business processes to the classic project model (e.g., [10]). Furthermore, many activities, e.g., regarding e-business/e-commerce trends, are performed as project work.

Due to the rapid growth of organizations (in particular in the software engineering domain), the number of people with long and extensive experiences in daily project work is small and insufficient. Nowadays, project management skills are a crucial factor in job placements. Numerous studies (e.g., [11]) have shown that specialists in this field are desperately needed. For example, the deficit of IT employees in Germany is estimated at 300,000 open positions for the next few years [7].

To deal with these problems, better project management training before the job has to be ensured first. Nowadays, numerous universities consider this and provide project

K.-D. Althoff, R.L. Feldmann, and W. Müller (Eds.): LSO 2001, LNCS 2176, pp. 178-189, 2001.

management courses in their curricula. Further PM training courses are established. They are offered by different institutions that train and certify qualified specialists (e.g., in Germany: GPM - Education to "Project Management Specialist"; international: PMI - "The Project Management Institute Certification Program"). Additionally, the application of the acquired skills can be supported by tools (e.g., SUMMIT Ascendant from Price Waterhouse Coopers, PMOffice from Systemcorp).

In a second step - learning on the job – companies must ensure that the knowledge of their experts in project management is made available, that reuse of this knowledge by members of other projects is possible, and that -at the same time- a continuous organizational learning process is supported. That is, the experiences of the experts (from individual learning processes) must be made available for learning processes within projects on project team level and across projects on company level.

For this purpose, these tacit experiences (which are only "stored" in the head of an expert) should be systematically recorded, structured, and distributed. All this is not a simple task (e.g., [15]), but it is possible, as reports from practice show [14]. Therefore, the Experience Factory approach (from software engineering domain) can be used [2].

The Experience Factory (EF) is a separate organizational unit that manages corporate knowledge and experience. An EF includes as its core element an experience base (EB), which is a repository for all kinds of project information (e.g., project plans, process descriptions) and experiences that are related to project work. Experiences are transformed into "experience packages". These packages are made available for reuse. Examples of such experience packages are process reference models, causes of errors and reasons for modifications, lessons learned, or quality models. Fig. 1 shows that the PM experience base (PM-EB) is helpful for the improvement of the PM practices and how the PM-EB supports the exchange of experience regarding these practices.

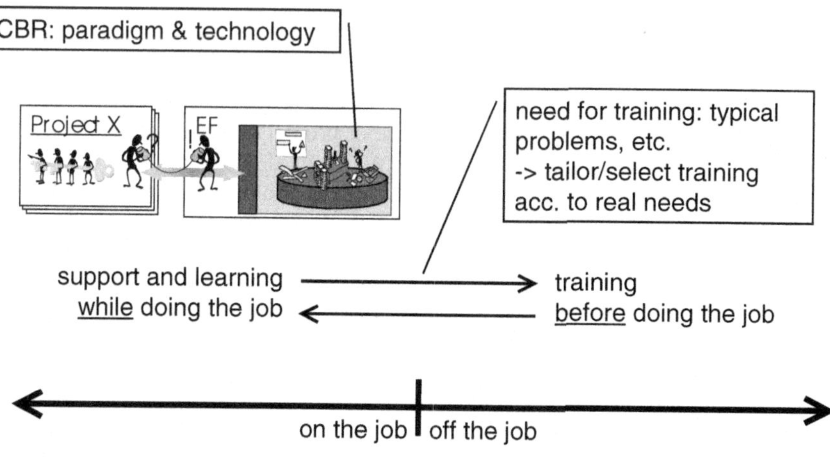

Fig. 1. The relationship of training and experience factory

However, the application of an EB for computer-supported reuse of project management experience can require high development effort for such a PM-EB if the PM-EB is developed from the scratch. Such a development from scratch can lead to an effort-benefit unbalance, which is mostly a knock out criterion for the buildup of such a PM-EB in a company.

Therefore, after a short presentation of general aspects of the reuse of experience in project management (Section 2), we present in this paper our approach COPER (Components for Project Management Experience Repositories), which can be useful to reduce such a expensive development process of company-specific PM-EBs by providing components of the conceptual knowledge model for reuse (Section 3). The result of our approach is a reference model for PM-EBs, which is currently under construction and has been validated in parts of Fraunhofer IESE's Corporate Information Network (COIN). This reference model for a project management experience base (PM-EB) forms the core of this paper. This model integrates a method for experience base (EB) development from software engineering and an internationally accepted PM standard (IEEE 1490-1998). Furthermore, we describe the steps in the development of this reference model. Finally, the paper closes with a summary (Section 4).

2 Procedure of Reuse of Experience in Project Management and Relevant Supporting Technologies

Although projects can be very different, the reuse of experience usually follows the same principle during project work. Before a new project starts, past experiences or lessons learned and a few similar projects are identified. These experiences are retrieved and adapted for the situation where the experiences are reused. The result of this reuse is checked for correctness and efficiency and (if needed) revised. At the end of a project, the newly gained knowledge is stored, characterized, qualified, and disseminated. In addition, the new knowledge is analyzed with respect to relevance for further or new knowledge areas, which can be made available for reuse by the company as well as by the project stakeholders [9]. This procedure has to be considered within a computer-supported reuse of project management experiences.

For this purpose, isolated approaches (e.g., method databases, checklists, expert systems) as well as project-libraries or experience bases can be used [4], but it is a well-known fact that there is an increasing tendency towards Project Information Systems (PIS) as well as Knowledge Management (KM) Systems for project work [9]. Numerous companies have developed or are developing such systems (e.g., Andersen Consulting: Knowledge Xchange; IBM: ICM AssetWeb; SAP: Knowledge Management with mySAP.com; Lotus: Lotus Development Server/K-Station/Knowledge Discovery System). Different knowledge management tools can be used within these systems. The technologies on which the knowledge management tools are based are of special interest because they have great influence on the performance of the respective knowledge management application. Nowadays, technologies from artificial intelligence (e.g., knowledge discovery in databases or case-based reasoning) are more and more in use because of their potential.

Case-based reasoning (CBR), in particular, is well suited as basic technology for computer-supported reuse of project management experiences. Numerous applications have shown the potential of CBR for parts of the PM domain (e.g., [6], [4]). One reason for using CBR is the similarity between the well-known CBR cycle [1] and the experience reuse procedure in project management. Another fact is that the concept of organizational learning based on an EF (see Section 1) is similar to the CBR cycle (see, e.g., the CBR-QIP comparison in [13]) and, therefore, can be supported by CBR technology (e.g., [12], [8]). At the technical level, requirements for tool support have been defined and technologies such as relational database systems, object-relational database systems, and CBR systems have been evaluated regarding their suitability for supporting experience management ([12], [3]). Both studies conclude that CBR is the most suitable technology.

3 Development of a Reference Model for Project Management Experience Bases

This section describes the reference model for PM-EBs in detail. First, we illustrate the term PM experiences with examples (Section 3.1). Then the basic elements of the reference model are described (Section 3.2). Using these elements, an overview on the contents of the reference model is given (Section 3.3). In addition, we outline how the contents of our reference model can be used for the buildup and improvement of PM-EBs. Finally, we describe how the reference model is built up stepwise.

3.1 Project Management Experiences

Following the EF approach, we assume that project management knowledge (knowledge in a project, knowledge about projects, knowledge from a project) in the form of processes, products, and technologies is enriched by explicit experience cases (e.g., explicitly documented lessons that were learned during the practical application of the knowledge). There are many kinds of experiences in PM (e.g., reports, process descriptions, lessons learned) that are connected to special aspects (e.g., associated business or project process, project description, project staff).

Fig. 2 shows an excerpt of an experience base on project management with lessons learned and business process descriptions as experience cases and their relationships. The lessons learned are represented in the form of guidelines, observations, and problems [12]. The guidelines act as solutions or mitigation strategies for the problems. An observation describes the results of an application of a guideline.

3.2 Basic Elements of the Reference Model

The idea of developing a reference model for project management experience bases (PM-EB) was triggered by (1) the existence of an internationally accepted standard for PM knowledge (IEEE 1490-1998) and (2) the research concerning PM-EBs at the Fraunhofer Institute for Experimental Software Engineering (IESE). Within the IESE research activities, a methodology for the systematic development of EB (DISER - Design and Implementation of Software Engineering Repositories) was developed [12], which can be used as a basis for the reference model.

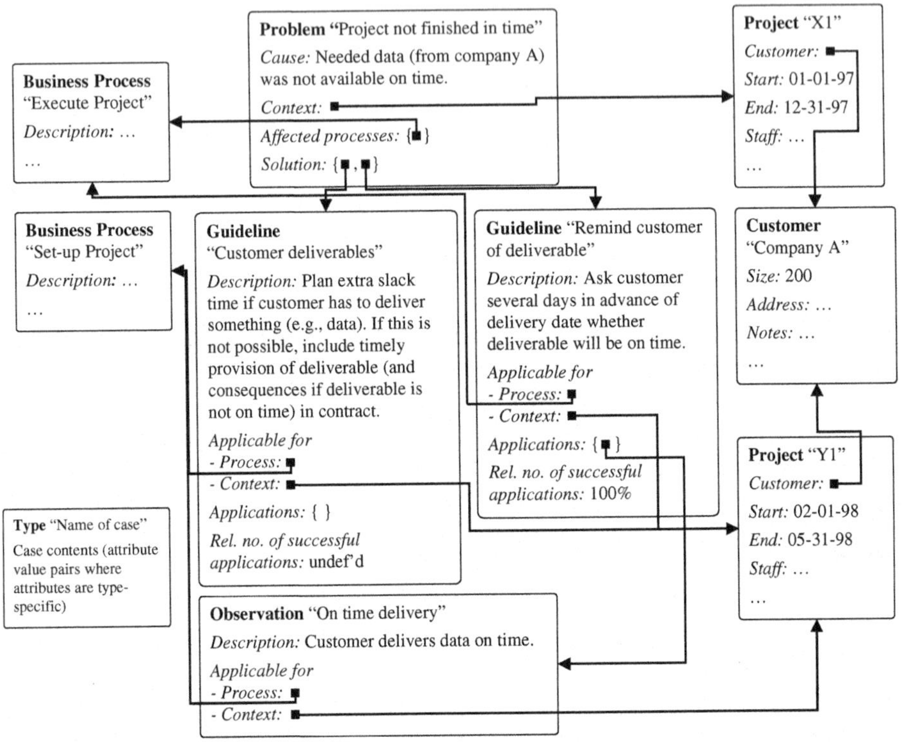

Fig. 2. Examples of experience cases and their connections

3.2.1 Experience Base Buildup Method

Using the DISER method, the systematic buildup of an experience base is performed in six main steps.

A vision of a *business model* (with focus on the aspect of the usage and production of knowledge and experiences) represents the starting point. This model shows, in particular, where the EF/EB can support the experience transfer. Based on this vision *concrete objectives* are defined, which are to be achieved by the EF. For the definition of the objectives, the interests of the stakeholders have to be considered. For each of these objectives, appropriate success criteria are defined, which allow measuring the progress concerning the objectives. Based on the business model and objectives, *relevant subject areas* are identified and selected, which are expected to contribute to the achievement of the objectives. As soon as objectives and relevant subject areas are known, acquisition and usage of experiences can be described with *scenarios*. In the context of the scenarios, the need for information is identified in more detail. This allows to develop a *conceptual model* for the experiences. In the last step, the knowledge acquisition is planned in detail and described in a *knowledge acquisition plan*.

A development using DISER creates a schematic top-down documentation for the implementation concept (i.e., conceptual model and knowledge acquisition plan). We call such a documentation *rationale*. Such a *rationale* documents the relationships of the components of the conceptual model and knowledge acquisition plan via scenarios and relevant subject areas to objectives and business model and makes the relationships traceable. Comprehensive documentation of these aspects is also the basis for reuse of the information on the aspects in the development and extension of EBs.

3.2.2 Project Management Body of Knowledge (PMBOK®) – A Standard for PM Knowledge (IEEE 1490-1998)

The experience stored in an EB is obviously in the context of the respective domain for which the EB is to be developed. Due to the complexity of the domain PM as well as specific conditions in individual companies, numerous standardization measures were performed concerning PM. Further general regulations were developed, which represent an overview on the substantial PM knowledge [16]. One summary that is also internationally accepted is the Project Management Body of Knowledge (PMBOK), published by the Project Management Institute (PMI). The PMBOK has the character of a standard in the USA and is one basis of the PM training in other countries as well. Based on the PMBOK , the PMI published the *PMBOK® Guide to the Project Management Body of Knowledge* [5] (subsequently called PMBOK Guide), which is standardized as IEEE standard (1490-1998). The primary purpose of the PMBOK Guide is to identify and describe the subset of the PMBOK that is generally accepted. Generally accepted means that the knowledge and practices described are applicable to most projects most of the time, and that there is widespread consensus about their value and usefulness. Generally accepted does not mean that the knowledge and practices described are or should be applied uniformly to all projects; the PM team is always responsible for determining what is appropriate for any given project [5].

The PMBOK Guide is also intended to provide a common lexicon within the profession of PM and can therefore also be used as the basis for the development of a PM-EB.

3.3 Our Vision: COPER - A Reference Model for PM-EBs

3.3.1 What Is COPER and What Is the Content of COPER ?

Our research efforts aim at developing a reference model for PM-specific EBs or the PM-specific parts of more general EBs (see Fig. 3). We call this reference model COPER (Components for Project Management Experience Repositories). COPER is based on tailoring the DISER methodology for the development of experience management systems in software engineering to the PM domain. This tailoring considers the PMBOK Guide (see also Section 3.2). The contents of COPER are structured using DISER's EB development steps accordingly, as presented in Section 3.2.1. COPER consists of five parts: (1) a business model that describes the relationship of the PM-EB and PMBOK project process; (2) a generic PM-EB consisting of parts of a conceptual model and retrieval goals; (3) information on the PM-EB development aspects (objectives, subject areas, detailed scenarios, knowledge acquisition techniques); (4) the rationale formed in the development; and (5) a "cookbook" on how to use the contents of COPER to build up a new EB or improve an existing EB (see right part of Fig. 3).

3.3.2 What Is the Purpose of COPER?

The reference model COPER will allow to develop "better" PM-EBs faster and easier. Our existing experiences with the development of an EB – e.g., (1) EB for software developers in a large insurance company, (2) EB in telecom sector, (3) EB for software/software engineering consultants in a large bank, (4) COIN at the Fraunhofer IESE – showed that EB development is complex and therefore a reference model like COPER can be useful.

This is made possible by the comprehensive reuse of suitable know-how from the development of COPER and other PM-EB projects. Comprehensive reuse means that all aspects regarding the development (e.g., objectives, relevant topics, scenarios, conceptual model) as well as the corresponding rationale can be reused. Based on the rationale, it is possible to detect which further elements of a later step could be interesting (depending on decisions made in an earlier step). For example, it is possible to analyze scenarios on specific topics of the reference model concerning

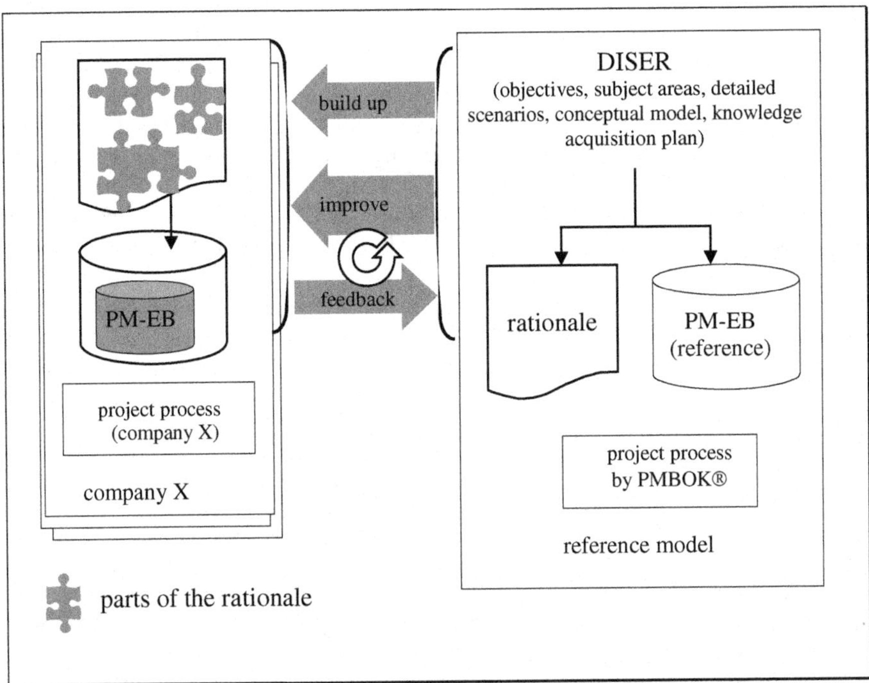

Fig. 3. An overview of the vision

their relevance for a company-specific EB installation. Based on the scenarios, one can detect which parts of the conceptual model in the reference model are needed for a company-specific EB installation.

3.3.3 How to Use COPER?

As a reference model, COPER covers the most important PM knowledge areas where reuse of experience is of special interest. For these knowledge areas, COPER provides patterns for a PM-EB that is developed for a company. Using COPER, we analyze if and how the project process of the company corresponds with the project process from the PMBOK® Guide. This mapping allows to identify the relevant PM knowledge areas. Using the mapping, the potentially relevant parts of the reference model can be identified (e.g., a specific part of the conceptual model, the respective rationale, single aspects of the development). These parts can be reused in the development of the company-specific PM-EB (see left part of Fig. 3).

3.3.4 Why and How to Improve COPER?

COPER must be improved and revised continuously. Improvement/revision can become necessary because, e.g., new insights in project management research or feedback from the application of COPER to the development of PM-EBs.

For the improvement and revision of COPER, a so-called improvement feedback loop is established. This feedback loop helps (1) collect experience on the applicability of COPER for the PM-EB buildup in a specific company, and (2) get feedback about the usage and efficiency of a PM-EB that was developed using COPER. Finally, this feedback has to be considered for the improvement and revision of COPER (see middle of Fig. 3).

3.4 The Stepwise Development of COPER

The contents of COPER -as described in Section 3.3.1- are developed stepwise. This addresses (1) the development of a business model that contains information on the relationships of PM-EB and PMBOK project process and (2) the development of a generic PM-EB using a tailored DISER methodology. Besides the generic PM-EB, this development also results in information on all aspects of the EB development as well as the corresponding rationale (see also 3.2.1 and 3.3.1). In the following, we give an overview on the steps in the development of COPER.

As a first step, we analyzed the PM domain for which the generic PM-EB of COPER is being developed. This analysis is based on the general PM knowledge areas, which are described in the PMBOK Guide. This analysis resulted in a model that represents the relations among the individual PM processes (see Fig. 4 and Table 1). We use this model to find out which aspects the experiences can refer to and how the knowledge is represented (e.g., work breakdown structure, collection of facts). Based on this we develop the business model of COPER.

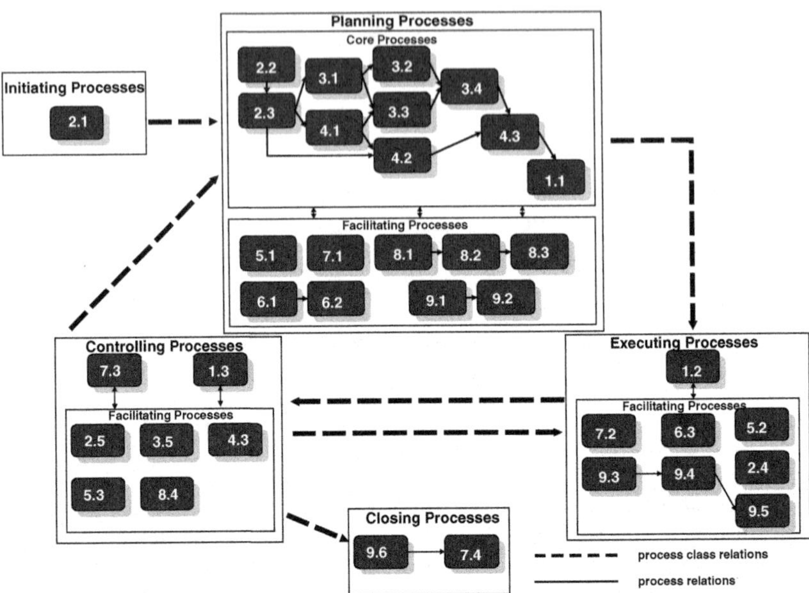

Fig. 4. Relations between the individual PM processes (following [5]). The numbers refer to the PM processes listed in Table 1.

Table 1. Overview of PM knowledge areas and PM processes (see [5])

PM knowledge areas	PM processes
1. Project Integration Management	1.1 Project Plan Development, 1.2 Project Plan Execution, 1.3 Overall Change Control
2.Project Scope Management	2.1 Initiation, 2.2 Scope Planning, 2.3 Scope Definition 2.4 Scope Verification, 2.5 Scope Change Control
3.Project Time Management	3.1 Activity Definition, 3.2 Activity Sequencing, 3.3 Activity Duration Estimating, 3.4 Schedule Development 3.5 Schedule Control
4.Project Cost Management	4.1 Resource Planning, 4.2 Cost Estimating, 4.3 Cost Budgeting, 4.4 Cost Control
5.Project Quality Management	5.1 Quality Planning, 5.2 Quality Assurance, 5.3 Quality Control
6.Project Human Resource Management	6.1 Organizational Planning, 6.2 Staff Acquisition, 6.3 Team Development
7.Project Communications Management	7.1 Communication Planning, 7.2 Information Distribution, 7.3 Performance Reporting, 7.4 Administrative Closure
8.Project Risk Management	8.1 Risk Identification, 8.2 Risk Quantification, 8.3 Risk Response Development, 8.4 Risk Response Control
9.Project Procurement Management	9.1 Procurement Planning, 9.2 Solicitation Planning 9.3 Solicitation, 9.4 Source Selection, 9.5 Contract Administration, 9.6 Contract Close-out

In this step, we also identified the relevant knowledge areas in which the reuse of experience can solve certain problems. We describe these problems or classes of problems and their relationship to the respective knowledge area and PM process. We derive related objectives and subject areas for the generic PM-EB. Table 2 illustrates this for an exemplary problem from the PM knowledge area cost management.

Table 2. Possible results of the first step (excerpt)

Knowledge Area: **Related PM Process:**	Project Cost Management Cost Estimation
Problem - situation: - description:	 Numerous cost estimation methods can be used in the early phase of the project Inaccuracy of cost estimation result due to dependence on the used estimation method and the input data.
Objective - description: - success criteria:	 Support of a more accurate cost estimation Average error computed lower than 30 %, result accepted by stakeholder
Subject Area	Experiences concerning the use of cost estimation methods at given project description (incl. available input data for the cost estimation)

In the next step, we define scenarios for knowledge reuse and acquisition with focus on the specific subject area. These are refined to specific retrieval goals (see DISER: *detailed scenarios*). Table 3 shows an example of such a scenario.

Respective parts of the conceptual model for the representation of PM-specific experiences are developed (see DISER: *conceptual model*).

Table 3. Example of a reuse scenario

Scenario: Use of cost estimation methods in the development of standard software	
Retrieval Goal	*Retrieve* guidelines, problems, and observations on cost estimation methods *for the purpose of* finding recommendations, comments, and notes *from the viewpoint of* the project manager *in the context of* making a cost estimation for the project at hand.
Trigger (When to use the EB?)	• When you want/have to make an offer during project acquisition • When project planning starts – scope definition and resource planning has finished (see Fig. 4) – and you want/have to perform a cost estimation
Actions	1. Using the EB you identify relevant guidelines and observations. Your search is based on the characterization of the current project (including the project scope, resource requirements, cost drivers – like products attributes, computer attributes, human attributes - , and project attributes) 2. Based on these guidelines and observations, decide which cost estimation method should be used in the project at hand. Note, if these experiences do not contain sufficient information to make a decision, then ask the EF team or the author of the experience. In addition, provide respective feedback to the EF team on problems with these experiences. 3. Use the "best" cost estimation method for the project at hand.

Finally, the knowledge acquisition (see DISER: *knowledge acquisition plan*) has to be planned. This concerns (1) the definition of the project processes or phases in which the knowledge acquisition should take place, and (2) the description of the respective acquisition steps. Fig. 5 shows – as an example - an acquisition process based on project analysis interviews, where the experiences are collected and summarized in a project analysis report. After review by the project team, the project analysis report is split into the actual experiences, which are then stored in the EB.

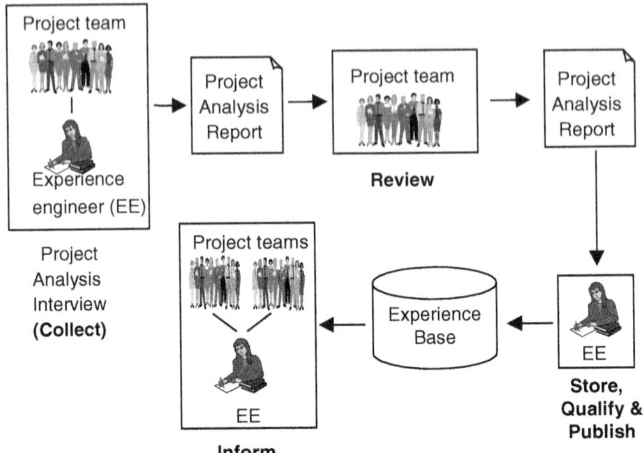

Fig. 5. Experience acquisition with project analysis interviews

3.5 Existing Results and the Validation of COPER in COIN

The Fraunhofer IESE project process forms the starting point of the validation of COPER in COIN. First we analyzed the matching between the IESE project process and our designed model that represents the relations among the individual PM processes (see Section 3.4) and which we use to find out which aspects the experiences can refer to. Within this analysis (IESE project process and the content of COIN), we have verified that COIN already includes a certain number of subject areas of COPER. We also use experiences of IESE in project work (1) to detect other relevant subject areas in which the reuse of PM-experiences is important and (2) improve the business model of COPER.

A number of scenarios for knowledge reuse and acquisition were designed at Fraunhofer IESE (see [12]). The scenarios are represented using the structure as shown in the example in Table 3. Currently, a more general scenario is implemented in COIN. We are creating additional scenarios, which are more aligned to specific PM processes (e.g., processes of cost management, processes of risk management) - within COPER. A detailed summary of the scenarios for COPER is being created during research activities at the university of Leipzig.

Finally, we use project analysis interviews (see Fig. 5) as technique for acquiring project management experiences for COIN's experience base.

4 Summary

In this paper, we have presented the newly designed approach COPER for computer-supported reuse of project management (PM) experience. COPER is based on tailoring the DISER methodology for the development of experience management systems in software engineering to the PM domain. We realized this adaptation on the basis of the PMBOK® Guide to the Project Management Body of Knowledge, internationally accepted as IEEE standard (1490-1998), which was developed at PMI [5]. The result is a methodology for the acquisition, modeling, and reuse of project experiences that is customized to the PM domain.

First experiences with COPER have been gained in the Corporate Information Network (COIN) project at the Fraunhofer Institute for Experimental Software Engineering. In this project, which has been running since January 2000, aspects of reuse of PM experiences are the focus of the research activities. Within an experiment for a typical planning situation, it was shown that the reuse of PM experiences supported by a case-based experience base system was more effective than manual activities like meetings or asking colleagues [12, p.285 f.].

Current work includes the further development of the knowledge model of COPER as well as the evaluation of the COIN system.

References

[1] Aamodt, A.; Plaza, E.: Case-Based Reasoning: Foundational Issues, Methodological Variations, and System Approaches. In: AI-Communications, Vol. 7, No. 1, 1994, S.39-59.

[2] Basili, V.R.; Caldiera, G.; Rombach, D.: Experience Factory; In Marciniak, J.J. ed., Encyclopedia of Software Engineering, vol 1, 469–476; John Wiley & Sons; 1994.

[3] Broomé, M.; Runeson, P.: Technical Requirements for the Implementation of an Experience Base. In Proceedings of the 11th International Conference on Software Engineering & Knowledge Engineering. Knowledge Systems Institute, Skokie, IL, 1999.

[4] Dornhoff, P.: Erfahrungswissen für das Management von Software-Entwicklungsprojekten. Reihe: Wirtschaftsinformatik, Band 4, Bergisch Gladbach 1993.

[5] Ducan, W. R.: A Guide to the Project Management Body of Knowledge, Project Management Institute, Upper Darby, PA, 1996.

[6] Kadoda, G.; Cartwright, M.; Chen, L.; Shepperd, M.: Experiences Using Case-Based Reasoning to Predict Software Project Effort, ESERG : Empirical Software Engineering Research Group at Bournemouth University, Technical Reports, TR00-01.

[7] Kossbiel, H.; Mülder, W.; Oberweis, A.: IT und Personal. In: Wirtschaftsinformatik Sonderheft (2000) Oktober , S. 7-8.

[8] Nick, M.; Althoff, K.-D.; Tautz, C.: Systematic Maintenance of Corporate Experience Repositories. In: Computational Intelligence – Special Issue on Maintaining Case-Based Reasoning System, 17 (2) 2001, S.364-386.

[9] Nebel, B.: Wissensmanagement in der Projektarbeit nutzen. In: GPM aktuell 3/00, S.15

[10] Lock, D.: Project Management, Gower Publishing Limited, Hampshire 1996.

[11] Scholz, C.: Personalarbeit im IT-Bereich: Erfolgskritische Aktionsfelder. In: Wirtschaftsinformatik Sonderheft (2000) Oktober , S. 7-8.

[12] Tautz, C.: Customizing Software Engineering Experience Management Systems to Organisational Needs. Dissertation am Fachbereich Informatik der Universität Kaiserslautern, 2000.

[13] Tautz, C. & Althoff, K.-D.: Using Case-Based Reasoning for Reusing Software Knowledge. In: D. Leake and E. Plaza (eds.), Case-Based Reasoning Research and Development, Second International Conference on Case-Based Reasoning (ICCBR97), Springer Verlag, 1997, pp156-165.

[14] Tautz, C., Althoff, K.-D., and Nick, M.: A case-based reasoning approach for managing qualitative experience. In AAAI-00 Workshop on Intelligent Lessons Learned Systems, 2000.

[15] von Krogh, G.; Ichijo, K.; Nonaka, I.: Enabling Knowledge Creation : How to Unlock the Mystery of Tacit Knowledge and Release the Power of Innovation, Oxford University Press 2000.

[16] Waschek, G.: Normen und Richtlinien. In: Projektmanagement-Fachmann Band 1, 6.Auflage, 2001, S.252-268.

Part 7:

Additional Papers: LSO 2001 Posters

The Integrated Corporate Information Network iCoIN: A Comprehensive, Web-Based Experience Factory

Björn Decker and Andreas Jedlitschka

Fraunhofer Institute for Experimental Software Engineering, Sauerwiesen 6, 67661 Kaiserslautern, Germany
{decker | jedl@iese.fhg.de}

Abstract. During execution of projects, Software Organizations gain experience in their business. However, timely, effective and efficient reuse of this experience in subsequent projects is often problematic. The concept of an Experience Factory (EF), an infrastructure for continuous learning from experience, was designed to tackle these problems in the software development business. To install such an EF at the Fraunhofer Institute for Experimental Software Engineering (IESE), the knowledge management initiative Corporate Information Network (CoIN) was started in 1999. This paper presents the vision for CoIN and the practical experiences gained in its business process modeling part.

1 Introduction

Work in Software Organizations (i.e., sub-organizations that earn most of their income based on software) is mostly structured in projects. The basic nature of a project is that it achieves specific and unique objectives [15]. However, due to specialization to a certain business area, Software Organizations will perform projects with similar objectives and thus, similar contents. For instance, a solution provider for eCommerce applications has to implement the business models of different customers; certain characteristics of those business models and thus, the approaches to implement them, are the same. Therefore, Software Organizations gain valuable, competition-relevant experience over time. In addition, Software Organizations are forced to use this experience in an efficient and effective way due to two characteristics of the software business: quick changes and the virtual nature of software artifacts: *Quick changes* in market and technology demand fast and efficient utilization of the experience gained. In particular, deviations from the project plan and mistakes have to be discovered early. The *virtual nature of software artifacts increases* the need to learn from real project experience, since the software artifacts cannot be tested like physical artifacts (e.g., the materials used in building construction).

When trying to utilize those project experiences in an efficient and effective way, organizations face several problems: Experience is (re-)used without regard to (a) whether it is applicable to the current situation and (b) how it was proven in similar situations. In addition, experience is not pre-processed to facilitate application to the current situation. As a result, experience is not re-used because of the effort needed to apply it, or similar actions during adaptation are repeated if applied in several projects [5]. The solution to those problems is (a) to compare the context of applicable past experience with the context of the

K.-D. Althoff, R.L. Feldmann, and W. Müller (Eds.): LSO 2001, LNCS 2176, pp. 192-206, 2001.

current project, (b) to evaluate the usage of each experience within a project, and (c) to use the results of these evaluations to process and consolidate the experiences [2]. One approach to define and implement the comparison of contexts, evaluation of content and processing of experience is the Quality Improvement Paradigm (QIP) [3] and its methodological refinement DISER (Design and Implementation of Software Engineering Repositories) [20].

An additional problem is that projects are burdened with knowledge-management-related activities. Those activities are often abandoned when conflicts with project objectives occur (e.g., effort, schedule). Therefore, the QIP demands to install a project-independent unit within an organization, called the Experience Factory (EF). Besides capturing and processing project experience of all kinds (e.g., project management documents), the EF actively supports the projects by providing suitable experience from past projects.

Such an EF was installed at IESE by the knowledge management initiative Corporate Information Network (CoIN). This paper presents (a) the underlying vision of this initiative and (b) the experiences gained with implementing and operating the business process part of CoIN, called the IESE Quality Management Systems (IQ). The paper itself is structured into three main sections: Subsequently, the vision and the parts of this vision already implemented are introduced. Then, IQ is described in detail. This description also covers the Lessons Learned gained during set-up and operation of IQ. Finally, a summary and outlook to upcoming developments in CoIN conclude the paper.

2 The Corporate Information Network CoIN: A Web-Based EF

Based on the "classical", project experience focused EF presented in the Introduction, the knowledge management initiative Corporate Information Network (CoIN) was initiated to (a) *create intranet-based access* to information and knowledge available within repositories for all members of an organization and (b) to *enlarge the scope* to general knowledge management related activities and content. The initial CoIN vision was presented in [20]. Based on the first developments to implement this vision, the initial vision was further developed to the iCoIN (for Integrated CoIN) vision: iCoIN implements an integrated personalized, multi-role-based information offer for uniform, controlled access to all information and applications of the organization: *Integrated* means that all functionalities and information needed for project or organizational work are accessible through a single point of login. This includes a uniform platform for the generation and distribution of information. This tight integration allows to derive the current situation of a user and present appropriate information. Furthermore, the integration makes it possible to detect and utilize situations where new information and knowledge is generated. *Personalized* means that the user is able to influence the presentation of the contents and the content he or she owns. *Multi-role-based* means that each employee has at least one organizational role and – in most cases - roles within several projects. In addition, special roles like "new organization member" are defined. The access rights and information presentation for every user are derived from those roles.

To implement those three properties of iCoIN, three aspects of the current user's context have to be regarded: The personal context, the role context, and the situated context. The *personal context* is the most static one, since it contains information about the user him-/herself (e.g., skills, personal data). The role context is the set of roles a user is currently performing, which may change over time. Finally, the situated context denominates the current situation of the user, i.e., the status of the business processes he or she is involved in. When those context attributes are combined with the three properties of iCoIN, several opportunities for knowledge management activities are created:

Minimally invasive, timely and context-sensitive knowledge collection
Due to integration, information can be collected where it is produced (i.e., context) or even derived as a by-product of daily work. This enables a timely and minimally invasive collection of information, which is particularly important for information and experience (e.g., Lessons Learned) that are small or highly volatile within the mind of members of an organization.

Pre-tailored information access and aggregation
For each role used broadly (like Project Member) or otherwise important role (e.g., Line Management) iCoIN provides pre-tailored aggregations and views to the content of CoIN. The user is able to instantiate and fine-tune those views. For those views, two different characteristics according to the roles of a user can be distinguished. The views for the operative working force focus on the details of the work based on the current situation. The views intended for *project and line management* will employ sophisticated aggregation methods, since those roles are normally interested in an overview and will access details only in case of exceptions (e.g., projects with schedule deviation). Therefore, the recognition of those exceptions has to be supported.

Comprehensive contents
The content covered within iCoIN covers consolidated documents as well as fine grained, context sensitive experiences like Lessons Learned [2]. Furthermore, capturing and offering information about the skills of the organization's members supports usage of tacit knowledge.

However, such comprehensive integration bears two dangers: *inflexibility*, since the creative nature of software business demands an opportunity to react to exceptions, and *misuse* of personal information. Therefore, two principles guide the integration within iCoIN: Flexibility and information sovereignty.

Flexibility: In general, all information offers and workflows are suggestions. If a user decides to choose another way, thus ignoring the suggestion, he or she is free to do so. Those exceptions are noticed by iCoIN and will trigger maintenance activities, since they indicate (a) an insufficient information or content (b) or insufficient knowledge or motivation to use this suggestion. (However, flexibility will not apply to all workflows, for instance due to legal restrictions.)

Information sovereignty: Some of the information and some aspects of information integration in iCoIN bear difficulties if they are distributed within the whole organization or some of their parts (e.g., effort recording, evaluation of personalized knowledge contributions). Therefore, the user (a) is in full control over the information he or she is willing to provide to the system and (b) the information distribution is communicated explicitly. Some regular settings are needed due to the work requirements (e.g., effort data for billing purposes), other will be negotiated with the employee representatives. (For information collection, in particular, GQM provides a powerful method for deriving measures in coordination with information providers (i.e., users) [16].)

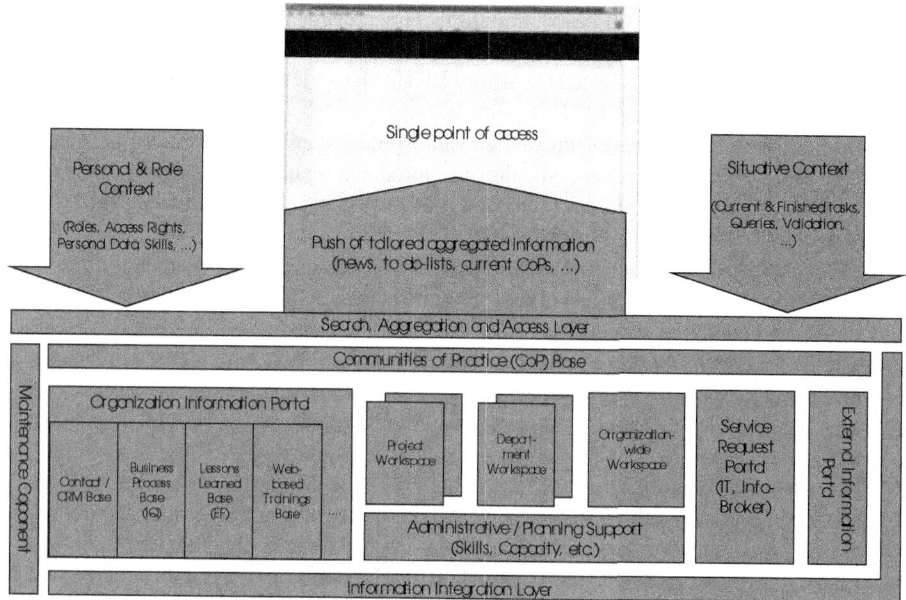

Fig. 1. Architecture of the iCoIN vision

To implement this integration, iCoIN will have an architecture like it is shown in Figure 1. Although it is mainly intended for the needs of IESE, it can be adapted to other organizations due to its modular components. The functionalities of the components are as follows:

The *Search, Aggregation and Access Layer* provides uniform access to the information sources within iCoIN. In particular, it provides (a) a single point of access and (b) overviews of news and relevant knowledge sources based on the personal, role and situated context (left and right arrows in Figure 1). Non-usage of those information offers or no results queries are reported to the Maintenance Component to trigger maintenance activities.

The *Communities of Practice (CoP) Base* handles two tasks within iCoIN: First, it acts as a platform for the exchange and discussion of ideas among the organization's members. In particular, questions that could not be answered by other information sources are featured as a discussion topic. Second, content of other parts of iCoIN can be subject to discussion or evaluation using the CoP Base. For example, users of the business process repository can evaluate the business process models and discuss exceptions. This collects a continuous stream of experiences, used for content and service maintenance activities.

The *Service Request Portal* is used to request in-house or supplier services. The integration of those requests into iCoIN offers opportunities to automatize (a) notification of affected roles and (b) billing of those services.

The *Organization Information Portal* provides uniform access to knowledge and other information restricted to exclusive usage by organization members like its contact address data base, business process models, Lessons Learned repository [6] and organization-adapted web-based trainings. The content accessible via this portal is unique to this organization. Therefore, the first efforts to build up iCoIN were made in this area: The Lessons Learned repository EF (for Experience Factory) and the business process model repository IQ [9].

Within the *Workspaces*, documents relevant to the organization or one of its sub-parts (like projects or line organization units) are stored and managed. Some areas of a project workspace may be accessible by customers or project partners to facilitate the exchange of ideas and documents within projects.

The *Administrative / Planning Support* provides functions used for planning of activities within the projects and for line organization like capacity planning, skill profiles, project status, accounting, or scheduling.

The *External Information Portal* is a collection of web sources (e.g., the homepages of international research organizations) that are relevant to the entire organization.

The *Maintenance Component* uses the continuous stream of experiences from the CoP Base to (a) evaluate content and (b) package interesting finalized discussions into the Lessons Learned Repository [13]. Furthermore, the Maintenance Component gives special overviews of those experiences and the other content to facilitate the definition of role- and situation-specific aggregations on the Search, Aggregation and Access Layer. Finally, it listens to the Information Integration Layer for status changes (e.g., when a project finishes) to trigger knowledge acquisition activities.

The *Information Integration Layer* is the backbone of iCoIN that enables the information exchange between the different services. In particular, the Aggregation, Search and Access Layer uses the Information Integration Layer to access the information to be searched or aggregated.

How these components of the iCoIN architecture work together is illustrated in examples for (1) project set-up and (2) for travel applications: During *project set-up*, the search for appropriate project staff is supported by the Administrative / Planning support by an overview of the available personnel capacity, together with the skills of potential project staff. If a project member is lacking needed skills, he or she can use Web-based trainings; the skill profile is updated after successful training. By using the Lessons Learned repository, experiences like best practices are used for project planning. *Travel applications* are distributed to the organization's members responsible for signing. Furthermore, the travel dates will be provided to the Administrative / Planning Support for billing (e.g., for accounting travel costs), scheduling (e.g., for planning appointment) and capacity planning. After the trip, a member of the organization turns in the expenses for accounting and is asked for experiences gained during the trip. This request is based on the type of trip, e.g., an organization member coming from an acquisition trip will be asked for new contact data, members coming from a scientific conference will be asked for scientific trends to be discussed in the CoP Base.

Within iCoIN, the role of the EF team is extended. At our institute, the EF team with such extended responsibilities is called the CoIN team. Besides active project support of the classical EF, the CoIN team is involved in general knowledge management related activities. This includes to coach, motivate and integrate the organization's members into the knowledge management activities (e.g., supporting scientists in providing information about their topic). Within iCoIN, one prominent task of this CoIN-Team will be to define and implement the aggregations used within iCoIN. The basic idea is to instantiate the DISER method for a combined, wide-scoped, and peer-based evaluation of the aggregation and its contents:

Before a new aggregation is implemented, the role context (i.e., which roles should be supported), the personal context (e.g., skilled or unskilled), and the situated context (i.e., which situation and information states will trigger usage) of a potential user of this aggregation and content is defined. Then, success criteria that define under which circumstance the new aggregation is regarded as successful are established and the content needs for the previously defined context are stated. Finally, the information sources, methods for aggregation of information, and the evaluation methods are selected.

During usage of these aggregations, feedback about the content and the aggregation is continuously collected via the CoP Base. This feedback includes tracking of acceptance and rejection of information offers. In general, each acceptance will be counted as a validation of the content and the aggregation, each rejection as a non-validation. This in-situ feedback is used for a permanently updated evaluation of the content and this aggregation visible to the user of iCoIN (e.g., score points).

In between, in-depth analyzes are performed for often rejected content and aggregations. The results of those analyzes are used to determine the reasons for rejection and to perform corrective actions. The following reasons and solutions can be distinguished:

1) The context of the aggregation was false: A new context has to be defined for the aggregation.
2) The contexts that led to rejections are exceptions: This indicates that those contexts may need a special aggregation.
3) The context was right, but the aggregation was inappropriate: A new or improved aggregation has to be defined.
4) Context and aggregation were right, but no appropriate content is currently available: Information acquisition has to be initiated.

Since an ambitious vision such as iCoIN cannot be implemented in one step, special regards have to be given to an evolutionary approach for the integration: At the starting point of iCoIN, the selected services will be loosely integrated (e.g., by regulations for information exchange and knowledge management-related procedure). In particular, this loose integration could be done by the COIN-Team "manually" to gain experience on how to integrate services. For instance, a member of the CoIN team could analyze discussions in the CoP-Base for potential Lessons Learned. Over time, further services can be added and promising opportunities for tighter integration of current and new services can be identified and implemented (e.g., support of this analysis by text-mining methods). This allows to adopt iCoIN to current developments in the state-of-art and state-of-practice in Information Technology and Knowledge Management. With tighter integration, opportunities for (partly) automated learning can be implemented. For instance, iCoIN could track actions of users that are evaluated as successful and present them to other users in similar contexts.

In the following, the already implemented sub-system of iCoIN that covers the business process models of IESE is presented. Started in January 2000, it was developed to implement a loose integration of services, since it describes the usage of the information and knowledge repositories and provides links to those repositories. This presentation will focus on the currently implemented version, but it will include potential for future development according to the iCoIN vision.

3 COIN-IQ: Business Process Descriptions

High quality procedural knowledge, i.e., "good" business processes, is a competitive edge of an organization, since it coordinates its members in an effective and efficient way. Therefore, one of the first efforts within CoIN was to build up a repository of business process descriptions of IESE. As already mentioned in the introduction, this part is called IESE Quality Management System, or IQ for short. Based on the results of a diploma thesis performed in advance, the build-up of IQ in 2000 took about ten person month of effort. This effort was equally distributed between the technical realization and the creation of content for IQ. About four person month of effort are allocated in 2001 for further content build-up and maintenance.

This section will present IQ as follows: *First*, the objectives of IQ are presented. *Second*, the content of IQ is presented in an overview and in detail, together with the way changes to this content are communicated. *Finally*, the Lessons Learned of the build-up and operating phase of IQ close the section.

The *objectives of IQ* can be positioned according to four criteria: (1) the purpose of process models, (2) the origin and (3) usage of the process models, and (4) the modeling techniques. In summary, IQ uses structured text describing empirical and theoretical process models to be executed by human agents. This is detailed in the following.

For the *general purpose of process models*, [8] identifies five different categories: Facilitate human understanding and communication, support process improvement, support process management, automate process guidance, and automate execution. According to this classification scheme, IQ fits into the first category of facilitating human understanding and communication: The processes are executed by human agents (i.e., IESE members), based on the process description. Supporting and enforcing process execution beyond this human-based approach (e.g., by workflow modeling and enactment as in [12]) was regarded as non-suitable for the purposes of IESE due to the creative nature of its Business Processes. Furthermore, processes according to the process models are executed rather infrequently (< 10 times per month), therefore (a) automation of the processes was not supposed to leverage a high cost/benefit and (b) tracking of process status can be done by asking the responsible process executor. In addition, the experience made with the Electronic Process Guide (EPG) [7] showed that web-based process descriptions are a feasible way of distributing process knowledge within creative environments such as Software Business. In particular, changes to web-based process models can be communicated much quicker than paper-based process models, thus enabling a quick integration of experience.

The *origin of process models* can be empirical (i.e., based on actual executed processes) and theoretical (i.e., reflecting a planned process execution). Process models in IQ have both origins: Some of the process models reflect well established processes (like, e.g., the administrative project set-up), others represent new procedures (e.g., the reflection of recent changes in the organizational structure of IESE).

The *usage of process* models can be descriptive (i.e., a description of a process) or prescriptive (i.e., intended to be used as an instruction for process execution). The process models within IQ are prescriptive with different degrees of obligation. In general, administrative procedures (e.g., project accounting) have to followed without exception; best-practice process models like project management procedure are to be seen as recommendations.

The *process modeling technique* of IQ is structured text, which is due to several reasons: zero effort training, straightforward modeling and perpetuation in industrial strength applications. *Zero effort* has to be spent on training, since any IESE member can read structured text without previous training. Furthermore, *straightforward modeling* means that any IESE members can model processes using structured text, if supported by guidelines and the CoIN team. This aspect is additionally fortified by the experience in scientific publishing of most of the IESE member. For the modeling itself, any word processing software can be used. Finally, structured text has proven its *industrial strength* in process models of quality management systems [10].

During the set-up phase, several other modeling techniques were evaluated: (1) extended programming languages like APPLA/A[21], (2) product-flow-based approaches like MVPL [4]), (3) petri-net-based approaches like EPKs [17], and Object-oriented approaches [23]. All those approaches are well suited for a detailed analysis to gain (a) executable models (e.g., for simulation or workflow execution) and (b) for handling comprehensive, extensive and complex models with many parties involved. However, both (a) and (b) are not applicable to the processes currently captured within IQ, since (a) due to the creative nature of the processes, detailed modeling would have consumed extensive effort and (b) the number and complexity of process models on the level currently described are rather low. Furthermore, effort would have had to be spent on educating IESE members in one of those modeling techniques or in processing the modeled information into structured text. However, compared to those formal methods, structured text cannot be checked automatically for consistency. Therefore, all process models are reviewed thoroughly by peers and the CoIN team. To facilitate this task, one potential development of IQ could be to enhance the process descriptions by integrating one of those formal modeling techniques that would allow sophisticated consistency checks.

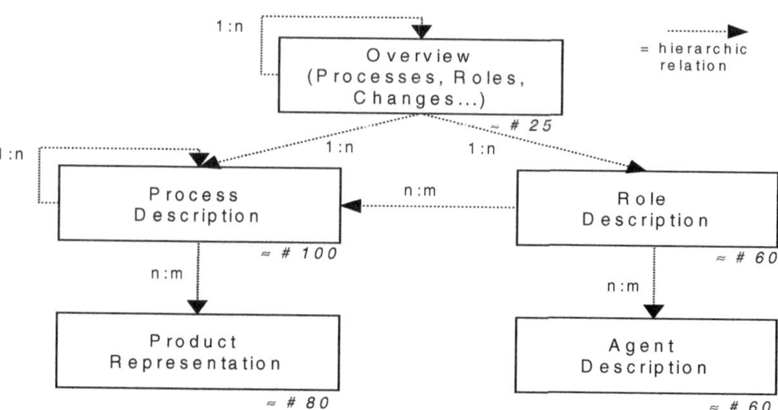

Fig. 2. Simplified structure of objects in IQ. Arrows show how objects are linked. The relations are to be read according to the direction of the arrows (e.g., one overview can refer to n other overviews, role descriptions or process descriptions). Italics denominate the number of elements of the respective type of objects within IQ.

To achieve those objectives, the following information is captured within IQ. Each of those information objects can be linked to other objects according to Figure 2:

Process Descriptions: Process descriptions describe the activities captured within CoIN (e.g., project management). Complex processes are structured into a hierarchy of super- and sub-processes.

Role Descriptions: Role descriptions describe the roles that are involved in the execution of processes.

Agent Descriptions: Agent Descriptions are used within role descriptions to name roles that are performed by a specific IESE member.

Product Representation: Product Representation represent documents to be used during process execution.

Overviews: Overviews structure the other objects within IQ to facilitate browsing.

The content of those objects is presented in detail in the following sections, followed by the Lessons Learned of the build-up and operation of IQ.

3.1 Process Descriptions

As depicted in Figure 3, a process within IQ is described according to the following structure: "Applicability Information", "Overview of Templates and Additional Information", "Objectives, Results, and Quality Measures", "Actions and Subprocesses" and "Guidelines". The content and purpose of these sections are described in the following:

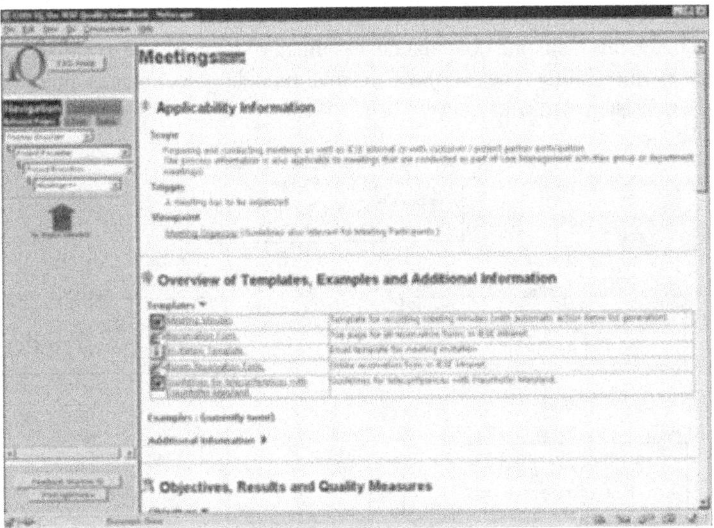

Fig. 3. Screenshot of a Process Description. The left frame provides functions applicable to all pages within IQ (help, printing, giving feedback) and navigation functions, including the current position within IQ.

"*Applicability Information*" gives a short overview of a process' context, thus helping the user to determine if the current process description is the desired one. To facilitate this overview even more, it is again structured into three sub-sections: Scope, Trigger and Viewpoint. "*Scope*" contains one or two sentences about the thematic range of a process and thus, the content of a process description. "*Trigger*" as the second sub-section describes the condition that starts the execution of a process. These triggering conditions can be events released from outside IESE (e.g., a customer telephone call), dependencies with other process executions (e.g., start or finish of a process) or dependencies from product states (e.g., a deliverable is about to be finished). "*Viewpoint*" contains the role from whose view the process is described.

"*Overview of Templates, Examples and Additional Information*" lists the products referenced by the process description. This overview is intended to support IESE members who are accustomed to the process and just need quick access to artifacts.

"*Objectives, Results and Quality Measures*" is information intended to guide the execution of a process. The difference between the three sub-sections is the increasing degree of quantification of quality information. *"Objectives"* are general objectives of the process (see Figure 5 for an example). *"Results"* are tangible outcomes of the process (e.g., meeting minutes). *"Quality Measures"* describe properties of such results (e.g., the number of pages of the meeting minutes should range between 10 and 20) or the process itself (e.g., the effort spent on preparing a meeting should not exceed one person day).

"Actions and Subprocesses" describe the steps of the process execution. In IQ, a distinction is made between actions and sub-processes. Actions are atomic steps that are not refined any further. Sub-processes are described in a separate process description according to this structure. The super-process contains a link to the sub-process, followed by a short explanation of the sub-process content.

"*Guidelines*" give hints for performing a process, like "do's and don'ts" or frequently asked questions about a process. Furthermore, frequently used variances of a process are modeled as guidelines. This reduces the number of similar process descriptions and lowers the effort to maintain the process description. Each guideline has a "speaking headline" in the form of a question or statement, followed by explanatory text.

Currently, those Process Descriptions have a particular function for the integration of services, in particular, knowledge management activities: (a) They are used to *define the point in the business processes* execution where services (like knowledge acquisition or access to sources) is performed. (b) They *describe the usage of services and knowledge management* activities themselves (e.g., like project touch down analyzes). When the CoP base is implemented, the collaboration will be guided by business process models within IQ. Vice Versa, the CoP Base will be used to refine and evaluate the business process models.

3.2 Role Descriptions

As depicted in Figure 4, Role Descriptions in IQ are structured into three main sections. "Role Description", "Processes Referring the Role X", and "Other Roles of Interest". The first section "*Role Description*" contains a general description of the role, who is able to perform this role, who can substitute this role if the respective agent is not available, and which roles support this role in their work. If an agent (i.e., a certain IESE member) can be assigned to one of the latter three sub-sections, the name, telephone and email are stated. For example, the role secretary is performed by several IESE members, each mentioned in this section. The second section "*Processes Referring the Role X*" lists the processes in which the role is involved. Therefore, it serves as a role-specific process overview that allows the performer of a role to gain quick access to relevant processes. The function of the third section "*Other Roles of Interest*" is straightforward; it contains links to other roles that can be relevant to the performer of the current role.

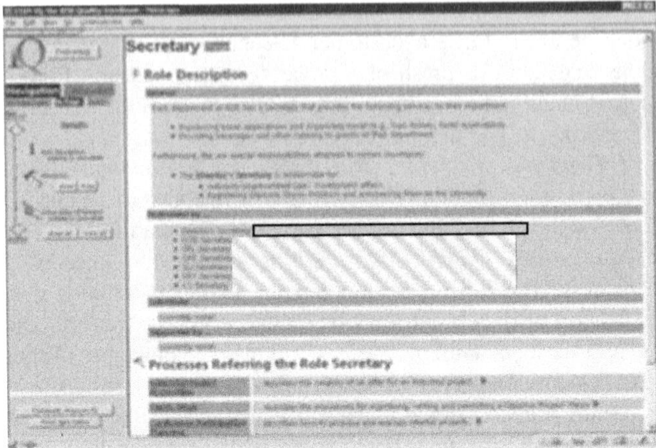

Fig. 4. Screenshot of a Role Description (Names are anonymized). The left frame now shows functions for navigating within a page.

3.3 Agent Descriptions

Within the section "Role Description", IESE members who perform specific roles are mentioned with their email, telephone number, and address (see Figure 4). Therefore - besides describing roles themselves - Role Descriptions serve as "yellow pages": A user of IQ can deduce from the role description whether the person mentioned in the contact information is the appropriate one and contact him or her directly. In particular, experts in certain areas are mentioned here to allow accessing the tacit knowledge of such an expert. The other way round of finding roles a certain agent performs is supported by the "Agent Overview". Since Agent Descriptions are only used as parts of Role Descriptions, they do not have separate pages.

3.4 Product Representations

Products within IQ are mostly referenced by processes. Since they are only referenced by other objects in IQ, they also do not have separate pages like Agent Descriptions. The products within IQ are structured according to two dimensions: representation and usage: *Representation* is relevant for how the product can be accessed: (1) As an html-document available online, (2) as a downloadable file (e.g., MS-Word file), or (3) as a description of where a document available only as hardcopy can be obtained. *Usage* of a product can be (a) as a template, (b) as an example document or (c) as additional information to a process or role description.

Those products are a particular area of interest for the CoIN team. In the course of the project analysis - primarily intended to capture Lessons Learned – re-usable documents are identified. If a document is of special interest for IQ users, it is processed further into a template to facilitate its application in future projects. Otherwise, it is brought into IQ as an example or as additional information. Furthermore, experiences with currently available documents are also captured for continuous improvement of those documents.

With the implementation of the organization-wide workspace, IQ can take over those Products Representations via the Information Integration Layer. Currently, the already mentioned loose integration of services by IQ is implemented by embedding them into the process descriptions as products (e.g., the reservation service for meeting rooms.)

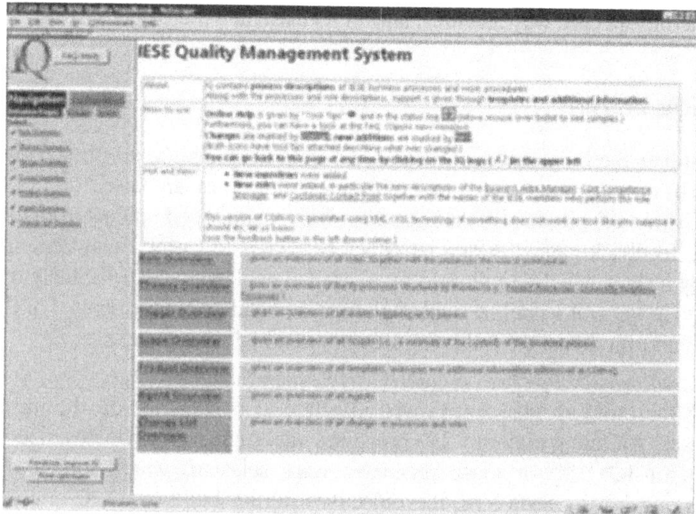

Fig. 5. Screenshot of the entry page of IQ as an example of an overview. Further overviews can be reached from this page.

3.5 Overview Descriptions

Overviews (see Figure 5) support a user in navigating through the elements mentioned before by (1) structuring the other objects (e.g., overviews for role or processes of a certain category) or (2) offering a certain view to those objects (e.g., overview of activities throughout the year). To structure the objects within IQ, those overviews are sufficient because (a) the topics of processes and the functions of roles are rather disjunctive and (b) – as pointed out in [11] - the overall number of objects is small enough for structuring it by overviews (see Figure 2).

3.6 Change Marking

One particular overview covers (a) the changes in and new additions of objects to IQ. Since each change is mentioned with the date and a short description of the change, a user can gain an overview of changes that have occurred since his or her last visit to IQ. In addition, the most recent changes are mentioned on the entry page of IQ (see Figure 5). This enables a quick access to those changes, which lowers the effort for propagating changes within the organization.

Furthermore, changes or new objects in IQ are marked by a "new" or "changed" icon (see Top of Figure 3 and 4). This change marking is sufficient for the information within IQ:

Process descriptions are not intended to be read on a daily basis. Therefore, a user will read the whole process description and focus his or her interest on the changed sections.

Besides listing and marking the changes in IQ itself, wide-scoped changes are communicated within IESE via email to all IESE members. In the future, IQ can utilize the news collected by the Search, Aggregation and Access Layer of iCoIN to summarize changes in a role-specific way and thus, inform IQ users in a more precise way.

3.7 Lessons Learned

This section lists the Lessons Learned gained during (a) the build-up phase (since begin of 2000) and (b) the operation (since mid of 2000) of IQ. They are based on (a) the authors' experience within the project, (b) on discussion with peers, (c) comments from the annual IQ reviews, (d) feedback gained during introductory classes to CoIN. Each Lesson Learned is described by a short headline followed by a detailed explanation. To facilitate reading, they are described as general guidelines, although they are validated in the context of IESE only.

During the build-up phase, the following Lessons Learned were gained:

Start small, revise objectives regularly, define increments
During the build-up phase, it proved effective to concentrate on the most important processes. An initial count of 250 processes was suggested to be described in the first version of IQ. 100 of those processes were selected, which turned out to be a challenging effort. Therefore, the objectives during build-up were revised regularly. Furthermore, stand-alone usable increments of the processes were defined.

Clear definition of target group of whole system and process
A clear definition of the target group helped to focus the effort, thus supporting the previous Lesson Learned. Furthermore, it facilitates finding review candidates among the organization's members.

Active and early feedback
Users should be involved early. Small increments support this early involvement. The build-up team should gain feedback actively, since in most cases users will not provide feedback on their own.

Consolidate roles early
Since role descriptions are used across all processes descriptions, they should be consolidated first and revised throughout the build-up phase. This avoids an uncontrolled growth of role descriptions, in particular, double, inconsistent or overlapping descriptions.

The following Lessons Learned are not only limited to the build-up, but also apply to the continuous operation of IQ:

High quality focus
Concentrate the effort on the relevant processes. If there are not enough resources to describe a process in a comprehensive way, it should not be described. A good indicator is to ask peers or organizational stakeholders whether they are interested in the definition of a particular process.

Be part of or support organizational changes
If organizational changes occur, they should be reflected in the business processes. Since those changes are a novelty to all organization members, the interest in the

changed process descriptions is high compared to established ones. Therefore, even experienced members have a higher motivation to read the process descriptions.

Peer review of descriptions
Peer review of process and role description is a simple, yet powerful procedure to identify blind spots and ambiguities. Furthermore, the process reviewer takes part in the distribution of process knowledge within the organization.

Take care of new organizations members
Since new organization members are also new to the business processes, they have a special interest in process descriptions. However, they could be annoyed by previously undiscovered blind spots in the process descriptions. Active help offered by the CoIN team allows (a) to overcome this annoyance and (b) to identify those blind spots. Furthermore, they should be supported by tutorials and online available guided tours.

Coach new processes
If new processes are described, one or two organization members executing these processes should be coached. This also allows feedback about the practical applicability of the process, thus improving the process description after the first executions.

4 Summary and Outlook

Web-based Business Process Descriptions using structured text are a means for loose integration of information and knowledge sources within an organization. Therefore, they are a first step towards the vision of a comprehensive EF named iCoIN. With increasing integration into the organization's flow of work, more information and knowledge will be used and captured as a by-product of the daily work. In particular, the evaluation of the information and knowledge can be done in a minimally invasive way. To implement this vision, work is currently ongoing or planned. Within IQ, those activities are:

- A web re-design according to usability criteria [14] is currently ongoing and will be finished in by mid -2002. This re-design will heavily involve IESE members by using a predecessor of the CoP base to collect experiences with this new design.
- The process models of IQ are migrated to be editable by SPEARMINT [19], a process modeling tool, which will offer opportunities for improved execution support.

The iCoIN vision will be implemented and further refined during the migration of the current IESE intranet to CoIN. In particular, the technical infrastructure to define and implement role specific access and aggregation is currently being implemented and will be finished by the end of 2001. It is planned to evaluate the "news"-functionality of the Search, Aggregation and Access Layer by implementing a change notification for changes in IQ.

References

[1] Althoff, K.-D.; Birk, A.; Hartkopf, S.; Müller, W.; Nick, M.; Surmann, D. Tautz, C.: Managing Software Engineering Experience for Comprehensive Reuse; Proceedings of the Eleventh Conference on Software Engineering and Knowledge Engineering, Kaiserslautern, Germany, June 1999; Knowledge Systems Institute; Skokie, Illinois, USA; 1999.

[2] Althoff, K.-D.; Bomarius, F.; Tautz, C.: Knowledge Management for Building Learning Software Organizations, Information Systems Frontiers; p. 349-367; Kluwer Academic Publishers; 2000.

[3] Basili, V.R.; Caldiera, G.; Rombach, D.: Experience Factory; In Marciniak, J.J. ed., Encyclopedia of Software Engineering, vol 1, 469–476; John Wiley & Sons; 1994.

[4] Bröckers, A.; Lott, C.M.; Rombach, H. D.: Verlage, M.: MVP-L Language Report Version 2; Technical Report University of Kaiserslautern, Department of Computer Science 265 / 95; 1995

[5] Basili, V.R.; Rombach, H.D.: Support for Comprehensive Reuse, Software Engineering Journal, September 1991

[6] Birk, A.; Tautz, C.: Knowledge Management of Software Engineering Lessons Learned; Proceedings of the Tenth Conference on Software Engineering and Knowledge Engineering; San Francisco Bay; USA. Skokie, Illinois, USA: Knowledge Systems Institute; 1998.

[7] Becker-Kornstaedt, U.; Verlage, M.: The V-Model Guide: Experience with a Web-based Approach for Process Support; Proceedings of Software Technology and Engineering Practice (STEP); 1999.

[8] Curtis, B.; Kellner, M. I., Over, J.: Process Modeling; Communications of the ACM; 1992.

[9] Decker, B.; Althoff, K.-D.; Nick, M.; Tautz, C.: Integrating Business Process Descriptions and Lessons Learned with an Experience Factory; 1st Workshop on business-process-oriented knowledge Management, http://SunSITE.Informatik.RWTH-Aachen.DE/Publications/CEUR-WS/Vol-37/Decker.pdf, 2001

[10] Dilg, P.: Praktisches Qualitätsmanagement in der Informationstechnologie; Carl Hanser Verlag, Wien; 1995.

[11] Griss M.L.; Software reuse: From library to factory. *IBM Systems Journal*, 32(4):548–566, November 1993.

[12] Maurer, F.; Holz, H.: Process-Oriented Knowledge Management For Learning Software Organizations, Proceedings of 12th Knowledge Acquisition For Knowledge-Based Systems Workshop 1999 (KAW99); Canada, Banff; 1999.

[13] Nick, M; Althoff, K.-D.; Tautz, C.: Systematic maintenance of corporate experience repositories; Computational Intelligence special issue on maintaining CBR systems, 2000 (to appear).

[14] Nielsen, Jakob, http://www.useit.com/alertbox/, 2001.

[15] Duncan, W. R. (Director of Standards): A Guide to the Project Management Body of Knowledge; Project Management Institute; PMI Publishing Division; North Carolina, USA; http://www.pmi.org/publictn/download/1996welcome.htm; 1996.

[16] Solingen, R. v.; Berghout, E.: The Goal/Questions/Metric Method; Mc Graw Hill Publishing Company;1999.

[17] Scheer, A.W.: Referenzmodelle für industrielle Geschäftsprozesse (siebte Auflage), Springer Verlag, 1997.

[18] Schindler, M., Seifried, P.: Projekte und Prozesse im Kontext des Wissensmanagement, Industrie Management 15 p.20-25; GITO-Verlag; 1999.

[19] Spearmint/EPG homepage, http://www.iese.fhg.de/Spearmint/index.html, 2001.

[20] Tautz, C.: Customizing Software Engineering Experience Management Systems to Organizational Needs; Ph. D. diss., Dept. of Computer Science, University of K aiserslautern, Germany; 2000.

[21] Osterweil, L.: Software Processes Are Software Too, Association for Computer Machinery (ACM); 1987

[22] Nonaka, Ikujori. The knowledge-creating company, in Harvard Business Review, November-December 1991

[23] Workflow Management Facility Specification, V1.2, Object Management Group; http://www.omg.org/, 2000

Reuse of Measurement Plans Based on Process and Quality Models

Christiane M. Differding

Fraunhofer Institute for Experimental Software Engineering,
Sauerwiesen 6,
D-67661 Kaiserslautern, Germany
differdi@iese.fhg.de

Abstract. Measurement is needed for project control, quality assurance, and process improvement activities in software development. Measurement planning is a difficult and time-consuming activity. Therefore, a great interest exists in reusing measurement plans. However, most measurement plans are structured intuitively and are written informally. Therefore, they are difficult to understand and to reuse. The contents of measurement plans strongly depend on the object being measured and the quality focus of measurement. Process models (describing the object) and quality models (describing the quality focus) change from project to project and over time. Therefore, in order to reuse measurement plans from one project to the next, relationships between measurement plans and process and quality models are needed. These relationships can be used to identify and adapt existing measurement plans to varying process and quality models. This paper presents a formal conceptual model of measurement plans including relationships to process and quality models and a development process for such measurement plans. This model and process build a sound basis for reuse of measurement plans. To further support reuse, a conceptual model for components of measurement plan elements is sketched. Components can be reused to build new measurement plans. A rudimentary reuse process is proposed that starts from a similarity analysis of the (reused and new) underlying process model and quality models.

1 Motivation

Measurement is needed for project control, quality assurance, and process improvement activities in software development. Measurement is a prerequisite to build quantitative empirical models of software products and processes. In a learning organization, these models can be used for characterizing, monitoring, estimating, predicting, and controlling software projects. There is a general acceptance that measurement should be goal-oriented. The Goal/Question/Metric (GQM) approach is an approach for goal-oriented measurement of software products and processes that is often used in industrial software organizations [3], [4]. It has been identified as the most flexible approach in [17] and in [16]. We use the GQM approach for measurement planning.

K.-D. Althoff, R.L. Feldmann, and W. Müller (Eds.): LSO 2001, LNCS 2176, pp. 207–221, 2001.

Measurement needs to be carefully planned, and measurement planning is a difficult and time-consuming task, see Subsection 1.1. Therefore, a strong interest exists in reusing measurement plans, see Subsection 1.2.

1.1 Measurement Planning

A measurement plan contains the rationale for measurement and measurement instruments. According to the GQM approach, a measurement plan consists of GQM plans (containing the measurement goal, a set of questions refining the goal, and measures needed to answer the questions), an abstraction sheet (an abstract view on the GQM plan), and data collection instruments (data collection forms).

Measurement planning is a difficult and time-consuming task. This is true for several reasons: In order to ensure successful usage of data, the goal of measurement needs to be clear from the beginning. This includes a clear definition of the object of measurement. Moreover, data collection needs to be optimized with respect to the data collector and the data collection point in time.

Successful data usage depends on careful selection of software measures. Measurement goals support a usage-oriented view on measurement. GQM goals define the parameters object, purpose, quality attribute, viewpoint, and context [2], [4].

- The object of measurement defines what should be measured. Examples are a project, code modules, inspection processes.
- The purpose of measurement defines what measurement will be used for. Examples are characterization, monitoring, estimation, prediction, and control. This paper is restricted to the purpose characterization.
- The quality focus of measurement defines the quality aspect to be determined through measurement. Examples are defect slippage, project effort, usability.
- The viewpoint determines the main customer of the measurement results. Examples are quality assurance, tester, department head.
- The context describes the main criteria of the environment where measurement takes place. Examples are application domain, department.

Each of these parameters influences which questions are relevant for the goal and which measures are needed to answer them. Object and quality focus can be considered as the two central parameters, while purpose, viewpoint, and context influence how object and quality focus are seen for a specific goal.

Successful data collection depends on the careful selection of data collector and collection point in time. To reduce collection effort, tools should be used wherever possible. When data collection is done by humans, the person who knows most about the data to be collected needs to be identified.

Data collection needs to be optimized with respect to the data collection point in time. If data are collected too early or too late, the information may be not yet available or already forgotten. Therefore, the data collected will be of bad quality.

All these aspects need to be considered during measurement planning. This indicates that measurement plans need to be consistent with existing project planning documentation, because such documentation contains the relevant information: Product structure, development processes used, resource allocation, quality models (e.g., for effort distribution or defect slippage). Such information may be available in the form of process models and quality models.

1.2 Reusing Measurement Plans

Measurement plans can be reused from project to project. Often, only part of one of the goal parameters changes from one project to the next, e.g., a process is added to the project plan, and the measurement plan can be easily reused with slight adaptations. This is beneficial for several reasons: First, it saves effort. Second, existing measurement plans of good quality that are reused are less error-prone than new measurement plans. And third, the number of data points available for a measurement plan influence the validity of the models derived from the data. Therefore, the more often a measurement plan is used in the same environment, the more valid models can be developed and reused for similar projects in a learning organization.

1.3 Prerequisites for Measurement Plan Reuse

Most measurement plans are structured intuitively and are written in an informal way. Therefore, they are difficult to understand and to reuse. To reuse measurement plans and adapt them easily to the new context, some prerequisites need to be met:

- Measurement plans need some degree of formality: Their elements and relationships need to be defined as formally as possible.
- Measurement plans strongly depend on the object and the quality focus they measure. Measures differ depending on the object measured (e.g., size of objects with different notations will often be measured in a different ways), and measures differ depending on the quality model to be provided (e.g., prediction models require more sophisticated measures than simple characterization models). Therefore, it is important that relationships exist between measurement plans and the process models describing the object, and between measurement plans and the quality models describing the quality focus. Such relationships are used to adapt measurement plans if process models and quality models change from one project to the next. To define such relationships, process and quality models also need to be defined in a formal way.

1.4 Tool Support

This paper has its focus on requirements and basic concepts for measurement plan reuse, and does not elaborate on tool support. Ideas for tool support go in the direction of conversational case-based planning system as described in [14], for example.

1.5 Other Approaches for Measurement Plan Reuse

Gresse von Wangenheim and colleagues work on reuse support for measurement planning with focus on storage and retrieval of measurement plans during planning [8], [10], [11], [12]. They use the measurement plan definition in [4] as a basis, develop the structures appropriate to store relevant knowledge in an experience base, retrieve the knowledge using similarity functions, and present it to the measurement planner as needed during different measurement planning steps. Their concept includes the introduction of new knowledge, which may be gained while planning measurement, to the experience base. Gresse von Wangenheim implemented a tool supporting reuse during measurement planning based on case-based reasoning [7]. In comparison to the approach described in this paper, they do not consider explicitly the relationships of measurement plans to process models and do not use these relationships for adapting measurement plans elements to a new context. Moreover, their measurement plan model is less fine-granular than the model described here.

2 Measurement Planning Based on Process Models and Quality Models

One prerequisite for measurement planning is the formality of measurement plans, and the formality of relationships to other models that are relevant for measurement plans, i.e., process models and quality models. The following sections give an overview of an approach for measurement planning that defines measurement plans in a formal way, and proposes and validates a process to develop such measurement plans. The approach is defined in detail in [6].

2.1 Formal Conceptual Model for Measurement Plans, Process, and Quality Models

This section gives an overview of a formal conceptual model for measurement plans and its relationships to process and quality models. The model has been defined using ConceptBase [13], an object-oriented conceptual modelling tool that implements O-Telos [15], a first order predicate logic language. For a detailed description and a full formal definition of the model, refer to [6].

2.1.1 Requirements for a Conceptual Model of Measurement Plans

The conceptual model should fulfil the requirements listed in the following:

1. It is comprehensive: All information considered necessary for measurement planning and derivable at planning time is contained in the measurement plan.
2. It is based on measurement plans as defined in [9].
3. It is traceable: Dependencies among different parts of the measurement plan are captured. Emphasis is given on dependencies supporting consistency checks of the measurement plan.
4. It integrates existing information from project and quality assurance plans: The conceptual model reflects the fact that various kinds of project information are taken into account in the measurement plan.
5. It is designed in a way that supports checks for completeness and consistency, automatically or manually (by verification activities). Checks are designed for easy automation, as far as possible.
6. It is designed in a way that a measurement plan can be built using a systematic development process.

2.1.2 Overview of Conceptual Model for Measurement Plans

This section defines a conceptual model that meets the requirements defined in Section 2.1.1. A measurement plan consists of a GQM plan and measurement procedures. Measurement procedures model data collection instruments and will not be further described here, we focus on GQM plans. A GQM plan consists of a goal, three types of questions, measures, and dependency relationships. Questions are split up into three question types because questions play different roles in the GQM plan: quality questions further describe the main quality attribute, variation questions refer to aspects that influence the main quality attribute, and dependency questions refer to relationships among quality questions and variation questions. Dependency questions are related to dependency relationships, which model the dependencies between quality questions and variation questions. All questions refine the goal. Quality and variation questions can refine themselves and are refined by measures at the lowest refinement level. Figure 1 gives a graphical overview of the concepts and their relationships.

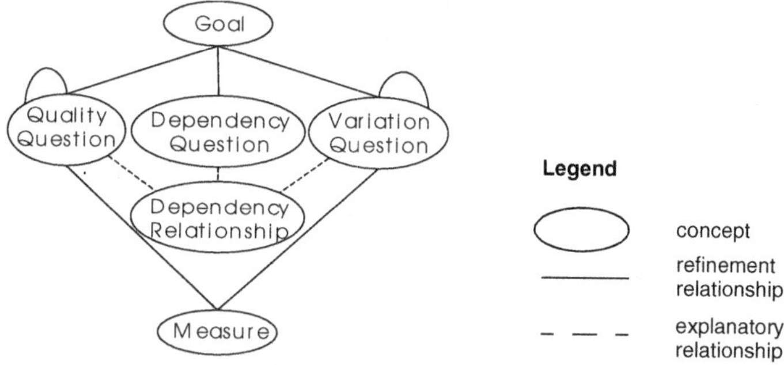

Figure 1 Conceptual model for measurement plans

All these concepts are further described by attributes. These attributes refer to the aspects that are relevant to describe a concrete instance of a concept (e.g., the parameter of the goal), to information that is needed to compute, represent, and interpret measurement results (e.g., how to represent the results of questions for a goal), and to the structure of the GQM plan (e.g., which questions refine the goal). Figure 2 shows attributes of a quality question. Additionally, constraints are defined on the level of concepts, but also on the level of concept attributes. These constraints allow us to model consistency and completeness aspects (e.g., a goal always needs five parameters and is refined by at least one quality question).

Structured template sentences show the role of some of the attributes in the question. In the templates, the attribute values are set in brackets <>, the attribute names are set in brackets and in *italics*.

- Question template 1: Which is the *<quality-attribute>* of the *<object>*?
  Examples: Which is the <effort> of the <process>? Which is the <experience> of the <developers>?
- Question template 2: Which is the *<quality-attribute>* of the *<object>* *<relating-operation>* *<related-aspect>*?

Examples: Which is the <effort> of the <process> <distributed over> <its sub processes>? Which is the <experience> of the <developers> <distributed over> <sub projects>?

Attributes of quality question:

- *name*: short, intuitive name of the question, used for abstract views on the question.
- *quality-attribute:* specifies the attribute of the object referred to by the question (e.g., number of failures),
- *object:* specifies the object the question refers to (e.g., acceptance test),
- *related-aspect:* specifies a quality aspect or a structural aspect related to the quality-attribute (e.g., subsystem, week).
- *relating-operation:* specifies the operation that relates the related-aspect to the quality-attribute (e.g, distribution, comparison, any other relation).
- *customer-relevance:* indicates if a question is of primary relevance to the customer of the GQM plan.
- *domain:* specifies the domain of measurement results expected for the measurement goal.
- *estimated-value:* is an exemplary instance of the n-dimensional vector defined as domain. It contains the value(s) expected as results for a specific measurement goal. An example for the domain vector previously introduced is < high, 5, 7.5 >.
- *determine-result:* specifies how the measurement result is combined from the results of the lower level elements (i.e., the questions and measures refining the question).
- *visualize-result:* specifies how the measurement results can be visualized for presentation. Takes the result as input and produces chart(s) or table(s) as output.

Figure 2 Quality question attributes

2.1.3 Constraints between Measurement Plans and Process and Quality Models

In order to fulfil the prerequisites for measurement described in Section 1.3, the conceptual model for measurement plans needs to be integrated with conceptual models for process models and quality models. Thus, conceptual models for process and quality models need to be developed. The conceptual model for process models is based on the conceptual model proposed by Armitage and Kellner [1]. The exact definition of process models and quality models can be found in [6]:

Relationships between measurement plans and process models and between measurement plans and quality models allow us to define constraints, see dotted lines in Figure 3. These constraints relate to consistency and completeness of a measurement plan concerning process models and quality models. An example for a completeness constraint is that each element of the GQM plan is related to an object of the process model, i.e., a process, a product, or a resource. An example for a consistency constraint is that in the case of one question refining another question, the question object (i.e., a process or a product) of the refining question refines the object of the refined question or is related to the object of the refined question through a product flow relationship (i.e., a consume or produce relationship).

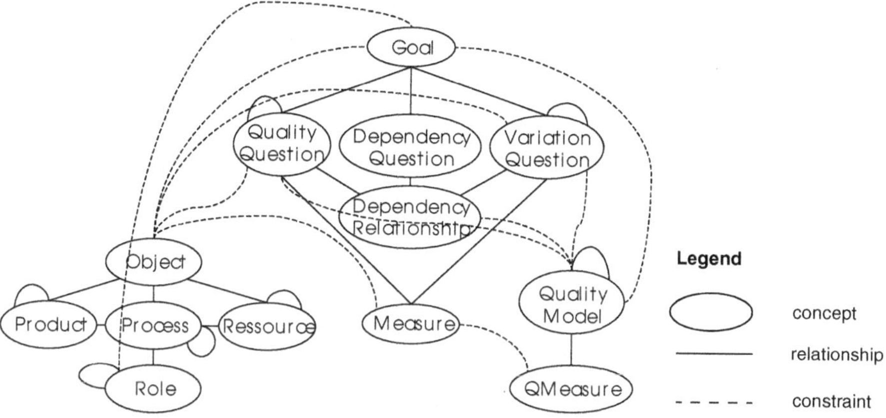

Figure 3 Constraints between measurement plans, process models, and quality models

2.2 Measurement Planning Process

This section describes the measurement planning process reduced to the development of a GQM plan. The development of measurement procedures is omitted. Section 2.2.1 lists the requirements for the process, Section 2.2.2 gives an overview of the process.

2.2.1 Requirements for a Measurement Planning Process

The development process fulfils the requirements listed in the following.

1. It builds on the measurement planning process as defined in [9].
2. It is designed to build measurement plans according to the conceptual model described in Section 2.1.
3. It is well-defined: The goal of the process, the expected inputs and outputs, constraints on inputs and outputs, and guidelines on how to perform the process are described for each step of the process.
4. It is systematic: The process is systematic for several reasons: First, it builds on existing project information. Second, it comprises constructive and analytic activities. Third, it supports modular measurement plan development.
5. It takes into account existing project information (i.e., process models and quality models) early during the development process of the measurement plan.

2.2.2 Overview of the Measurement Planning Process

This section gives an overview of a measurement planning process that produces measurement plans according to the conceptual model defined in Section 2.1. The process to develop GQM plans and its sub processes are depicted in Figure 4 using the graphical notation of the process modelling language MVP-L [5]. The process is supported by a tool that checks the structure of the plans and performs automatic completeness and consistency checks [6]. The process consists of four sub processes: hold interviews, develop high-level questions, develop refining questions, and review GQM plan. They are described in the following.

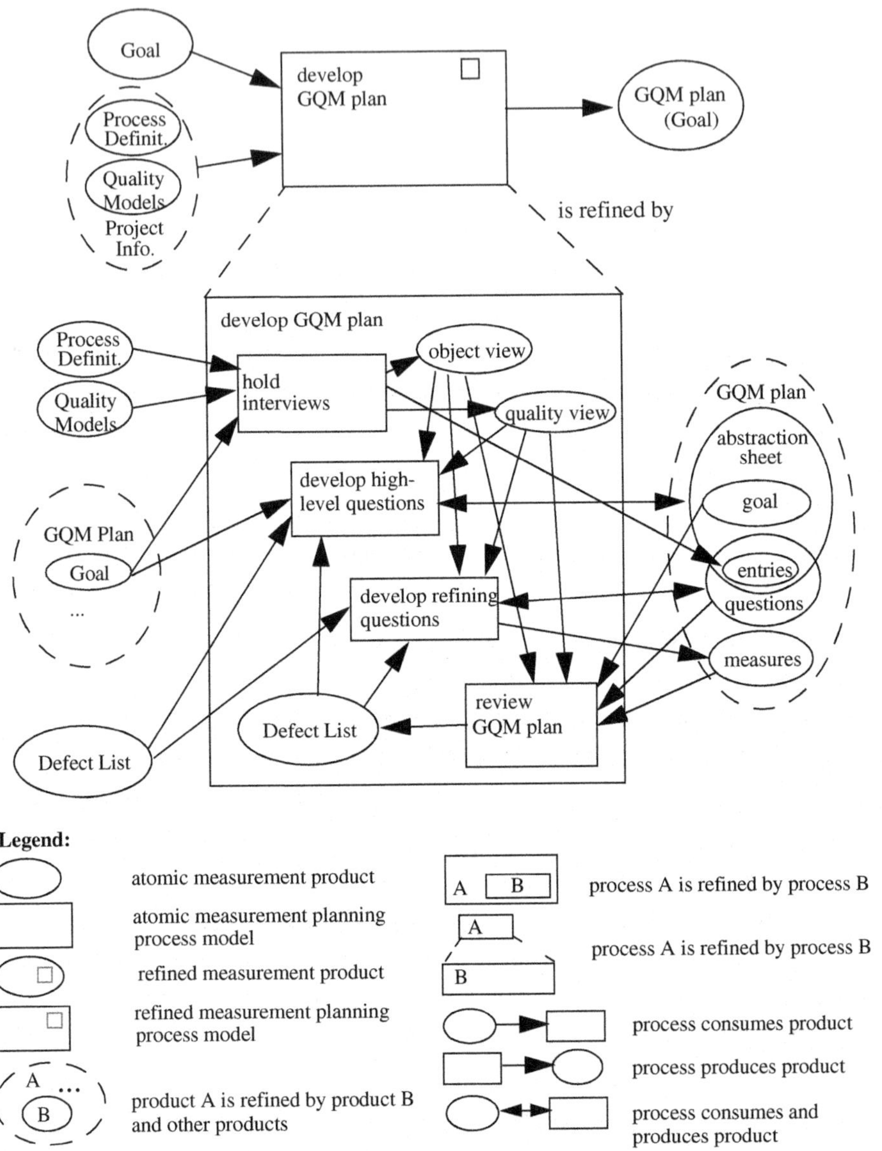

Figure 4 'Develop GQM plan'

- Hold interviews
  The process 'hold interviews' consumes project information (i.e., existing process models and quality models) and produces three intermediate products needed for the other sub processes of 'develop GQM plan': object view, quality view, and abstraction sheet. The object view contains a reduced view on the process de-

finition, i.e., only those processes and products that describe the object from the goal's viewpoint. The object view may contain information additionally to the process definition, if this information is crucial for developing the measurement plan. The quality view contains a view of the overall quality models for the project. This view reflects the viewpoint's models of the quality focus of the goal. The quality view may contain information additionally to the overall quality models, if this information is crucial for developing the measurement plan. The abstraction sheet, a GQM technique first introduced in [9], now combines object view and quality view in each of its entries.

- Develop high-level questions

  The information captured in the three intermediate products (i.e., object view, quality view, and abstraction sheet) are used to develop the high-level questions of the GQM plan in the process 'develop high-level questions'. Each abstraction sheet entry is detailed by a question in the GQM plan. The high-level questions of the GQM plan are those that are directly related to the goal. They belong to three different types: quality questions, variation questions, and dependency questions. They define the structure of the GQM plan. In case a defect list from a review is input for this process, the defects in the high-level questions are corrected.
- Develop refining questions

  The process 'develop refining questions' uses the high-level questions as input. It refines the GQM plan by breaking down its high-level quality and variation questions into sub quality- and sub variation questions and measures. Additionally, it defines dependency relationships and relates them to the dependency questions. This refining process uses the object view and the quality view. Definition of all measurement plan elements is supported by a tool that allows to check all measurement plan internal constraints. In case a defect list from a review exists as input for this process, the defects in the refined questions are corrected.
- Review GQM plan

  When the GQM plan is completely refined, it is reviewed in the process 'review GQM plan' by the representative of the goal's viewpoint and another measurement planner. Detailed checklists are available to guide the reviews. The checklists support the detection of semantic consistency defects that cannot be automated as constraints. If defects are detected, the GQM plan is reworked.

3 Reuse of Measurement Plans

Section 2 describes an approach for measurement planning that satisfies the preconditions for measurement plan reuse listed in Section 1.3. This section investigates reuse of measurement plans. Sections 3.1 to 3.4 investigate typical variations that occur from one project to the next and, thus, are the basis for reuse. The purpose parameter will not be considered here. Section 3.5 states the need for similarity models to identify the most appropriate reuse candidates. Section 3.6 sketches a conceptual model for reusable parts of measurement plans. Section 3.7 proposes a reuse process based on this conceptual model and similarity models.

3.1 Variation of Object to Be Measured

If the goal parameter 'object' changes, the object view changes. The name of the object may be the same, but its refinement in terms of processes, products, resources, and flows may be different. The differences of the existing to the new object views is a combination of:

- addition/deletion of a process, product, or resource model
- addition/deletion of an aggregation refinement relationship among product or process models
- addition/deletion of a product flow relationship between products and processes
- addition/deletion of a resource assignment
- change of a process, product, or resource model name

3.2 Variation of Quality Focus to Be Measured

If the goal parameter 'quality focus' changes, the quality view changes. The name of the quality focus may be the same, but its refinement in terms of quality models and measures may be different. The differences of the existing to the new quality views is a combination of:

- addition/deletion of a quality model
- addition/deletion of a measure
- addition/deletion of an input parameter for a quality model (relationship)
- change of the input parameter definition
- change of the model definition
- change of the assumptions
- change of a quality model or measure name

3.3 Variation of Viewpoint of Measurement

For the viewpoint parameter, only full changes are possible. The representative of the viewpoint parameter defines the contents of object and quality view. Therefore, if the viewpoint changes, object and quality view usually change with it. Thus, a view change can be reduced to a change of object and quality view at the same time and does not need to be considered as special case.

3.4 Variation of Context of Measurement

If the context parameter is modified, the meaning of all the other parameters may change. New object and quality views may become relevant to the viewpoint. Context parameter changes can be rather complex and will not be considered here.

3.5 Similarity Models

Similarity models are needed to identify the best match for a reuse candidate. Similarity models are not only needed for measurement plans and parts of measurement plans, but also for process models and quality models. Process and quality models directly influence the structure of a measurement plan and can be used to identify the best reuse candidate. A similarity model for the process modelling language MVP-L is described in

[18]. Similarity models of measurement plan elements can be based on equality of their attribute values. Therefore, a high degree of formality is needed also on the attribute level of measurement plan element.

3.6 Conceptual Model for Reusable Measurement Plans

This section sketches a conceptual model of measurement plans for a composition-based reuse approach. The components to be reused are templates of measurement plan elements, instantiated templates, and interrelated sets of instantiated templates, all of which need to be modifiable. The components are situated on four different levels of detail: abstraction sheet level, question refinement tree level, measurement plan element level, and entry for measurement plan element attribute level, see Figure 5.

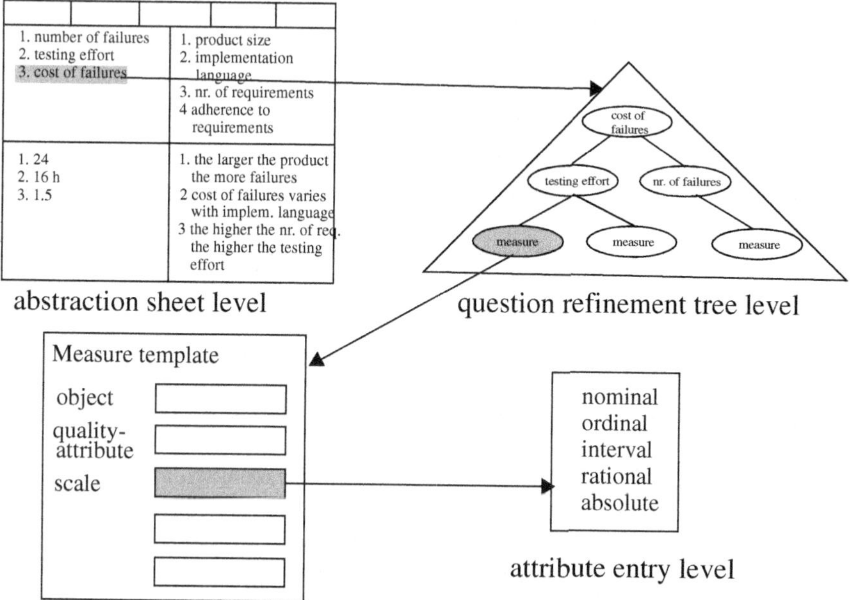

Figure 5 Four levels of measurement plan reuse

Different levels of detail of reusable components call for different reuse techniques, so that they can be reused effectively. The reusable components represent parts of GQM plans:

- Abstraction sheet level

  Abstraction sheets can be identified and selected based on the similarity of goals, and of object and quality view that refine the goal parameters object and quality focus, respectively. (Object and quality views can also be reused.) The abstraction sheets then can be modified systematically based on the differences of goals, and of object and quality views.

- Question refinement tree level

  Question refinement trees can be identified and selected based on the similarity of the attributes' entries of the questions, and of the object and quality views that are used to refine the question. The question refinement trees then can be modified based on the differences of questions, and of object and quality views. Question refinement trees do not contain dependency relationships that relate them to other question refinement trees. Such interrelationships among question refinement trees are only contained in the abstraction sheets and have to be modified there.

- Measurement plan element level

  Measurement plan elements (goals, questions, dependency relationships, and measures) can be reused as templates, but also as instantiated templates, i.e., templates with attributes' entries. Templates are selected and evaluated based on refinement process guidelines. For details, see [6].

- Attribute entries for measurement plan elements level

  Attribute entries for measurement plan elements' attributes can be reused. This is already done in case of the attribute entries for some of the attributes (e.g., object, quality-attribute, and scale), where the potential attribute entries can be selected from a set of values. Moreover, entry reuse pools for other attributes could be developed (e.g., domain, range), as well as languages to build entries for some specific attributes (e.g., determine-result, interpret-result, and visualise-result).

In the following, we assume that searchable sets of reusable components of each level of detail are available. We call these sets '<name of component> pool', e.g., abstraction sheet pool. Moreover, we assume the availability of similarity models.

3.7 Sketch of the Process Model 'Develop Systematically with Reuse'

The previous section presented different levels of detail of measurement plan components. The process sketched in this section describes a reuse-based development process for measurement plans, which is based on the reuse process described in Section 2.2, Figure 4 'develop GQM plan', and on the different levels of details introduced previously. Figure 6 gives an overview of the products and processes involved in development with reuse. Additionally to the products already known, searchable pools of components are used as input for the processes. The processes are arranged based on increasing levels of detail of the reused components: abstraction sheet level, question refinement tree level, measurement plan element level, and attribute entry component level. The processes are a restricted view on the overall development with reuse process: The view is restricted to the processes implementing reuse aspects. The view omits the development part. The processes can easily be integrated with the overall development process described by 'develop GQM plan', see Figure 4 in the following way: 'Reuse abstraction sheets' is integrated within 'hold interviews', 'reuse question refinement trees' within 'develop high-level questions', 'reuse questions' and 'reuse measures' within 'develop refining questions'. A detailed description of the integration is omitted here, as the goal of this section is to communicate the main ideas behind the proposed reuse approach.

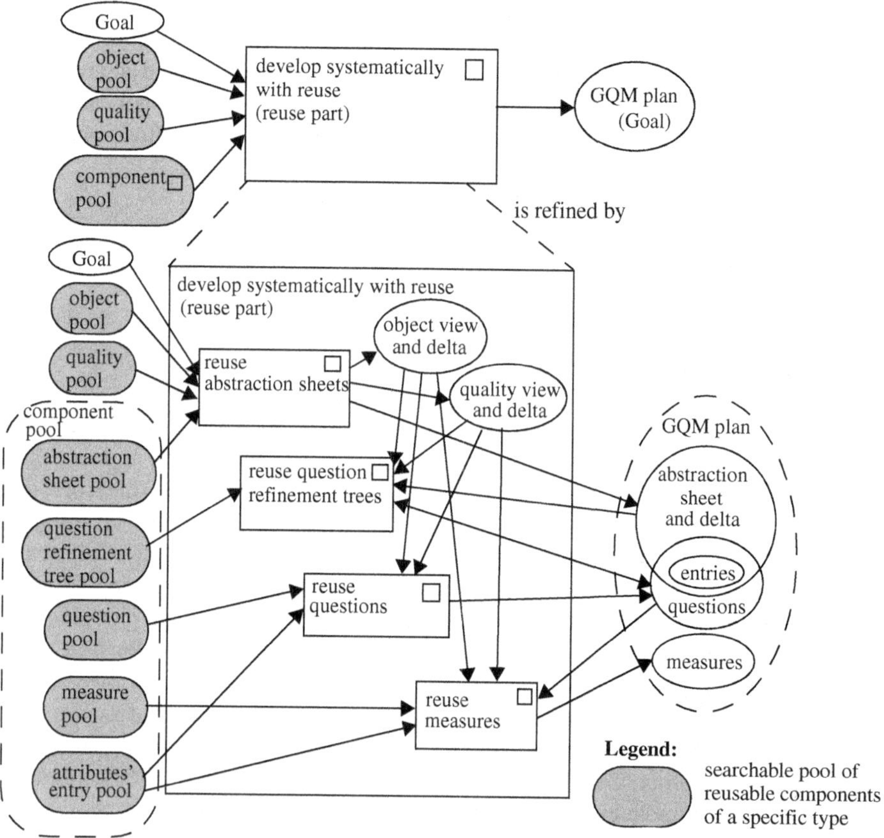

Figure 6 'Develop systematically with reuse'

Process description

- Reuse abstraction sheets

  Based on the measurement goal, the available object views, quality views, and abstraction sheets are identified, selected, and modified. The modification information for object view, quality view, and abstraction sheet is captured and stored together with these documents. This information is used as input for the following process.

- Reuse question refinement trees

  Based on the modified abstraction sheet, object view, and quality view, question refinement trees are identified, selected, and modified. For unmodified abstraction sheet entries, the question refinement trees associated to the originally reused abstraction sheet are the most probable reuse candidates. For new or modified abstraction sheet entries, question refinement trees from the pool are reused.

- Reuse questions

  If question refinement trees need to be modified, or if no fitting question refinement tree can be identified and selected, new questions are created and refined according to the development process. In this case, the question pool can be searched for existing questions similar to the needed one. For modifications of questions, the attributes' entry pool can be searched for entries.
- Reuse measures

  Depending on the availability of reusable question refinement trees, in the same way as questions, measures can be reused. For modifications of measures, the attributes' entry pool can be searched for entries.

4 Conclusion

The contents of measurement plans strongly depends on process models of the object that is measured and quality models of the quality focus of measurement. Process models and quality models change from project to project and over time. Therefore, in order to reuse measurement plans in a learning organization, relationships between measurement plans and process and quality models are needed. These relationships can be used to identify and adapt existing measurement plans to varying process and quality models. This paper presents a formal conceptual model of measurement plans including relationships to process and quality models and a development process for such measurement plans. This model and process build a sound basis for reuse of measurement plans. To further support reuse, a conceptual model for components of measurement plan elements is sketched. Components can be reused to build new measurement plans. A reuse process is proposed that starts from a similarity analysis of the (reused and new) underlying process model and quality models.

Acknowledgements. I want to thank Niniek Angkasaputra, Eric Ras and the anonymous reviewers for their comments on this paper.

References

[1] James W. Armitage and Marc I. Kellner. A conceptual schema for process definitions and models. In Dewayne E. Perry, editor, *Proceedings of the Third International Conference on the Software Process*, pages 153–165. IEEE Computer Society Press, October 1994.

[2] Victor R. Basili. Applying the Goal/Question/Metric paradigm in the experience factory. In Norman Fenton, Robin Whitty, and Yoshinori Iizuka, editors, *Software Quality Assurance and Measurement: A Worldwide Perspective*, pages 21–44. International Thompson Computer Press, 1995

[3] Victor R. Basili and David M. Weiss. A methodology for collecting valid software engineering data. *IEEE Transactions on Software Engineering*, SE-10(6):728–738, November 1984

[4] Lionel C. Briand, Christiane M. Differding, and H. Dieter Rombach. Practical guidelines for measurement-based process improvement. *Software Process*, 2(4):253–280, December 1996.

[5] Alfred Bröckers, Christiane Differding, Barbara Hoisl, Frank Kollnischko, Christopher M. Lott, Jürgen Münch, Martin Verlage, and Stefan Vorwieger. A graphical representation schema for the software process modeling language MVP–L. Technischer Bericht 270/95, Fachbereich Informatik, Universität Kaiserslautern, 67653 Kaiserslautern, June 1995.

[6] Christiane Differding. Adaptive Measurement Plans for Software development. Dissertation. Department of Computer Science, University of Kaiserslautern, Germany, November 2000.

[7] Christiane Gresse von Wangenheim. Remex – a case-based approach for reusing software measurement experience. In *Case-Besed Reasoning Research and Development. Third International Conference on Case-based reasoning ICCBR'99. Proceedings*, pages 173–187, 1999.

[8] Christiane Gresse and Lionel Briand. Requirements for the Knowledge-Based Support of Software Engineering Measurement Plans. In *Proceedings of the Ninth International Software Engineering and Knowledge Engineering Conference (SEKE'97)*, pages 559–568, Madrid, Spain, June 1997.

[9] Christiane Gresse, Barbara Hoisl, and Jürgen Wüst. A process model for GQM-based measurement. Technical Report STTI-95-04-E, Software Technologie Transfer Initiative Kaiserslautern, Fachbereich Informatik, Universität Kaiserslautern, D-67653 Kaiserslautern, 1995.

[10] Christiane Gresse von Wangenheim, Alexandre Moraes Ramos, Klaus-Dieter Althoff, Ricardo M. Barcia, Rosina Weber, and Alejandro Martins. Case-based reasoning approach to reuse of experiential knowledge in software measurement programs. In Lothar Gierl, editor, *Proceedings of the Sixth German Workshop on Case-Based Reasoning*, Berlin, Germany, 1998.

[11] Christiane Gresse von Wangenheim, Klaus-Dieter Althoff, and Ricardo M. Barcia. Intelligent retrieval of software engineering experienceware. In *Proceedings of the Eleventh Conference on Software Engineering and Knowledge Engineering*, pages 128–135, Kaiserslautern, Germany, June 1999. Knowledge Systems Institute, Skokie, IL, USA.

[12] Christiane Gresse von Wangenheim, Klaus-Dieter Althoff, and Ricardo M. Barcia. Goal-oriented and similarity-based retrieval of software engineering experienceware. In Guenther Ruhe and Frank Bomarius, editors, *Learning Software Organizations – Methodology and Applications*. Springer-Verlag, 2000.

[13] Matthias Jarke, Manfred Jeusfeld, and Christoph Quix. Conceptbase 5.0 user manual. http://www-i5.informatik.rwth-aachen.de/CBdoc/userManual, March 1998. viewed in 1998.

[14] Hector Munoz-Avila, David W. Aha, Leonard A. Breslow, Dana S. Nau and Rosina Weber.Integrating Conversational Case retrieval with generative planning. To appear in *Proceedings of the Fourth European Workshop on Case-Based Reasoning (EWCBR-2000)*. Trento, Italy, Springer-Verlag.

[15] John Mylopoulos, Alex Borgida, Matthias Jerke, and Manolis Koubrakis. Telos: Representing knowledge about information systems. *ACM Transactions on information systems*, 8(4):325–362, oct 1990.

[16] John Roche and Mike Jackson. Software measurement methods: recipes for success? *Information and Software Technology*, 36(3):173–189, 1994

[17] H. Dieter Rombach. Practical benefits of goal-oriented measurement. In N. Fenton and B. Littlewood, editors, *Software Reliability and Metrics*, pages 217–235. Elsevier Applied Science, London, 1991.

[18] Martin Verlage. *Ein Ansatz zur Modellierung großer Softwareentwicklungsprozesse durch Integration unabhängig erfaßter rollenspezifischer Sichten*. PhD thesis, Universität Kaiserslautern, 1997

Engineering Experience Base Maintenance Knowledge

Markus Nick and Klaus-Dieter Althoff

Fraunhofer Institut Experimentelles Software Engineering (IESE)
Sauerwiesen 6, 67661 Kaiserslautern, Germany
{nick, althoff}@iese.fhg.de

Abstract. The value of a corporate information system such as an experience base tends to degrade with time. To keep the value of such a system, maintenance is an essential. Maintenance should not simply happen ad-hoc but systematically and based on specific maintenance knowledge. As a jump-start for maintenance, maintenance knowledge should be available right from the start of continuous operation. This paper describes how to systematically develop ("to engineer") such maintenance knowledge during buildup of the corporate information system.

1 Introduction

The value of a corporate information system tends to degrade with time, be it by external impacts on the organization's environment or by changes within an organization (e.g., the development of a new product). This is particularly true if exemplary knowledge (experience, case-specific knowledge) is stored in the information system, as is typically done in experience bases (EBs), lessons learned systems, best practice databases, or case-based reasoning (CBR) systems, because such knowledge is gained almost continuously in daily work [10, 1, 31]. In the recent past the new field "Experience Management" [30, 8] appears to establish itself. Experience Management deals with all the relevant research and development issues for this kind of information systems. The ingredients of experience management stem from different scientific fields, among others experience factory (EF)/learning software organization [28, 7, 6], CBR [2], and knowledge management [27].

In this paper we deal with experience management approaches. While the term "management" underlines the "process" aspects of such approaches, we subsume the "product" aspects under the notion of EB systems (or EBs, CBR systems, case bases, organizational memory systems, organizational memory, corporate information system). Experience management includes methods for identifying, collecting, documenting, packaging, storing, generalizing, reusing, tailoring, and evaluating of experience (experience packages, cases) based on an EB.

EB systems must be maintained on a continuous basis [9, 21]. Such maintenance should not be performed ad-hoc. Instead, a systematic approach is required to ensure "good", well-controlled maintenance. For this purpose, knowledge-focused and technical issues as well as organizational issues have to be considered. To deal with the organizational issues, a dedicated role - e.g., a Chief Information Officer (CIO) - and/or a

K.-D. Althoff, R.L. Feldmann, and W. Müller (Eds.): LSO 2001, LNCS 2176, pp. 222–236, 2001.

dedicated organizational unit - e.g., an EF - should be established [9, 3, 7, 6]. To support the actual maintenance of the EB, specific maintenance experience and its conceptual structure has to be included [17, 18, 14, 21].

Maintenance knowledge has been partly discussed in the literature: Leake & Wilson [15] introduced the concept of "maintenance policies" for maintaining the EB. These "maintenance policies" can be viewed as maintenance knowledge. Rombach [26] discussed principles for the maintenance of cost models, which were based on the dimensions of software maintenance by Swanson [29]. Minor & Hanft [19] presented a life-cycle model for test cases and a life-cycle model for lessons learned is available in [4]. McKenna & Smyth [16] presented competence-preserving maintenance strategies for planning tasks.

Another type of knowledge that is related to maintenance, is quality knowledge. Quality knowledge describes how the quality of the EB is defined and how to measure quality as well as the rationale for the quality knowledge [17]. Quality knowledge deals with quality aspects of the EB system as a whole, i.e., the EB's contents and conceptual model as well as retrieval mechanisms and usability of the user interface. An example for content-related quality knowledge is a definition of metrics for the utility or value of single experience packages [23].

In [21], we presented the EMSIG framework and an integrated technical solution operationalizing the (decision) support for the maintenance of an EB regarding experience packages and conceptual model using specific maintenance and quality knowledge. While the quality knowledge can be acquired and improved using a systematic approach [22, 23], the maintenance knowledge is rather acquired "by chance" during continuous operation (with the exception of maintenance strategies such as competence-preserving case base maintenance strategies for planning tasks [16]). Thus, it might take long to learn the required maintenance knowledge. The problem is that existing methods such as INRECA [9] or DISER[1] [30] only fill the "standard" knowledge containers of CBR/EB systems (vocabulary, cases, similarity measures, adaptation [25]) and do not address the acquisition and usage of maintenance and quality knowledge.

This brings us to three open issues that are subject of this paper: (1) How to acquire and develop maintenance knowledge systematically. Our approach derives operational maintenance knowledge from artifacts and information gained during EB buildup and from a knowledge/experience life-cycle model. (2) After the maintenance and quality knowledge has been developed, it has to be integrated into the operational EB system. (3) Such systematic maintenance and quality knowledge acquisition must be integrated into a buildup method.

The development of the required maintenance and quality knowledge during EB buildup ensures that the maintenance and evaluation needs are considered during the development of the EB. This aims at avoiding more expensive future changes due to maintenance needs identified later than possible.

---

[1] DISER is a methodology for **d**esigning and **i**mplementing **s**oftware **e**ngineering **r**epositories

The paper is structured as follows. Section 2 states some assumptions about the EB buildup and evaluation, and gives a glimpse on our in-house EF COIN. Section 3 presents our approach to systematically developing maintenance knowledge and illustrates this with examples from COIN and industrial projects. Section 4 describes how to integrate this maintenance and quality knowledge into an EB system using currently available CBR tools such as Orenge from tec:inno/empolis and how to integrate evaluation into the usage of the EB. Section 5 discusses how to integrate the method into an EB buildup methodology. Finally, some conclusions are drawn (Section 6).

2 Assumption about EB Buildup

During buildup, the following artifacts and information are developed: Objectives (including high-level success criteria) and subject areas of the EB need to be identified. For these, detailed experience reuse and record scenarios are developed. Based on the scenarios, the conceptual model underlying the experience packages is developed. Processes/methods for recording and utilizing experience are defined/selected. A knowledge collection plan describes when which artifact has to be collected how by whom. Finally, the actual technical and non-technical infrastructure must be implemented according to the organization's needs. All these parts and intermediate artifacts/ information should be developed using some methodology such as INRECA or DISER (see [30] for an industrial-strength case study and a detailed description). Usually, these parts are not developed from scratch. Instead, they are tailored from similar parts used in other organizations.

The result of the initial acquisition of quality knowledge (i.e., of the planning phase of an evaluation program) are (1) a measurement plan that describes which measurement data is collected when, how, by whom, and who validates and stores the data; and (2) an evaluation plan that defines when to conduct analyses of the collected measurement data and when to involve users in the interpretation of the analysed data. This should be developed in a systematic manner, e.g., with the goal-oriented Goal-Question-Metric (GQM) method for the measurement plan (see [22, 23] for details). With GQM, the evaluation can be linked to business goals, e.g., from the learning-and-growth part of a balanced scorecard [11, 13]. To jump-start evaluation, GQM allows to reuse and validate existing quality models [22, 5] and quality measures [24]. Still, there are open issues: integration into usage and the integration of lessons learned from the evaluation program into the EB (e.g., guideline/rule about relationships between variation and quality factors). These issues will be addressed in Section 4.

Our in-house-EF COIN (**Co**rporate **I**nformation **N**etwork) was launched -due to the rapid growth of the IESE- to (a) provide the less experienced people with default processes and guidelines to jump-start them and (b) to facilitate experience sharing among them to build up their expertise more quickly [30, 21]. Since the size of our institute does not allow to talk to all people on a weekly basis, experience sharing on a personal basis does not work. The EB was developed using the DISER method. Fig. 1 shows an excerpt of COIN's EB, which will be used in examples in the remainder of this paper. The focus in the excerpt is on lessons learned in the form of guidelines, observations, and problems. The guidelines act as solutions or mitigation strategies for the problems.

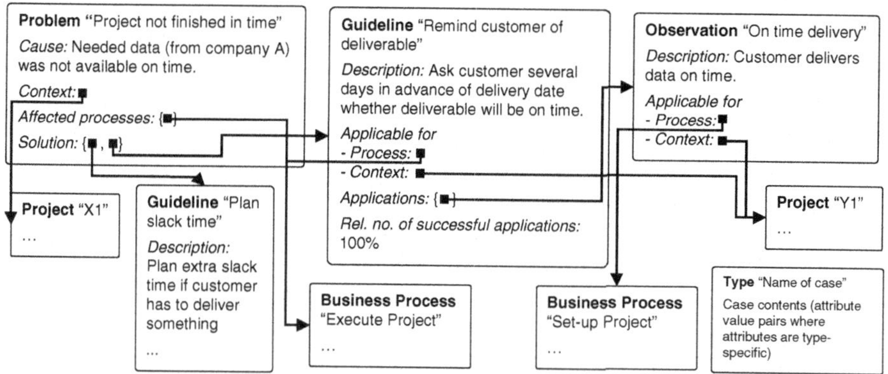

Fig. 1. Excerpt of COIN experience base (8 experience packages)

An observation describes either the results of an application of a guideline or something interesting that has been observed without related experiences.

3 A Method for Engineering Maintenance Knowledge

The principle of engineering maintenance knowledge during buildup (Fig. 2) is to derive operational maintenance knowledge from three major sources: (1) a knowledge/experience life-cycle model, (2) artifacts and information gained during EB buildup, and (3) the measurement plan for the evaluation. From these sources, we derive rather informal maintenance policies and more formal maintenance guidelines. The maintenance policies are further formalized as maintenance guidelines. The maintenance guidelines can be automated using EMSIG's maintenance decision support components (i.e., maintenance assistance and maintenance management component [21]).

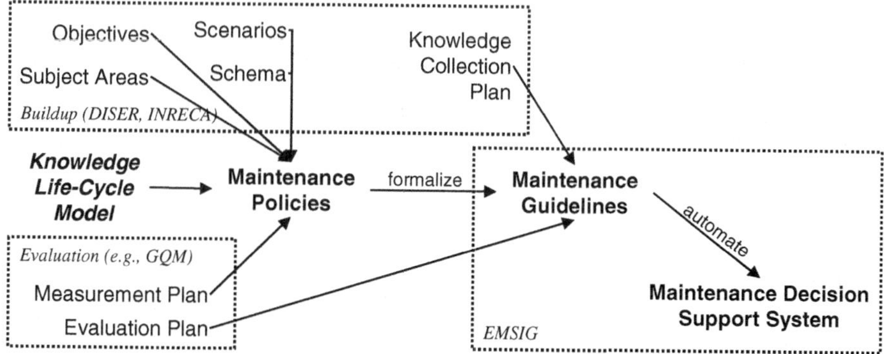

Fig. 2. Systematically developing maintenance knowledge and support during EB buildup.

The following sections describe the definition of a knowledge life-cycle model and the deriving of maintenance policies in detail and illustrate this with examples from our in-house-EF COIN and from industrial projects. Furthermore, the formalization of the maintenance policies into maintenance guidelines and the automation using EMSIG's tools are summarized.

3.1 Defining a Knowledge Life-Cycle Model

A *knowledge/experience life-cycle model* describes the basic idea of how to maintain and improve knowledge and experience over time. Thus, it is the basis of any further refinement of the maintenance process, in particular, with respect to the EB content. The life-cycle model also addresses issues such as validity and degree of maturity of the knowledge and experience stored. All this is the starting point for a systematic maintenance and improvement of the knowledge and experience.

A generic knowledge life-cycle model is depicted in Fig. 3 [4]. This model has been used for COIN and industrial projects. Explicitly documented knowledge is developed and matured over time: In the beginning, very context-dependent experiences are collected, e.g., from measurement data analyses or expert interviews. Examples for such experiences on very specific issues are the observations, guidelines, and problems in COIN (Fig. 1). By reuse in similar contexts, these experiences are more and more validated. Furthermore, more experiences are collected that are on similar or related issues like the experiences already stored. In addition, these experiences are further aggregated and generalized. When these experiences cover a sufficiently wide area and are mature enough, they can be combine in order to derive a comprehensive best-practice description (e.g., a business process description as in COIN - see Fig. 1).[2] Such a best-practice description is enriched with further experiences, which are integrated into the best-practice description from time to time. This closes the loop.

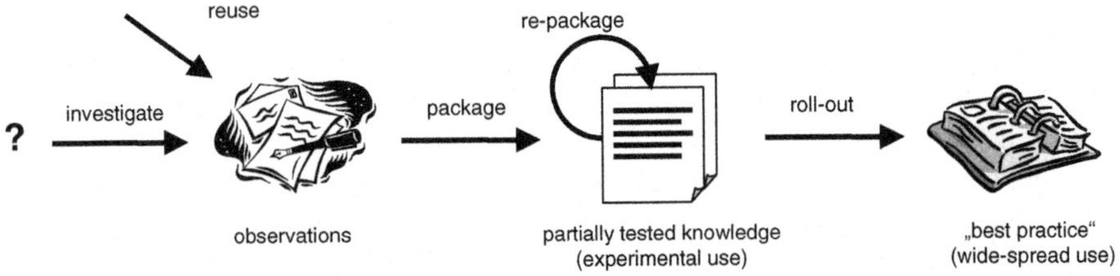

Fig. 3. Generic knowledge life-cycle model. [4]

In parallel or triggered by the evolution of the knowledge, the conceptual model of the knowledge is also improved: Knowledge and experience can be more formalized. This leads to defining more attributes and extending existing attribute types.

While the form/type of the knowledge in the life-cycle model (i.e., first sample, lesson learned, best practice) deals with the maturity of the knowledge, more in-depth issues address validity.

Validity describes how general an experience is and how much one can trust the experience to be successfully reused in its anticipated application context. To integrate validity issues into the life-cycle model, an operational definition of validity is required. This definition can be in a qualitative [20] or quantitative manner (COIN).

---

[2] When tacit best practice is available (e.g., knowledge about a business process that has not been made explicit), best-practice descriptions are also elicited directly using suitable knowledge acquisition methods (e.g., business process elicitation & modelling [12]).

If the reuse of experiences can be measured, a quantitative validity can be defined using the number of successful and failed reuse attempts. The validity increases after successful reuse and decreases after failed reuse - at least temporarily until the experience is maintained respectively. Such a quantitative definition is particularly suitable for "new" experiences, i.e., experiences that are recorded directly in the EB when becoming known.

For already known experiences that are entered into the EB later, a purely quantitative definition of validity obviously cannot be complete because the number of applications before the recording in the EB cannot be determined. Instead, a qualitative definition of validity is appropriate.

Based on the ideas made explicit in the knowledge life-cycle model, the maintenance can be defined in more detail.

3.2 Deriving Maintenance Policies

The objective of deriving maintenance policies is to describe –in an informal manner– when, why, and how to do maintenance on an EB system.

This is done by deriving so-called "maintenance policies". For our purposes, we extend the definition of [15]:[3] *Maintenance policies* determine when, why, and how maintenance is performed for an EB system. The "why" addresses the reason of maintenance including the expected benefits of the maintenance operation, which should be related to the objectives of the EB system or to the general goal of maintenance (i.e., to preserve and improve the EB's value [21]).

When DISER is used, the action refers to one task or a combination of tasks from DISER. Relevant tasks are record/update/forget experience package and restructure EB as well as their respective sub-tasks.

Maintenance policies can be derived from various sources (Fig. 2): the knowledge/ experience life-cycle model; artifacts and information gained during EB buildup; and the measurement plan for the evaluation. In addition, generic, well-tested maintenance policies from CBR research and practice should be reused for general aspects (see [15] for an overview). In the following, we describe how to derive maintenance policies from these sources and illustrate this with examples from COIN or industrial projects. For reasons of space, some maintenance policies are only outlined.

Deriving maintenance policies from the knowledge life-cycle model. There are two major issues in the knowledge life-cycle model that are refined using maintenance policies:

1. The transformation of experience of one type into another is performed under specific conditions and for certain reasons. These conditions and reasons have to be

[3] The original definition of [15] is as follows: "*Maintenance policies* determine when and how a CBR system performs *case base maintenance*. Maintenance policies are described in terms of how they gather data relevant to maintenance, how they decide when to trigger maintenance, the types of maintenance operations available, and how selected maintenance operations are executed."

identified and related actions are outlined. Together reason and related action form a maintenance policy. Fig. 4 shows an example of such a maintenance policy for transforming partially tested knowledge such as lessons learned into best practice.

Trigger: Number of lessons learned attached to a best practice description is more than X
Actions: Aggregate best practice description with (some of the) lessons learned.
Expected benefits: The description is more comprehensive and easier to understand.

Fig. 4. Example maintenance policy for transforming experience from one type into another.

2. The ways of dealing with failed reuse attempts have to be defined. This is defined by a combination of monitoring the quality/validity of the knowledge in the EB and proposing respective actions. These maintenance policies mainly refer to corrective actions and fix problems that were encountered during reuse of an experience.
   For example, an experience was misunderstood and applied incorrectly several times, which requires two actions: rephrasing and checking if the recording is unreliable or inaccurate (see Fig. 5).

Trigger: validity ratio < X% and
number of related observations "phrasing not comprehensible or misunderstood" > N
Actions:
(a) The experience package has to be rephrased and tested regarding its understandability. The observations that are considered during rephrasing are deleted. The latter implies an increase of the validity ratio of the experience package.
(b) The quality criteria for recording the knowledge have to be checked regarding their effectiveness for ensuring the comprehensibility of the recorded experiences.
Expected benefits:The description is easier to comprehend.

Fig. 5. Example of a maintenance policy derived from the knowledge life-cycle model.

   For another example, the application context was too different from the contexts where the experience was gained and applied so far. Then the experience has to be split, i.e., rewritten and newly recorded for the context where it failed.

Although adding negative observations about the application of an experience decreases the validity ratio of the applied experience, this does not decrease the overall competence of the EB in every case: The knowledge about a context where an experience is not applicable is useful to avoid making the same mistake twice and, thus, contributes to the EB's overall competence and value.

The content-triggered maintenance policies (e.g., Fig. 4 and Fig. 5) benefit in particular from the learning about maintenance. After an initial good guess for the trigger regarding X%, N, etc., these policies can be improved and validated based on the evaluation [21].

Deriving maintenance policies from conceptual model and scenarios. From the scenarios and the conceptual model, maintenance policies are derived that analyse if the different types of experience are used as intended and not "abused." Abuse is mainly possible for experience types or subject areas where users can enter items that are published without further reviewing by the EF staff.

For example: The EF allows every user to add comments to experience packages in order to make the EB more interactive. These comments should only deal with minor problems such as typos, misunderstandings, etc. A respective maintenance policy is as follows: A larger average number of larger comments indicates that the commenting feature might be abused to store actual experience without further reviews. Thus, the comments are checked. If abuse has happened, the respective comments are rewritten as experience packages and the commenting feature is deactivated. Furthermore, a more "in-time" recording of experiences could be considered because such an abuse can demonstrate the need for such a change.

Deriving maintenance policies from evaluation, user feedback, and scenarios. Maintenance policies can be stated for the different types of user feedback [5]. For example, if users do not select any experience in the query results as useful in more then X% of the queries, then the coverage could be too low or the EB might focus on the wrong subject area. Thus, the users should be interviewed respectively and the respective measure should be taken (i.e., record more experiences or change focus of EB).

For each of the reuse scenarios, the expected usage is estimated by the number of times the scenario will happen. This serves as a baseline for an evaluation of the usage of the EB.

Using strategies from CBR research and practice. Besides the tailored and more EB-specific maintenance policies that were addressed so far, maintenance strategies from CBR research and practice should be considered. Before using these, their application constraints must be checked and analysed carefully. For example, a competence-preserving approach to case deletion has been tested for planning tasks [16]. This could we reused for EB/CBR systems with a similar task.

The impact of EB objectives on the maintenance policies. The "expected benefits" section of the maintenance policies should be related to the EB's objectives or the general goal of maintenance. Since these objectives are typically very high-level, it is not very meaningful to address the EB objectives directly. Instead, we use a refinement of the objectives: the quality criteria from the evaluation program or the recording methods (e.g., see Fig. 4 and Fig. 5).

3.3 Formalizing Maintenance Policies

The maintenance policies are formalized as *maintenance guidelines* [21]. Because maintenance guidelines still describe a typical task or pattern of maintenance activities, they usually refer to classes/groups of experience packages and not directly to experience packages. These maintenance guidelines are used for generating change requests for the experience packages that require maintenance. For this purpose, the following changes and extensions are made with respect to maintenance policies:

For the automatic generation of change requests, a partial or complete formalization of the "trigger" is required to allow an automatic tool-based checking of the trigger. The formalized parts of the trigger can refer to EB's conceptual model and contents as well as evaluation results. The part of the trigger than cannot be formalized is included in the maintenance guideline for manual checks by the responsible role. In case the actual trigger cannot be formalized at all, then the respective guideline can be triggered periodically as a reminder and the actual condition check is done manually by an EF staff member.

The "actions" now refer to the existing descriptions of "standard" maintenance activities as modules (if the required description already exists). EMSIG provides these modules with its maintenance primitive component. Simple text is used as glue among the modules or for the remaining parts that are not "standard."

The "expected benefits" help justify the instantiation of the guideline as change request (e.g., by cost-benefit issues, quality improvements, the importance of a scenario) and provide – at least hints – for assigning a priority or importance level to the change request. In addition, the related record and reuse scenarios are stated to support the estimation of the expected benefits.

The responsible role is stated, to increase flexibility instead of a fixed assignment of experience package changes to the experience engineer and changes of the conceptual model to the experience manager. If different roles are responsible for a maintenance policy, this has to be split into several dependent maintenance guidelines to allow the assignment of the task to several persons.

Since maintenance guidelines usually refer to generic items from the EB (e.g., "process descriptions") or to a generic configuration of items. Therefore, it is necessary to generate a separate change request for each single experience package or configuration that is affected.

3.4 Tool Support for Maintenance Policies

To allow the automatic generation of change requests, tool support is essential for the maintenance guidelines. For this purpose, the maintenance assistance component of the EB maintenance and evaluation framework EMSIG [21] can be used. The reader is referred to [21] for details on the EMSIG framework and its components.

4 Integrating Evaluation and Maintenance for the EB System

The maintenance and quality knowledge engineering leads to additional conceptual knowledge and cases that have to be harmonized and integrated with the conceptual model, the knowledge collection plan, and the evaluation program before the EB system is implemented.

Section 4.1 describes the integration of the conceptual model, knowledge collection plan, measurement program, and evaluation plan. The actual representation of such an integrated, more comprehensive conceptual model and the respective tool architecture can be found in [21]. Section 4.2 describes exemplary how to embed measurement data collection for evaluation into the usage on an EB system.

4.1 Harmonize & Integrate Conceptual Knowledge, Knowledge Collection Plan, and Evaluation Program

The task of harmonizing conceptual knowledge, maintenance knowledge, and quality knowledge has the objective of integrating maintenance and quality knowledge into the EB system (i.e., into conceptual model and case base).

The integration of the knowledge collection plan and of the evaluation plan is quite simple. The knowledge collection plan defines when which artifact has to be collected how by whom [30]. Thus, each entry can be represented as a maintenance guideline: "when" and "which artifact" describe the condition, "how to collect" the action, and "by whom" the responsible role. For example, if "project[X].end < 'today'" then "notify experience engineer about task 'record project experience' for project[X]".

The evaluation plan describes when which evaluation of the collected measurement data is performed how and by whom (e.g., when to analyse the collected data using a certain statistical method and when to hold a feedback session on the data analysis results with representatives of the users). Thus, the evaluation plan's structure is very similar to the knowledge collection plan's and it can be represented in the same way.

The measurement plan defines quality metrics as well as manual and automatic data collection procedures. These metrics and data collection procedures have to be integrated into conceptual model as well as usage and record scenarios (e.g., see Section 4.2). The measurement plan itself is not stored in the EB. There are two reasons: (1) The measurement plan might be kept in a separate evaluation tool (e.g., a GQM tool). (2) The measurement plan also refers to EB aspects that are not part of the conceptual model or case base (e.g., user interface).

In the evaluation, general knowledge is identified about relationships between variation factors and quality factors. Such knowledge is attached as lessons learned to the respective parts of the record process/method description. Thus, the experience engineers are informed about these lessons when they perform the respective recording.

4.2 Embedding Evaluation into Usage

Practice has shown that the users' motivation for entering measurement data during usage is rather low. A reason for that is certainly that it is not practically possible to involve all users in the development/definition of the measurement program.

This means that (a) if possible, measurement data should be collected automatically (i.e., without further user interaction), and (b) the collection of measurement data that can only be collected manually has to be combined with useful add-on features according to the principle "we want measurement data from the user, we offer him something."

An opportunity to smartly combine the collection of measurement data as feedback with the usage process is to establish a so-called "feedback loop" (Fig. 6). In the presented example, the collection of feedback is integrated into the project process in a simple manner. It is part of the project planning, in the beginning of the project, to identify the existing, relevant experiences in COIN. This is done using similarity-based retrieval over IESE's intranet. The project manager receives as an answer to his query a list of 30 similar experiences, which he can classify as useful or not useful. With a click, he composes a checklist of these useful experience for his project. This checklist can be printed or emailed.

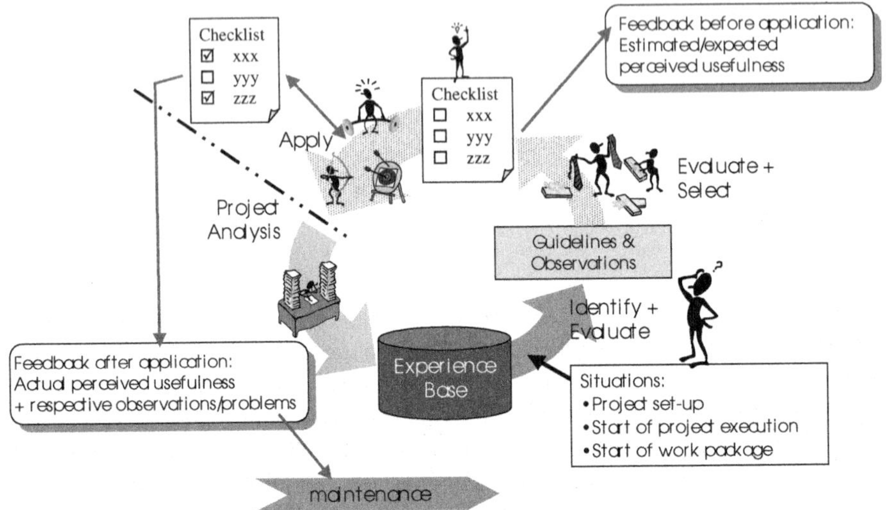

Fig. 6. Embedding the collection of measurement data in the usage process (example).

While this classification collects feedback on the estimated/expected usefulness before the application of the experiences, the project analysis interview is used for asking about the actual usefulness of the respective experiences. The analysis of usage and usefulness of the experience packages delivers information that is used for (1) empirically validating the experience packages and (2) maintaining the EB.

5 Discussion: Engineering Maintenance and Quality Knowledge during EB Buildup

This section discusses how to integrate the method into an EB buildup methodology (namely DISER [30] and INCREA [9]). This allows to systematically develop the required maintenance and quality knowledge during EB buildup. On the one hand, this ensures that the maintenance and quality knowledge is acquired as early as possible and that the maintenance and quality needs are considered during the development of the EB in order to avoid future changes due to maintenance needs identified later than possible. On the other hand, we observed that the conceptualization usually is not stable during buildup and prototypical usage [22]. Thus, evaluation and maintenance should be addressed with low-effort solutions, i.e., generic or standard components should be used for maintenance and evaluation where possible and feasible.

Since the development of the EB itself is iterative and does not follow a waterfall approach, it is not very useful to link the definition and elicitation of maintenance and quality knowledge too strictly to the EB development process. In addition, mixing everything can lead to a "cognitive overload" for the experts involved because they have to make too many decisions with different background (experience itself, maintenance, evaluation/quality). Therefore, the development information and artifacts are grouped into three levels:[4] high-level information dealing with the objectives, success criteria, and subject areas (*reference level* acc. to [6]); mid-level information dealing with detailed scenarios, conceptual model, and record methods (*conceptual level* acc. to [6]); and low-level information dealing with the technical implementation including the design of the user interface (*implementation level* acc. to [6]).

The knowledge life-cycle model is considered as high-level information. In particular, it should be discussed and defined after the subject areas and before the detailed scenarios because the life-cycle model defines together with the subject areas –at an abstract level– which types of knowledge and experience are in the focus of the EB and, thus, have to be addressed by the detailed scenarios.

The maintenance policies (related to the knowledge life-cycle model or to the scenarios and conceptual model) are conceptual information. Obviously, they require that the conceptual model of the actual experience is settled. Therefore, they should be derived after the definition of the conceptual model for the actual experience.

The formalization of the maintenance policies into maintenance guidelines and the automation is part of the technical implementation of the EB system.

A feedback loop -as presented in Section 4.2- obviously has an impact on the design of the EB's user interface and on the knowledge collection. Thus, a decision on a feedback loop should be made before addressing the latter two issues.

The measurement plan must be completed before doing the harmonizing task from Section 4.1 because it is input for this task. For the reasons mentioned above, a generic standard measurement plan should be used. Such a measurement program was outlined in [21]. It uses two indicators for the EB value: sustained usage of the EB and perceived usefulness of the retrieved cases. Together with the feedback loop from Section 4.2, it has been implemented for COIN.

A measurement program also includes the definition of a baseline or an estimation of the quality criteria under focus. For the usage, the expected number can be determined after defining the scenarios. This also helps to decide on scenarios that are not relevant due to a low number of expected uses.

6 Conclusion

In [21], we presented an evaluation and maintenance methodology for experience bases (EBs). This methodology is based on two ideas: (1) EB maintenance is driven by systematically conducting and exploiting evaluation. (2) EB maintenance itself is performed systematically by recording and using experience gained during maintenance in the form of special maintenance guidelines.

This paper extends this maintenance and evaluation methodology with a method for the systematic development of maintenance and evaluation knowledge during EB buildup. Operational maintenance knowledge is systematically derived from various sources such as artifacts and information gained during EB buildup, a knowledge/ experience life-cycle model, and the evaluation program for the EB. In addition, gener-

---

4 The terminology is taken from DISER. However, the terms in INRECA are almost the same.

ic, well-tested maintenance policies from CBR research and practice should be reused for general aspects (see [15] for an overview). The maintenance knowledge is formalized further to enable automated support. For the implementation, the maintenance and quality knowledge is integrated into the EB. The collection of quality/measurement data is embedded into the usage to increase the motivation of the users for providing quality/measurement data. The systematic development has the benefit that the maintenance knowledge can be traced to its roots and that a detailed operational maintenance plan/strategy is developed. This explicit relation of the maintenance policies and guidelines to the EF/EB's objectives and quality criteria ensures that the maintenance knowledge addresses relevant issues of maintenance. The fine-tuning of the maintenance knowledge for an EB is an issue of learning about EB maintenance [21].

We used the presented method for systematically developing maintenance knowledge for COIN and an industrial EF project in the telecommunication section. Here we could also transfer maintenance knowledge (in form of maintenance policies) from one EB to another. This transfer and reuse was simplified by the similarity of knowledge life-cycle model and conceptual model (at a coarse-grained level).

We also used the GQM method for developing quality knowledge and transferring this quality knowledge across EFs. We used our experience gained in [22, 23] to set up evaluation programs for COIN and industrial projects faster and cheaper. The standard set of metrics allows better comparison of evaluation results across EFs.

As a next step, the proposed integration of the maintenance and quality engineering methods into the buildup method DISER will be tested. Furthermore, future work will deal with a systematic analysis of maintenance reasons and respective actions in a generic knowledge life-cycle model for all kinds of knowledge and experience (i.e., set of generic maintenance policies related to the life-cycle model) considering existing maintenance knowledge and its dimensions [26, 15, 29]. A collection of such knowledge will jump-start the definition of maintenance policies related to the knowledge life-cycle model of EBs.

Acknowledgements. The COIN project has been funded as an internal project at IESE since January 2000.

References

1. Aha, D., and Weber, R., editors. *Proceedings of the Workshop on Intelligent Lessons Learned Systems at 17th National Conference on AI (AAAI-00)*, 2000.
2. Althoff, K.-D. Case-based reasoning. In Chang, S. K., editor, *Handbook of Software Engineering and Knowledge Engineering*, volume 1. World Scientific, 2001. (to appear).
3. Althoff, K.-D., Birk, A., Hartkopf, S., Müller, W., Nick, M., Surmann, D., and Tautz, C. Systematic population, utilization, and maintenance of a repository for comprehensive reuse. In Ruhe, G., and Bomarius, F., editors, *Learning Software Organizations - Methodology and Applications*, number 1756 in Lecture Notes in Computer Science, pages 25–50. Springer Verlag, Heidelberg, Germany, 2000.

4. Althoff, K.-D., Bomarius, F., and Tautz, C. Using case-based reasoning technology to build learning organizations. In *Proceedings of the the Workshop on Organizational Memories at the European Conference on Artificial Intelligence '98*, Brighton, England, Aug. 1998.
5. Althoff, K.-D., Nick, M., and Tautz, C. Improving organizational memories through user feedback. In *Workshop on Learning Software Organisations at SEKE'99*, Kaiserslautern, Germany, June 1999.
6. Basili, V. R., Caldiera, G., and Cantone, G. A reference architecture for the component factory. *ACM Transactions on Software Engineering and Methodology*, 1(1), 1992.
7. Basili, V. R., Caldiera, G., and Rombach, H. D. Experience Factory. In Marciniak, J. J., editor, *Encyclopedia of Software Engineering*, volume 1, pages 469–476. John Wiley & Sons, 1994.
8. Bergmann, R. Experience management - foundations, development methodology, and internet-based applications. Postdoctoral thesis, Department of Computer Science, University of Kaiserslautern, 2001.
9. Bergmann, R., Breen, S., Göker, M., Manago, M., and Wess, S. *Developing Industrial Case-Based Reasoning Applications – The INRECA Methodology*. Springer Verlag, 1999.
10. Birk, A., and Tautz, C. Knowledge management of software engineering lessons learned. In *Proceedings of the Tenth Conference on Software Engineering and Knowledge Engineering*, San Francisco Bay, CA, USA, June 1998. Knowledge Systems Institute, Skokie, Illinois, USA.
11. Buglione, L., and Abran, A. Balanced scorecards and GQM: What are the differences? In *Proceedings of the Third European Software Measurement Conference (FESMA-AEMES 2000)*, Madrid, Spain, Oct. 2000.
12. Hammer, M., and Champy, J. *Reengineering the Corporation*. Nicolas Brealey Publishing, London, 1993.
13. Kaplan, R. S., and Norton, D. P. *The Balanced Scorecard. Translating Strategy into Action*. Harvard Business School Press, Boston, 1996.
14. Leake, D. B., Smyth, B., Wilson, D. C., and Yang, Q., editors. *Computational Intelligence special is¦sue on maintaining CBR systems*, 2001. (to appear).
15. Leake, D. B., and Wilson, D. C. Categorizing case-base maintenance: Dimensions and directions. In Smyth, B., and Cunningham, P., editors, *Advances in Case-Based Reasoning:Proceedings of the Fourth European Workshop on Case-Based Reasoning*, pages 196–207, Berlin, Germany, Sept. 1998. Springer-Verlag.
16. McKenna, E., and Smyth, B. Competence-guided editing methods for lazy learning. In Horn, W., editor, *Proceedings of the 14th European Conference on Artificial Intelligence*. IOS Press, Berlin, Germany, 2000.
17. Menzies, T. Knowledge maintenance: The state of the art. *The Knowledge Engineering Review*, 1998.
18. Minor, M., Funk, P., Roth-Berghofer, T., and Wilson, D., editors. *Proceedings of the Workshop on Flexible Strategies for Maintaining Knowledge Containers at the 14th European Conference on Artificial Intelligence (ECAI 2000)*, Aug. 2000.
19. Minor, M., and Hanft, A. Corporate knowledge editing with a life cycle model. In *Proceedings of the Eighth German Workshop on Case-Based Reasoning*, Laemmerbuckel, Germany, 2000.
20. Müller, M. Interestingness during the discovery of knowledge in databases (in German). *Künstliche Intelligenz*, pages 40–42, Sept. 1999.

21. Nick, M., Althoff, K.-D., and Tautz, C. Systematic maintenance of corporate experience repositories. *Computational Intelligence special issue on maintaining CBR systems*, 2000. (to appear).
22. Nick, M., and Feldmann, R. Guidelines for evaluation and improvement of reuse and experience repository systems through measurement programs. In *FESMA-AEMES 2000*, Madrid, Spain, Oct. 2000.
23. Nick, M., and Tautz, C. Practical evaluation of an organizational memory using the goal-question-metric technique. In *XPS'99: Knowledge-Based Systems - Survey and Future Directions*. Springer Verlag, Würzburg, Germany, Mar. 1999. LNAI Nr. 1570.
24. Reinartz, T., Iglezakis, I., and Roth-Berghofer, T. On quality measures for case base maintenance. In Blanzieri, E., and Portinale, L., editors, *Advances in Case-Based Reasoning:Proceedings of the Fifth European Workshop on Case-Based Reasoning*, pages 247–259. Springer-Verlag, 2000.
25. Richter, M. M. Introduction. In Lenz, M., Bartsch-Spörl, B., Burkhard, H.-D., and Wess, S., editors, *Case-Based Reasoning Technologies: From Foundations to Applications*, number 1400 in Lecture Notes in Artificial Intelligence, chapter 1, pages 1–15. Springer-Verlag, Berlin, Germany, 1998.
26. Rombach, H. D. Keynote: Maintenance of software development/maintenance know-how. In *Proceedings of the International Conference on Software Maintenance*, 1995.
27. Romhardt, K. *Die Organisation aus der Wissensperspektive - Möglichkeiten und Grenzen der Intervention*. Gabler Verlag, Wiesbaden, 1998.
28. Ruhe, G. Learning software organisations. In Chang, S. K., editor, *Handbook of Software Engineering and Knowledge Engineering*, volume 1. World Scientific, 2001. (to appear).
29. Swanson, E. B. The dimensions of maintenance. In *Proceedings of the Second International Conference on Software Engineering*, pages 492–497, 1976.
30. Tautz, C. *Customizing Software Engineering Experience Management Systems to Organizational Needs*. PhD thesis, University of Kaiserslautern, Germany, 2000.
31. Tautz, C., Althoff, K.-D., and Nick, M. A case-based reasoning approach for managing qualitative experience. In *AAAI-00 Workshop on Intelligent Lessons Learned Systems*, 2000.

Part 8

Announcements

Announcement of LSO Discussion Forum

LSO Workshop Advisory Committee

c/o Fraunhofer Institute for Experimental Software Engineering, Sauerwiesen 6, D-67661 Kaiserslautern, Germany
www.forumromanum.de/member/forum/forum.cgi?USER=user_42473

As requested at the LSO 2000 workshop in Oulu, Finland, we have installed a discussion forum for sharing and discussion of topics related to learning software organizations. Topics of interest include, but are not limited to:

Success stories and failures - what can we learn?
Knowledge acquisition in improvement programs
Activation and distribution of explicit knowledge
Establishing continuous improvement - the role of experts
Establishing learning cycles and feedback mechanisms
Making tacit knowledge explicit
Cultural changes for successful organizational learning
Evaluation of knowledge management activities
Knowledge sharing between different groups
WWW-based knowledge management
Building, adaptation, and evolution of corporate repositories
Technical infrastructures and technologies for supporting LSOs

The forum addresses researchers and practitioners who are concerned with knowledge management, organizational learning, or experience handling in software process improvement. Currently, the forum is not moderated. However, your comments and help are welcomed. Either post directly to the forum or contacted us at the above address.

Hopefully, the forum will establish as a communication platform between the LSO workshops for members from all communities who are interested in LSOs. Therefore, let others with similar interests know about this discussion forum, encourage people to participate, and get involved!

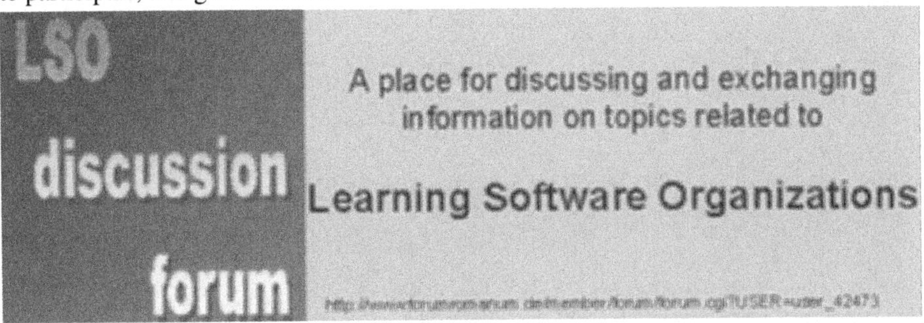

LSO
discussion
forum
A place for discussing and exchanging information on topics related to
Learning Software Organizations

K.-D. Althoff, R.L. Feldmann, and W. Müller (Eds.): LSO 2001, LNCS 2176, p. 238, 2001.

Announcement for LSO 2002

Scott Henninger

Department of Computer Science & Engineering
University of Nebraska-Lincoln
Lincoln, NE 68588-0115
+1-402-472-8394
scotth@cse.unl.edu

As the organizer for LSO 2002, I would like to invite people to participate in next year's workshop. At the time of publication, the venue and has not yet been set, but we are inquiring about conferences to co-locate with and looking into the possibility of workshop support from the ACM and IEEE. Keep an eye on the LSO 2002 Web site (http://cse.unl.edu/LSO2002/) for key dates and location!

Having three successful years behind us, we look forward to the fourth consecutive year of LSO being the premiere venue for research, discussion and collaboration on issues and questions of organizational learning from the software perspective. This and past workshops have built on existing work in knowledge management, organizational memory and learning, experience factories, and information systems. We hope these ties will continue and that related topics from other fields are explored and further investigated, such as computer-supported cooperative work and groupware, workflow and process engineering, and other subjects relevant to the overall theme of software support for organizational learning.

Remember, keep an eye of the Web page, let others with similar interests know about this workshop, encourage people to participate, and get involved! Your comments and help are welcomed and I can be contacted at the above e-mail address and/or phone number.

See you in 2002!

Remember the LSO 2002 Web site: http://cse.unl.edu/LSO2002/

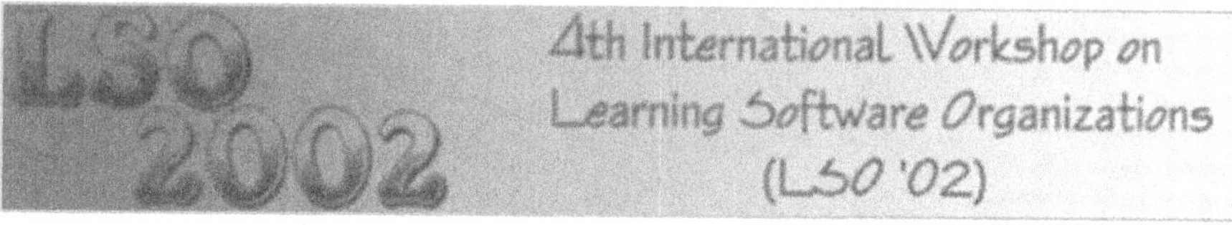

LSO
2002
4th International Workshop on
Learning Software Organizations
(LSO '02)

K.-D. Althoff, R.L. Feldmann, and W. Müller (Eds.): LSO 2001, LNCS 2176, p. 239, 2001.

Author Index

Lecture Notes in Computer Science

For information about Vols. 1–2084
please contact your bookseller or Springer-Verlag

Vol. 1982: S. Näher, D. Wagner (Eds.), Algorithm Engineering. Proceedings, 2000. VIII, 243 pages. 2001.

Vol. 1996: P.L. Lanzi, W. Stolzmann, S.W. Wilson (Eds.), Advances in Learning Classifier Systems. Proceedings, 2000. VIII, 273 pages. 2001. (Subseries LNAI).

Vol. 2085: J. Mira, A. Prieto (Eds.), Bio-Inspired Applications of Connectionism. Proceedings, 2001. Part II. XXVII, 848 pages. 2001.

Vol. 2086: M. Luck, V. Mařík, O. Stěpánková, R. Trappl (Eds.), Multi-Agent Systems and Applications. Proceedings, 2001. X, 437 pages. 2001. (Subseries LNAI).

Vol. 2087: G. Kern-Isberner, Conditionals in Nonmonotonic Reasoning and Belief Revision. X, 190 pages. 2001. (Subseries LNAI).

Vol. 2088: S. Yu, A. Păun (Eds.), Implementation and Application of Automata. Proceedings, 2000. XI, 343 pages. 2001.

Vol. 2089: A. Amir, G.M. Landau (Eds.), Combinatorial Pattern Matching. Proceedings, 2001. VIII, 273 pages. 2001.

Vol. 2090: E. Brinksma, H. Hermanns, J.-P. Katoen (Eds.), Lectures on Formal Methods and Performance Analysis. Proceedings, 2000. VII, 431 pages. 2001.

Vol. 2091: J. Bigun, F. Smeraldi (Eds.), Audio- and Video-Based Biometric Person Authentication. Proceedings, 2001. XIII, 374 pages. 2001.

Vol. 2092: L. Wolf, D. Hutchison, R. Steinmetz (Eds.), Quality of Service – IWQoS 2001. Proceedings, 2001. XII, 435 pages. 2001.

Vol. 2093: P. Lorenz (Ed.), Networking – ICN 2001. Proceedings, 2001. Part I. XXV, 843 pages. 2001.

Vol. 2094: P. Lorenz (Ed.), Networking – ICN 2001. Proceedings, 2001. Part II. XXV, 899 pages. 2001.

Vol. 2095: B. Schiele, G. Sagerer (Eds.), Computer Vision Systems. Proceedings, 2001. X, 313 pages. 2001.

Vol. 2096: J. Kittler, F. Roli (Eds.), Multiple Classifier Systems. Proceedings, 2001. XII, 456 pages. 2001.

Vol. 2097: B. Read (Ed.), Advances in Databases. Proceedings, 2001. X, 219 pages. 2001.

Vol. 2098: J. Akiyama, M. Kano, M. Urabe (Eds.), Discrete and Computational Geometry. Proceedings, 2000. XI, 381 pages. 2001.

Vol. 2099: P. de Groote, G. Morrill, C. Retoré (Eds.), Logical Aspects of Computational Linguistics. Proceedings, 2001. VIII, 311 pages. 2001. (Subseries LNAI).

Vol. 2100: R. Küsters, Non-Standard Inferences in Description Logocs. X, 250 pages. 2001. (Subseries LNAI).

Vol. 2101: S. Quaglini, P. Barahona, S. Andreassen (Eds.), Artificial Intelligence in Medicine. Proceedings, 2001. XIV, 469 pages. 2001. (Subseries LNAI).

Vol. 2102: G. Berry, H. Comon, A. Finkel (Eds.), Computer-Aided Verification. Proceedings, 2001. XIII, 520 pages. 2001.

Vol. 2103: M. Hannebauer, J. Wendler, E. Pagello (Eds.), Balancing Reactivity and Social Deliberation in Multi-Agent Systems. VIII, 237 pages. 2001. (Subseries LNAI).

Vol. 2104: R. Eigenmann, M.J. Voss (Eds.), OpenMP Shared Memory Parallel Programming. Proceedings, 2001. X, 185 pages. 2001.

Vol. 2105: W. Kim, T.-W. Ling, Y-J. Lee, S.-S. Park (Eds.), The Human Society and the Internet. Proceedings, 2001. XVI, 470 pages. 2001.

Vol. 2106: M. Kerckhove (Ed.), Scale-Space and Morphology in Computer Vision. Proceedings, 2001. XI, 435 pages. 2001.

Vol. 2107: F.T. Chong, C. Kozyrakis, M. Oskin (Eds.), Intelligent Memory Systems. Proceedings, 2000. VIII, 193 pages. 2001.

Vol. 2108: J. Wang (Ed.), Computing and Combinatorics. Proceedings, 2001. XIII, 602 pages. 2001.

Vol. 2109: M. Bauer, P.J. Gymtrasiewicz, J. Vassileva (Eds.), User Modelind 2001. Proceedings, 2001. XIII, 318 pages. 2001. (Subseries LNAI).

Vol. 2110: B. Hertzberger, A. Hoekstra, R. Williams (Eds.), High-Performance Computing and Networking. Proceedings, 2001. XVII, 733 pages. 2001.

Vol. 2111: D. Helmbold, B. Williamson (Eds.), Computational Learning Theory. Proceedings, 2001. IX, 631 pages. 2001. (Subseries LNAI).

Vol. 2116: V. Akman, P. Bouquet, R. Thomason, R.A. Young (Eds.), Modeling and Using Context. Proceedings, 2001. XII, 472 pages. 2001. (Subseries LNAI).

Vol. 2117: M. Beynon, C.L. Nehaniv, K. Dautenhahn (Eds.), Cognitive Technology: Instruments of Mind. Proceedings, 2001. XV, 522 pages. 2001. (Subseries LNAI).

Vol. 2118: X.S. Wang, G. Yu, H. Lu (Eds.), Advances in Web-Age Information Management. Proceedings, 2001. XV, 418 pages. 2001.

Vol. 2119: V. Varadharajan, Y. Mu (Eds.), Information Security and Privacy. Proceedings, 2001. XI, 522 pages. 2001.

Vol. 2120: H.S. Delugach, G. Stumme (Eds.), Conceptual Structures: Broadening the Base. Proceedings, 2001. X, 377 pages. 2001. (Subseries LNAI).

Vol. 2121: C.S. Jensen, M. Schneider, B. Seeger, V.J. Tsotras (Eds.), Advances in Spatial and Temporal Databases. Proceedings, 2001. XI, 543 pages. 2001.

Vol. 2123: P. Perner (Ed.), Machine Learning and Data Mining in Pattern Recognition. Proceedings, 2001. XI, 363 pages. 2001. (Subseries LNAI).

Vol. 2124: W. Skarbek (Ed.), Computer Analysis of Images and Patterns. Proceedings, 2001. XV, 743 pages. 2001.

Vol. 2125: F. Dehne, J.-R. Sack, R. Tamassia (Eds.), Algorithms and Data Structures. Proceedings, 2001. XII, 484 pages. 2001.

Vol. 2126: P. Cousot (Ed.), Static Analysis. Proceedings, 2001. XI, 439 pages. 2001.

Vol. 2127: V. Malyshkin (Ed.), Parallel Computing Technologies. Proceedings, 2001. XII, 516 pages. 2001.

Vol. 2129: M. Goemans, K. Jansen, J.D.P. Rolim, L. Trevisan (Eds.), Approximation, Randomization, and Combinatorial Optimization. Proceedings, 2001. IX, 297 pages. 2001.

Vol. 2130: G. Dorffner, H. Bischof, K. Hornik (Eds.), Artificial Neural Networks – ICANN 2001. Proceedings, 2001. XXII, 1259 pages. 2001.

Vol. 2132: S.-T. Yuan, M. Yokoo (Eds.), Intelligent Agents. Specification. Modeling, and Application. Proceedings, 2001. X, 237 pages. 2001. (Subseries LNAI).

Vol. 2136: J. Sgall, A. Pultr, P. Kolman (Eds.), Mathematical Foundations of Computer Science 2001. Proceedings, 2001. XII, 716 pages. 2001.

Vol. 2138: R. Freivalds (Ed.), Fundamentals of Computation Theory. Proceedings, 2001. XIII, 542 pages. 2001.

Vol. 2139: J. Kilian (Ed.), Advances in Cryptology – CRYPTO 2001. Proceedings, 2001. XI, 599 pages. 2001.

Vol. 2141: G.S. Brodal, D. Frigioni, A. Marchetti-Spaccamela (Eds.), Algorithm Engineering. Proceedings, 2001. X, 199 pages. 2001.

Vol. 2142: L. Fribourg (Ed.), Computer Science Logic. Proceedings, 2001. XII, 615 pages. 2001.

Vol. 2143: S. Benferhat, P. Besnard (Eds.), Symbolic and Quantitative Approaches to Reasoning with Uncertainty. Proceedings, 2001. XIV, 818 pages. 2001. (Subseries LNAI).

Vol. 2146: J.H. Silverman (Eds.), Cryptography and Lattices. Proceedings, 2001. VII, 219 pages. 2001.

Vol. 2147: G. Brebner, R. Woods (Eds.), Field-Programmable Logic and Applications. Proceedings, 2001. XV, 665 pages. 2001.

Vol. 2149: O. Gascuel, B.M.E. Moret (Eds.), Algorithms in Bioinformatics. Proceedings, 2001. X, 307 pages. 2001.

Vol. 2150: R. Sakellariou, J. Keane, J. Gurd, L. Freeman (Eds.), Euro-Par 2001 Parallel Processing. Proceedings, 2001. XXX, 943 pages. 2001.

Vol. 2151: A. Caplinskas, J. Eder (Eds.), Advances in Databases and Information Systems. Proceedings, 2001. XIII, 381 pages. 2001.

Vol. 2152: R.J. Boulton, P.B. Jackson (Eds.), Theorem Proving in Higher Order Logics. Proceedings, 2001. X, 395 pages. 2001.

Vol. 2153: A.L. Buchsbaum, J. Snoeyink (Eds.), Algorithm Engineering and Experimentation. Proceedings, 2001. VIII, 231 pages. 2001.

Vol. 2154: K.G. Larsen, M. Nielsen (Eds.), CONCUR 2001 – Concurrency Theory. Proceedings, 2001. XI, 583 pages. 2001.

Vol. 2157: C. Rouveirol, M. Sebag (Eds.), Inductive Logic Programming. Proceedings, 2001. X, 261 pages. 2001. (Subseries LNAI).

Vol. 2158: D. Shepherd, J. Finney, L. Mathy, N. Race (Eds.), Interactive Distributed Multimedia Systems. Proceedings, 2001. XIII, 258 pages. 2001.

Vol. 2159: J. Kelemen, P. Sosík (Eds.), Advances in Artificial Life. Proceedings, 2001. XIX, 724 pages. 2001. (Subseries LNAI).

Vol. 2161: F. Meyer auf der Heide (Ed.), Algorithms – ESA 2001. Proceedings, 2001. XII, 538 pages. 2001.

Vol. 2162: Ç. K. Koç, D. Naccache, C. Paar (Eds.), Cryptographic Hardware and Embedded Systems – CHES 2001. Proceedings, 2001. XIV, 411 pages. 2001.

Vol. 2164: S. Pierre, R. Glitho (Eds.), Mobile Agents for Telecommunication Applications. Proceedings, 2001. XI, 292 pages. 2001.

Vol. 2165: L. de Alfaro, S. Gilmore (Eds.), Process Algebra and Probabilistic Methods. Proceedings, 2001. XII, 217 pages. 2001.

Vol. 2166: V. Matoušek, P. Mautner, R. Mouček, K. Taušer (Eds.), Text, Speech and Dialogue. Proceedings, 2001. XIII, 452 pages. 2001. (Subseries LNAI).

Vol. 2170: S. Palazzo (Ed.), Evolutionary Trends of the Internet. Proceedings, 2001. XIII, 722 pages. 2001.

Vol. 2172: C. Batini, F. Giunchiglia, P. Giorgini, M. Mecella (Eds.), Cooperative Information Systems. Proceedings, 2001. XI, 450 pages. 2001.

Vol. 2176: K.-D. Althoff, R.L. Feldmann, W. Müller (Eds.), Advances in Learning Software Organizations. Proceedings, 2001. XI, 241 pages. 2001.

Vol. 2177: G. Butler, S. Jarzabek (Eds.), Generative and Component-Based Software Engineering. Proceedings, 2001. X, 203 pages. 2001.

Vol. 2181: C. Y. Westort (Eds.), Digital Earth Moving. Proceedings, 2001. XII, 117 pages. 2001.

Vol. 2184: M. Tucci (Ed.), Multimedia Databases and Image Communication. Proceedings, 2001. X, 225 pages. 2001.

Vol. 2186: J. Bosch (Ed.), Generative and Component-Based Software Engineering. Proceedings, 2001. VIII, 177 pages. 2001.

Vol. 2188: F. Bomarius, S. Komi-Sirviö (Eds.), Product Focused Software Process Improvement. Proceedings, 2001. XI, 382 pages. 2001.

Vol. 2189: F. Hoffmann, D.J. Hand, N. Adams, D. Fisher, G. Guimaraes (Eds.), Advances in Intelligent Data Analysis. Proceedings, 2001. XII, 384 pages. 2001.

Vol. 2190: A. de Antonio, R. Aylett, D. Ballin (Eds.), Intelligent Virtual Agents. Proceedings, 2001. VIII, 245 pages. 2001. (Subseries LNAI).

Vol. 2191: B. Radig, S. Florczyk (Eds.), Pattern Recognition. Proceedings, 2001. XVI, 452 pages. 2001.

Vol. 2193: F. Casati, D. Georgakopoulos, M.-C. Shan (Eds.), Technologies for E-Services. Proceedings, 2001. X, 213 pages. 2001.